Democracy
by
Disclosure

Democracy
by
Disclosure

The Rise of Technopopulism

Mary Graham

GOVERNANCE INSTITUTE
BROOKINGS INSTITUTION PRESS
Washington, D.C.

Copyright © 2002
THE BROOKINGS INSTITUTION
1775 Massachusetts Avenue, N.W., Washington, D.C. 20036
www.brookings.edu

Library of Congress Cataloging-in-Publication data

Graham, Mary, 1944–
  Democracy by disclosure : the rise of technopopulism / Mary Graham.
  p. cm.
Includes bibliographical references and index.
  ISBN 0-8157-3234-1 (cloth : alk. paper)
  1. United States—Social policy—1980–1993. 2. United States—Social
policy—1993– 3. Disclosure of information—Government policy—United
States. 4. Disclosure of information—Government policy—United
States—States. I. Title.
  HN59.2 .G72 2002   2002009667
  361.6'1'0973—dc21   CIP

9 8 7 6 5 4 3 2 1

The paper used in this publication meets minimum requirements of the
American National Standard for Information Sciences—Permanence of Paper for
Printed Library Materials: ANSI Z39.48-1992.

Typeset in Sabon

Composition by Cynthia Stock
Silver Spring, Maryland

Printed by R. R. Donnelley and Sons
Harrisonburg, Virginia

THE BROOKINGS INSTITUTION

The Brookings Institution is an independent organization devoted to nonpartisan research, education, and publication in economics, government, foreign policy, and the social sciences generally. Its principal purposes are to aid in the development of sound public policies and to promote public understanding of issues of national importance. The Institution was founded on December 8, 1927, to merge the activities of the Institute for Government Research, founded in 1916, the Institute of Economics, founded in 1922, and the Robert Brookings Graduate School of Economics and Government, founded in 1924.

The Institution maintains a position of neutrality on issues of public policy to safeguard the intellectual freedom of the staff. Interpretations or conclusions in Brookings publications should be understood to be solely those of the authors.

THE GOVERNANCE INSTITUTE

The Governance Institute, a nonprofit organization incorporated in 1986, is concerned with exploring, explaining, and easing problems associated with both the separation and the division of powers in the American federal system. It is interested in how the levels and branches of government can best work with one another. It is attentive to the problems within an organization or between institutions that frustrate the functioning of government. The Governance Institute is concerned as well with those professions and mediating groups that significantly affect the delivery and quality of public services. The Institute's focus is on institutional process, a nexus linking law, institutions, and policy. The Institute believes that problem solving should integrate research and discussion. This is why the Institute endeavors to work with those decisionmakers who play a role in making changes in process and policy. The Institute currently has four program areas: problems of the judiciary; problems of the administrative state; problems in criminal justice; and challenges to the legal profession.

For my husband, Don,
and my children,
Molly, Will, Laura, and Liza.

Preface

This book explores some of the complicated issues behind the seemingly simple idea of transparency. At the beginning of the twenty-first century, the United States seeks to teach by example the value of an open society, promoting the idea that reliable information empowers citizens to participate in government and provides an underpinning for healthy markets. Developing countries have been attentive. Many are experimenting with structured systems of transparency as a substitute for more conventional regulation. Likewise, international organizations have begun to promote transparency as a means of furthering global priorities.

Yet our own systems of legislated transparency remain far from perfect. Nearly seventy years ago, after the stock market crash of 1929, Congress created what would become the nation's most venerated program of structured disclosure, in order to reduce financial risks to investors. In 2001 the collapse of Enron, the world's largest energy trader, became the latest crisis to reveal that this system still suffers from serious and persistent flaws.

Now legislators have created scores of new disclosure regimes to reduce other kinds of risks—from toxic chemicals and contaminants in drinking water to ingredients in processed foods and medical mistakes. Huge amounts of previously proprietary information have been transferred permenantly to the public domain. The explosive growth of information technology has placed this information in the hands of ordinary citizens for use in making political and economic choices, creating a new technopopulism.

During the last decade, government's authority to compel the disclosure of information has taken a legitimate place beside its authority to set rules and redistribute financial resources as a means of furthering public priorities. Transparency has become an instrument of public policy. However, providing the public with facts that translate into the reduction of risk has proved surprisingly difficult—and there are serious dangers in doing it badly. The question now is whether the lessons learned from early experience will be applied to bring practice more into line with promise.

I am grateful to the John F. Kennedy School of Government at Harvard University for providing an intellectually rich environment for pursuing this work. Alan Altshuler, Ruth and Frank Stanton Professor in Urban Policy and Planning and director of the A. Alfred Taubman Center for State and Local Government, offered insights and support at every step of the way. Henry Lee, director of the Environment and Natural Resources Program, encouraged this work from the start and was extraordinarily generous with his time when problems arose. Ira A. Jackson, director of the school's Center for Business and Government, offered fresh ideas and shared lessons from his experience in the private sector. Deborah Hurley, director of the Harvard Information Infrastructure Project, helped to place this work in the context of new developments in information technology. David Luberoff, associate director of the Taubman Center, and Arnold Howitt, its executive director, offered ideas, encouragement, and comments on early drafts. Gail Christopher, executive director of the Institute for Government Innovation, provided an invaluable opportunity to outline transparency issues in an early paper, and Cary Coglianese, director of the Regulatory Policy Program, allowed me to try out ideas in one of his stimulating seminars. There is no adequate way to thank Archon Fung and David Weil, my fellow codirectors of the Transparency Policy Project, for their inspiration and for the great pleasure of our ongoing collaboration. David Greenberg provided outstanding research assistance. I am also grateful to Georgetown University Law Center for generously providing a base for research in Washington, D.C. Dean Judith Areen and Professors Richard Lazarus, Lisa Heinzerling, and Donald Langevoort helped to clarify legal issues and offered comments on early articles and papers. Tracey Bridgman and her team of researchers in the center's library provided invaluable assistance with document gathering and checking references. In addition, I am grateful to expert readers who offered meticulous comments on each profile: Bradley Karkkainen of Columbia Law School; Michael Taylor of Resources for the Future; and Janet Corrigan of the Institute of Medicine. I am indebted, too, to Catherine Miller of the Hampshire Research Institute for her collaboration in analyzing trends related to the disclosure of toxic releases and in producing an article and workshop presentation. Any errors, of course, are the responsibility of the author and not of those who worked to minimize them.

A number of individuals with special understanding of information issues offered generously of their time and insights. Senator Daniel Patrick Moynihan, whose book *Secrecy* examined obstacles to openness in the national security context, provided wise counsel at several critical points in the project. Paul Portney, president of Resources for the Future, offered an unbeatable combination of unwavering support and skeptical questioning. Lois Schiffer, assistant attorney general, provided the benefit of her wide experience in analyzing information issues. Once again, my longtime friend Bob Samuelson encouraged, edited, questioned, and advised. I never found the limits of his patience. Finally, this book would not have been possible without the support of Bob Katzmann and the Board of Directors of the Governance Institute. The institute believed in the project from the start, and Bob, its president when this work began, continued to provide sage advice despite his busy schedule as a newly appointed judge on the U.S. Court of Appeals for the Second Circuit.

At Brookings, I am grateful to Paul C. Light, senior fellow and director of the Center for Public Service, and Carol Graham, vice president and director of Governance Studies, for their interest in this book and their enthusiasm for its publication. I owe special thanks to Janet Walker, managing editor of Brookings Institution Press, both for her efficient oversight of the publication process and for making that process a pleasure for the author. Kerry Kern provided meticulous editing and made many helpful suggestions. Enid Zafran prepared the index, and Tanjam Jacobson proofread the pages. It was a delight to work again with Susan Woollen, who directed the development of the cover design

Contents

Democracy
by
Disclosure

1   The Power of Publicity

Publicity is justly commended as a remedy for social and industrial diseases. Sunlight is said to be the best of disinfectants; electric light the most efficient policeman.

—LOUIS D. BRANDEIS*

I n 1913 Louis D. Brandeis, known as the "people's attorney" for his fights against the predatory practices of big business, had a simple but revolutionary idea. In a series of articles in *Harper's Weekly*, he proposed that requiring businesses to reveal basic financial information could encourage them to reduce risks to the public. His immediate targets were the hidden fees and commissions exacted by J. P. Morgan and other investment bankers on purchases of publicly traded stocks. Brandeis was years ahead of his time, as it turned out. It was not until nearly two decades later, in the midst of a national crisis, that his idea became the cornerstone of a new president's initiative. The stock market crash of 1929 left millions of people holding worthless securities. Accepting the Democratic Party's nomination in 1932, Franklin D. Roosevelt, who had long admired Brandeis, called for the "letting in of the light of day on

---

*Louis D. Brandeis, *Other People's Money*, 2d ed. (Frederick A. Stockes Company, 1932), p. 92.

issues of securities, foreign and domestic, which are offered for sale to the investing public." During the campaign he often repeated the theme: "Let in the light."[1] In response, Congress passed the Securities Act of 1933 and the Securities and Exchange Act of 1934. They required companies that sold securities to the public to reveal detailed information about their officers, earnings, and liabilities. As this reporting system matured, it would form a foundation for investor confidence for the rest of the century. Disclosure had become a form of regulation.

There was a second half to Brandeis's agenda, however. He believed that requiring businesses to reveal information could help reduce social risks as well. The archaic doctrine of *caveat emptor* was vanishing, he argued. Government-mandated disclosure in ordinary commercial transactions could remedy "social diseases." In the Pure Food and Drug Act of 1906, Congress already had required processors to inform the public about ingredients in foods shipped in interstate commerce. This idea, however, proved to be much farther ahead of its time. Brandeis's social agenda lay dormant for many more decades. Federal and state governments gradually increased their efforts to protect health and safety, but they did so mainly by issuing rules and imposing penalties.[2]

Now that is changing. In recent years the use of government authority to command the disclosure of information has taken a legitimate place beside the authority to set standards and redistribute resources as a means of reducing social as well as financial risks. Since the mid-1980s Congress and state legislatures have approved scores of laws that require systematic disclosure by corporations and other large organizations of risks they create to the public. They aim to prevent deaths and injuries from toxic chemicals, drinking water contaminants, overconsumption of fat, medical errors, and many other perils in everyday life simply by mandating that companies reveal detailed information about their contribution to those risks.

These measures employ publicity in the way that Brandeis envisioned: not as a one-time spur to action but as a means of creating continuing economic and political pressure for change. Brandeis noted that government rules and penalties inevitably were limited in effect, whereas the potent force of publicity could be used "as a continuous remedial measure."[3] He argued that "[p]ublicity offers [a] more promising remedy . . .

which would apply automatically to railroad, public-service and industrial corporations alike."[4] Like the established financial disclosure laws, new systems of social disclosure require organizations to produce standardized factual information at regular intervals, and they identify companies, facilities, or products that are sources of risk. Just as investors have long compared companies' earnings, travelers can compare airline safety records, shoppers can compare the healthfulness of cereals and canned soups, and community residents can compare toxic releases from nearby factories.

New disclosure systems follow another Brandeis precept. He emphasized that the way information was communicated was as important as its substance. It was crucial that disclosure be made directly to investors or purchasers in a format that they could understand. "It will not suffice to require merely the filing of a statement" of commissions and fees with the government, just as it would not suffice to file a statement of food ingredients with a government department. "To be effective, knowledge of the facts must be actually brought home . . . and this can best be done by requiring the facts to be stated in good, large type in every notice, circular, letter and advertisement."[5] Instead of collecting information for the government to use in making rules, these systems have followed populist and progressive tenets. They have placed in the hands of a public that is increasingly distrustful of giant corporations and their influence on the political process a means of directly applying political and economic pressure for change.

Yet the sudden prominence of the second half of Brandeis's agenda is also puzzling for several reasons. First, disclosure programs have become mainstream policy in the United States without the guidance of any central plan. Separate initiatives have percolated up through the legislative process as pragmatic approaches to diverse problems during a time characterized by regulatory retrenchment and frequent policy stalemate. Second, it is hard to imagine what forces would cause large and powerful corporations to willingly give up substantial amounts of proprietary information or empower opponents to overcome their resistance. Revealing risks affects one of the most valuable assets of any organization: its reputation. Finally, it is odd that these policy initiatives have attracted so little attention. Commercial appropriation of information about individuals has become an increasingly contentious privacy issue, as retailers, banks, and health care providers strive to learn more about their customers. The reverse phenomenon—public appropriation of unprecedented amounts of commercial information—has barely been noticed.

Surprisingly, giving ordinary citizens systematic factual information about health and safety risks in their everyday lives has never before been a dominant theme of U.S. policy. Government rules and economic incentives have been framed mainly through debates among experts. In principle, the public has a right to much of the information that has been collected from factories, neighborhood businesses, and other community institutions to inform these mandates. But in practice, most of it has made a one-way trip to Washington or state capitals, where it has remained scattered in government files.

Many deaths and injuries have occurred in situations where facts known by company executives and small groups of experts were not communicated to individuals at risk.[6] Experts know that people who live in some neighborhoods are more vulnerable than others to risks associated with exposure to toxic pollution. Yet, until recently, no public source of information gave residents the facts to compare those health hazards. Experts know that some workplaces have much higher rates of accident or chemical contamination than others. Yet no public source of information warns prospective employees about the character and seriousness of those risks. And experts know that some hospitals are many times safer than others. Yet no public source of information tells prospective patients which nearby facility is more likely to perform surgery or administer chemotherapy without serious errors.

In the last decade, government by disclosure has emerged as a third wave of modern risk regulation.[7] Health and safety regulation in the 1960s and 1970s, a time of optimism about the capacity of government, emphasized rules and penalties, creating pressures for improvement through collective action. Regulation in the 1980s, a time of unusual optimism about market mechanisms, embraced taxes, subsidies, and trading systems (government-created markets) to further national priorities. It is not surprising, then, that regulation in the late 1980s and 1990s, a time of optimism about enormous advances in communication and information technology, produced an unprecedented array of disclosure systems.[8]

Now, advances in computer power and the growth of the Internet are transforming disclosure into a new kind of technopopulism. Acceptable levels of societal risk are established by the actions of millions of ordinary citizens, armed with factual information made accessible by the World Wide Web, instead of by legislative deliberations. The Internet has enhanced the power of disclosure by shattering a seemingly immutable law of communication: in-depth information about risks could be shared among experts; only superficial information could be shared with broad audiences. Trade-offs were inevitable between the richness of information and its reach.[9] The Internet has provided easy and fast access to layers of information that might influence economic choices or spur collective action. It has fostered integration of data from many sources to produce a more comprehensive picture of relative risks. It has created the potential for diverse users to customize information to serve their particular needs. Five years after the American public began seeking information on the web, users could quickly survey environmental problems in their neighborhoods, violations of labor laws by specific companies, or safety records of specific airlines in as little or as much detail as they chose.

However, the sudden multitude of efforts to employ transparency as an agent of social change has also shed light on the formidable challenges involved in constructing systems that work. Disclosure is inevitably a product of political compromise. Public access to information often conflicts with protection of trade secrets, personal privacy, national security, or powerful political interests. As a result, some systems define risks too narrowly, apply inappropriate metrics, or require disclosure from only a limited number of sources. Others fail to communicate effectively or lack mechanisms that encourage adaptation to market changes.

Flaws matter because disclosure can increase as well as decrease risks. If revelations are distorted, incomplete, or misunderstood, they can misinform, mislead, or cause unwarranted panic. If most facts are already known or reliable data are unobtainable, disclosure can waste public and private resources. If health risks are minor, it can draw undue attention to problems that do not warrant such scrutiny. If risks are immediate and serious, banning products or outlawing practices may be more appropriate. To be effective as an instrument of public policy, transparency requires careful design and continuing oversight.

Flaws are also important because the United States promotes transparency as a core value. Maintaining its credibility means not only patrolling the boundaries of official secrecy but also assuring that claims of transparency are legitimate. In the Oxford Amnesty lecture in 1999, Joseph Stiglitz, then chief economist of the World Bank, underscored the importance of such legitimacy: "[I]f we are truly to set an example for the rest of the world, we must confront our own issues of transparency and openness head on."[10] Disclosure systems that miss the mark create perverse results and reduce trust in government not only at home but also abroad. The sudden collapse of Enron, the nation's largest energy trader, provided a case in point. The crisis it sparked in December 2001 may ultimately be remembered as a constructive midcourse correction in the financial disclosure system. But its immediate impact was to shake the public's trust in the legitimacy of government-mandated transparency. It not only led federal regulators, members of Congress, and institutional purchasers to demand more accurate disclosure but also undermined foreign confidence in U.S. securities.

Some of the conflicts inherent in using public disclosure to reduce risks were placed in bold relief by responses to the terrorist attacks of September 11, 2001. Officials quickly dismantled user-friendly disclosure systems on government websites. They censored information designed to tell community residents about risks from nearby chemical factories; maps that identified the location of pipelines carrying oil, gas and hazardous substances; and reports about risks associated with nuclear power plants. The importance of providing public access to information about everyday risks clashed with the importance of keeping that information away from terrorists. Whether temporary measures would grow into a longer-term shift in the balance between openness and national security remained uncertain.

Emerging systems of social disclosure provide laboratories for understanding and improving the role of transparency in public policy. Each has been designed as a pragmatic response to a pressing problem. All remain works in progress. Together, they offer an opportunity to understand the scope, unique characteristics, origins, and problems associated with this promising policy tool.

Reducing Social Risks

The scope of government-mandated disclosure systems has proven remarkably broad. They have addressed risks from *products* or man-made structures; manufacturing or other *processes*; and errors, accidents, crimes and other *unanticipated events*.[11] While the list that follows is not meant to be exhaustive, the point should be clear: once viewed as an underpinning for government rules or as a public right, information is now employed by public authorities in a wide variety of situations as an instrument of social change.

Reducing Risks from Products

New laws require companies to disclose risks associated with consumer products and residential structures. In the summer of 2000 mounting evidence indicated that more than 100 people had died in automobile accidents in the 1990s, due to a combination of sudden tread separation on specific models of Firestone tires and an apparent tendency of Ford Explorers and other sport utility vehicles to roll over. In response, federal regulators proposed new tire labeling to improve safety and a warning system for tire underinflation on new models.[12] They also expedited a rating system of one to five stars that measured the likelihood of rollovers when drivers lost control. Models with one star had a risk of rollover greater than 40 percent, while those awarded five stars had a risk of less than 10 percent. Safety implications were significant, since rollovers accounted for more than 10,000 fatalities in 1999, more than side and rear collisions combined.[13]

The same year, the Federal Communications Commission responded to the growing fears of cell phone users that radio waves emitted by the phones might be associated with brain cancer. Under pressure from members of Congress and the General Accounting Office, regulators posted on the agency's website amounts of radiation absorbed from each phone model.[14]

After reports indicated that lead poisoning had harmed the health of as many as 3 million children, Congress searched for ways to create incentives for minimizing risks. A new law approved in 1992 required that sellers, landlords, and realtors disclose known lead-based paint hazards when housing was sold or leased.[15]

New laws also established disclosure systems to reduce risks from food and drinking water. In addition to requiring nutritional labeling to reduce risks of chronic disease in 1990, Congress responded to persistent fears about the health effects of pesticide residues in foods. New regulations finalized in 2000 standardized labeling of organic fruits and vegetables so shoppers could make their own judgments about their relative safety. In 1996 Congress required that the nation's 55,000 public water systems send their customers annual "consumer confidence reports" that listed all detectable amounts of contaminants. Three years earlier, cryptosporidium, a microbe from animal waste, invaded the water supply of Milwaukee, Wisconsin. More than 400,000 people got sick, 4,400 went to the hospital, and more than 50 died. Scores of less serious incidents in the 1990s shook the public's confidence in their water supply. The new reports disclosed contaminants even in small amounts that did not violate any state or federal law. The first reports were sent to customers in October 1999.[16]

Reducing Risks from Processes

New disclosure systems also focused on ways in which food, clothing, and other familiar items were produced. Growing public concern about food safety has led regulators to consider requiring revelations about food processes as well as contents. In 2001 surveys showed that most Americans were worried about the effects of adding genes from other organisms to familiar foods. Pressure built for labeling foods that contained ingredients derived from genetically modified organisms, even if the foods themselves were chemically identical to earlier versions. (The European Union adopted such a labeling provision in 1998.)

Responding to allegations in 1996 that "sweatshops" in the United States and abroad supplied merchandise to major fashion houses like Donna Karan and Ralph Lauren, regulators employed disclosure strategies to improve working conditions. Officials at the U.S. Department of Labor established a "trendsetter list" of companies that maintained high standards and encouraged retailers to release supplier information. National rules adopted in the mid-1980s already required employers to label known hazards in the workplace and provide detailed explanations of health problems associated with them to employees.[17]

In addition to the federal requirement that manufacturers reveal toxic releases from industrial processes, Massachusetts, New Jersey, and other states constructed their own mandates that manufacturers disclose amounts of toxic substances used in production or released into the environment.[18] In 1985 California voters approved Proposition 65, a ballot initiative that required anyone who exposed members of the public to carcinogens or reproductive toxins to issue a clear and reasonable warning unless they could demonstrate that the risk created was not significant.[19]

Reducing Risks from Unanticipated Events

A third cluster of requirements aimed to improve safety by creating incentives to minimize errors or other unanticipated events. Congress required commercial airlines to disclose serious safety incidents, which were then investigated by the National Transportation Safety Board.[20] Another federal requirement encouraged more limited sharing of information by pilots, flight attendants, mechanics, and others about near misses or minor problems for the purpose of uncovering patterns of errors that could be corrected before they caused serious harm.[21]

To reduce accidents on the job, Congress required companies to maintain records of workers' injuries and illnesses and make them available to government inspectors for use in government surveys and by employees themselves.[22] Congress also created requirements that manufacturers of prescription drugs and medical devices disclose deaths and injuries in standardized form.[23]

Improving Service Quality and Reducing Corruption

Disclosure systems have been constructed not only to reduce risks but also to improve the quality of services and reduce corruption. Congress required commercial airlines to reveal late arrivals and baggage-handling errors to create incentives for improved service.[24] After incidents in which planeloads of passengers were kept waiting on runways for hours, congressional leaders proposed a broader "passenger bill of rights" that would require standardized disclosure of reasons for flight delays or cancellations and information regarding ticket-pricing practices.[25]

To help ensure that customers received fair treatment from lending institutions, Congress required banks, savings and loans, and credit unions to disclose the geographical distribution of their loans and investments. Such disclosure was intended to reduce "red-lining" and other forms of racial or gender discrimination.[26]

Broadening requirements first adopted in the 1970s to limit the influence of special interests in political campaigns, Congress voted in July 2000 to require disclosure of campaign contributions by certain nonprofit organizations. Some legislators advocated going further, replacing government rules altogether with a "deregulate and disclose" strategy.[27]

Disclosure Differs from Other Forms of Regulation

Disclosure strategies differ from traditional government standards and financial incentives in at least three fundamental ways. First, they aim to establish levels of acceptable risk by means of public pressure rather than deliberation. Government standards specify acceptable design or performance by legislative and regulatory processes. Economic incentives specify a legislated price or quantity of acceptable risk. Disclosure, however, influences risk through the countless actions of consumers, suppliers, employees, investors, community residents, and voters that alter organizations' decisions. Only the scope and character of information about pollution or errors are set legislatively. Gaining prominence during the 1990s, when public distrust of political processes was high, these systems, like the financial disclosure mechanism adopted in the 1930s, reflected a desire to skirt legislative processes to empower ordinary citizens.

Second, they employ communication as a regulatory mechanism. Government standards rely on rules and the threat of sanctions to encourage organizations to reduce risks. Taxes, subsidies, and other economic incentives rely on the prospect of financial loss or gain. Information strategies, by contrast, depend on improving understanding in ways that lead to changed purchasing, investing, or employment, or collective action. Placing new data in the public domain is itself intended to produce changes in markets or politics in ways that ultimately reduce risks.

Finally, most of these systems extend the reach of government. They generally seek to influence activities beyond those that are the targets of government rules, taxes, and subsidies and they create the potential for impacts that are not circumscribed by state or national boundaries. Information required in one jurisdiction becomes available everywhere, unimpeded by political or geographical barriers.

The Roots of Democracy by Disclosure

Disclosure systems that aim to reduce risks have been products of expediency and frustration. Legislators have required organizations to reveal information to produce pragmatic compromises, correct market flaws, overcome perceived shortcomings of conventional regulation, and affirm core values.

Responding to Political Stalemate and Changing Agendas

During much of the 1980s and 1990s, Democrats and Republicans shared control of the White House and Congress but often differed in their approaches to risk regulation. Even when they agreed about the need for national action to address problems such as the quality of health care or the contamination of drinking water, divisions persisted about what form that action should take. In this political atmosphere, the idea of revealing information to the public sometimes provided common ground. It combined the ideas of corporate transparency and public participation often favored by Democrats with the lower cost, less intrusive, market-oriented approaches typically championed by Republicans.

It also suited changing public agendas. In the 1960s and 1970s Congress addressed high-profile risks with uniform rules. Government standards that promoted safer cars, cleaner air and water, and more effective drugs commanded broad support. By the 1980s and 1990s, however, public concern focused increasingly on risks that were less familiar and more variable in their impact. Consumption of processed foods influenced the risk of heart disease, cancer, and other chronic ailments in ways that were specific to individuals. Moderate levels of contaminants in drinking water created health problems for some people but not others. A shifting public agenda called for new regulatory tools.

Reducing Market Flaws

Disclosure also promised to correct market flaws. A generation of economists gradually abandoned the classical assumption that markets would
produce needed information. Instead, they explored the ways in which the
absence of information affected social and economic outcomes. Corporations and other organizations that had knowledge of facts of interest to
customers, employees, or investors often failed to produce them, due to
cost or possible impact on liability, competition, or reputation. Individuals who would benefit from additional information often did not collect it.
The result could be persistent information asymmetries. Companies may
have understood the public risks they were creating; customers, employees, and investors often did not.[28] Such disparities not only could increase
risks, they could stifle innovation. Information gaps could prevent firms
from being rewarded for new and healthier products and services. They
could perpetuate markets for low-quality or defective products, a theme
developed by economist George Akerlof in his renowned essay, "The Market for Lemons, Quality Uncertainty and the Market Mechanism."[29]

Minimizing Endemic Problems with Risk Regulation

In addition, disclosure systems responded to growing disenchantment
with the rigidities of traditional regulation. For three decades, widely
publicized instances of regulatory failure, increasingly unmanageable
agency workloads, reductions in federal grant funds, and growth in international commerce had highlighted limitations associated with strict standards. Optimism about the corrective power of government rules gave
way to pervasive concern about their shortcomings. Economic hard times
in the late 1970s and early 1980s amplified business objections to their
costs. Democratic president Jimmy Carter attempted to discipline the regulatory process by requiring federal agencies to justify proposed regulations and estimate their costs. Elected in 1980, Republican Ronald Reagan went further: government was not the solution to the nation's health,
safety, and environmental problems; government was the problem.

Telling the public about risks provided a middle ground. For businesses, collecting, processing, and disseminating information often seemed
simple compared to submitting to new government rules. For govern-

ment, it was viewed as less contentious and easier to administer. Legislators needed to decide only what information people needed, not what level of protection was appropriate. Proponents argued that such requirements were largely self-enforcing, with information about polluters and consumer products substituting for squads of government inspectors.

Following Earlier Examples

The idea of requiring that the public be informed about risks as a means of reducing them also drew strength from historic precedent. When Congress adopted disclosure requirements to reduce financial risks seventy years earlier, no public or private organization defined accounting standards and only one-quarter of the firms listed on the New York Stock Exchange provided investors with quarterly or annual reports. Investigations revealed a network of deceptive practices. Insiders bought stock at preferred prices, managers hid liabilities, and owners made secret deals.[30] When President Franklin D. Roosevelt endorsed public disclosure, he and his advisers understood that it would transform American capitalism. What was at stake, declared one adviser, was "whether the elements of power . . . now tied to finance remain in the hands of the financial group or whether they pass . . . into the hands of the community."[31]

The Securities Act of 1933 and the Securities and Exchange Act of 1934 required companies that sold stocks to the public to disclose, in standardized form and at regular intervals, detailed information about their officers and financial practices and gave the government new authority to set accounting standards. They made corporate officers and directors, as well as outside accountants and investment bankers, liable for untrue statements or omissions of material fact. An extraordinary crisis had made possible an extraordinary transfer of previously proprietary information to the public domain. In the words of Joel Seligman, a leading historian of securities regulation, the early days of the Roosevelt administration were a rare time "when money talked and nobody listened."[32]

Starting with a narrow scope and relatively primitive metrics, that system gained credibility. Its scope broadened and its measures became more accurate. Changing markets and technology as well as searches by target companies for loopholes in existing rules led to crises that improved disclosure.

Even earlier, in the first decade of the twentieth century, Congress employed public disclosure to improve food safety. Sensational revelations by muckraking journalists created a demand for better information. In *The Jungle,* novelist Upton Sinclair had described sausage making in the Chicago stockyards: "There was never the least attention paid to what was cut up for sausage. . . . There would be meat stored in great piles . . . and thousands of rats would race about on it. . . . A man could run his hand over these piles of meat and sweep off handfuls of the dried dung of rats."[33] The same year *The Jungle* was published, Congress passed the Pure Food and Drug Act of 1906 to require accurate labeling of packaged foods shipped in interstate commerce.

Later, health, safety, and environmental laws occasionally added disclosure requirements to national standards. For example, in 1966 the National Highway and Traffic Safety Act required that automobile manufacturers provide purchasers with standardized information concerning the crashworthiness of the new models.[34] In 1969 the National Environmental Policy Act directed federal agencies to tell the public about environmental consequences of major federal actions.[35] In 1973 the Food and Drug Administration required nutritional labeling whenever food manufacturers added nutrients or made nutritional claims.[36] In 1975 the Energy Policy and Conservation Act mandated energy efficiency labels on household appliances.[37] For the most part, however, members of Congress and state legislators continued to rely on design or performance standards to reduce risks.

Building on the Duty to Warn and the Right to Know

Disclosure systems were also constructed on a foundation of American common law, which had long held manufacturers responsible for warning the public about foreseeable harm from their products.[38] To this duty, Congress had added scores of statutory provisions that mandated warnings for specific products, including cigarettes and alcoholic beverages.[39]

Beginning in the 1960s, Congress and state legislatures supplemented these requirements with the idea that the public had a "right to know" about any information held by the government, including information about risks in everyday life. Reforms to protect workers and consumers from some of the harshest consequences of industrialization called on businesses to report to government agencies about working conditions, food processing, and other practices previously considered private. In the 1960s and 1970s union demands for information about workplace hazards and citizen groups' demands for information about neighborhood toxins inspired community "right-to-know" laws. The Freedom of Information Act, adopted in 1966 and amended several times, created a presumption that the public had a right to any information in the hands of executive branch agencies unless disclosure threatened national security, personal privacy, or other specified interests. A 1996 amendment required that new records be available electronically within a year of their creation and that agencies establish electronic reading rooms to make frequently sought records generally available on the Internet.[40]

As a practical means of providing ordinary citizens with useful information, both duty-to-warn and right-to-know requirements proved quite limited, however. Information was fragmentary. It did not help users compare products, rank risks, or judge their own exposure. Also, facts were accessible in principle but could be difficult to obtain in practice. Under the Freedom of Information Act, people had to request information piece by piece, meaning that knowledge of its existence and location was usually necessary, and they often had to wait months or years for results. For many potential users, bureaucracy and secrecy became synonymous.

New disclosure systems differed from these earlier right-to-know requirements in several respects. First, they collected information primarily to inform the public. Most right-to-know requirements had simply passed on information collected primarily to inform government actions. Second, disclosure systems served regulatory rather than normative purposes. Information was viewed as a way to change behavior, not simply as a public right. Format, timeliness, and completeness of data therefore became critical issues. Third, the new disclosure systems held creators of risks accountable. Instead of reports aggregated by industry or geographical area, the public received information about named facilities, companies, and products.

This book explores the puzzles and potential of democracy by disclosure. It sounds a cautionary note. Disclosure systems resonate with current efforts to improve public participation in government, correct market flaws due to information asymmetries, and reap the benefits of information technology. These perspectives emphasize the promise of such systems. This book aims to add another, more skeptical dimension to our understanding of their workings. Disclosure systems are inevitably products of the political process. They result from compromises that reconcile competing values and interests. Universally acclaimed in principle, disclosure often conflicts with protection of trade secrets, personal privacy, minimization of regulatory burdens, and guarding of national security. Compromises among such values can lead to fragmentation, distorted incentives, and excessive costs. In practice, communication, too, is complicated not only by political imperatives but also by cognitive distortions and the self-interested motivations of intermediaries who add their own interpretations. Like financial disclosure, social disclosure is a simple idea that has proven extraordinarily complicated in practice.

The book's scope is limited. It focuses on the most ambitious of the new disclosure systems, those that aim to reduce health, safety, and environmental risks. It does not examine in detail the many systems constructed to improve services or reduce corruption. Its focus is also limited to government-required disclosure. The scores of voluntary certification and report card systems initiated in recent years by trade associations, consumer groups, and companies themselves deserve separate attention. Their politics and mechanics differ in fundamental ways from disclosure systems that start with a public mandate. The book's focus is also limited to an examination of disclosure policies in the United States. Developing countries have begun to employ disclosure systems as alternatives to conventional health and safety standards, and international organizations have begun to employ them as alternatives to sanctions. However, the dynamics of those systems also deserve separate analysis.

I have chosen to explore this new and varied policy terrain by constructing detailed profiles of three of the most important new disclosure systems, those that make public toxic releases, nutrients in processed foods, and medical errors. Profiles are useful mechanisms that permit readers to follow unfolding events, observe the interaction of political and economic forces, and appreciate the influence of individuals and the role of serendipity in the development of new policies. They are well suited to capture the nuances of conflicts among values and interests and provide a sense of how those issues influence the design and evolution of particular strategies. Profiles also provide a context for understanding obstacles to effective communication, the emerging role of information technology, and complexities involved in evaluating the effectiveness of government by disclosure. They encourage readers to examine the evidence and construct their own interpretations of unfolding events. These systems are dynamic. They evolve as political and economic forces change and interact.

I have chosen these profiles to illustrate the breadth and versatility of regulation by disclosure. One addresses risks from industrial processes. A second addresses risks from consumer products. A third addresses risks from systematic errors that occur when humans and technology interact. One system influences companies' practices mainly through political pressures. A second works mainly through economic pressures. A third invokes both. The profiles also illustrate the growing sophistication of this regulatory mechanism. Disclosure of toxic chemicals—an evolutionary bridge between the idea of information as a public right and information as a means of reducing risks—took effect in 1988. Six years later a much more nuanced and explicitly regulatory system of nutritional labeling became law. Six years after that a particularly innovative effort to employ two-tier disclosure to reduce medical errors struggled for acceptance. Finally, each of these systems represents an important policy development in its own right. Each addresses what is perceived as a major societal problem and introduces innovative ways of approaching it. Each continues to be viewed as an important national initiative.

These studies are arranged in chronological sequence to highlight the evolution of this policy tool. Chapter 2 profiles the creation of one of the earliest and most important of the new disclosure programs. After a disastrous leak from a pesticide plant in Bhopal, India, in 1984 killed more than 2,000 people, Congress required U.S. manufacturers to begin revealing annually the amounts of dangerous chemicals they released into the environment, factory by factory and chemical by chemical. The profile traces the system's tumultuous course. Initially adopted as a right-to-know requirement, it was later recognized as one of the nation's most successful environmental regulations and was widely credited with encouraging target companies to cut toxic releases by nearly 50 percent in ten years. But from serendipitous beginnings, it produced clashes among values and interests that narrowed disclosure and compromised the accuracy and completeness of reporting. Initially, new information produced welcome surprises. Government officials and environmental groups were amazed when the first round of revelations prompted some corporate executives to promise to eliminate as much as 90 percent of toxic air releases. Next, disclosure produced disappointments, as design defects contributed to public misunderstanding. Soon, though, it benefited from new and remarkable applications of information technology, which showed promise for repairing some of its earlier defects. Finally, as those applications gained momentum, they produced new and forceful efforts by industry to rein in disclosure efforts on the web.

Chapter 3 profiles what is probably the nation's most familiar disclosure system. Every day Americans encounter Congress's effort to reduce risks of heart disease and cancer through nutritional labeling. Since 1994 makers of processed foods have been required to list nutrients in government-designed panels on each box of cereal and can of soup. In some respects, nutritional labeling represented a polar opposite of the disclosure system for toxic chemicals. It concerned valued features of widely used consumer products instead of wastes from little known manufacturing processes. It relied on company-produced labels instead of government-produced reports. It influenced companies' practices through markets rather than collective action. Nutritional labeling also illustrated the evolution of disclosure requirements and their growing sophistication. Unlike the system of toxic disclosure, which listed releases only in total pounds, nutritional labeling included a remarkable effort to calibrate amounts of fat, salt, and other nutrients to risks by recommending daily allowances. Despite these differences, the two systems had much in common. Both were characterized by government-mandated disclosure of standardized information that aimed to reduce risks to the public. Both produced battles over the need for accuracy and completeness of information versus the need to minimize regulatory burdens and the benefits of federal uniformity versus state discretion. In both instances, the architecture of disclosure pieced together by Congress limited the system's usefulness to the public.

The final profile points to the future. Six years after food companies adopted nutritional labels, the Clinton administration and leading members of Congress recommended a major new disclosure system to reduce another serious risk to public health. The Institute of Medicine shocked the nation by reporting that medical errors in hospitals killed between 44,000 and 98,000 Americans a year. Instead of new rules and penalties, the institute recommended that hospitals disclose serious errors to the public to increase pressures for safety and share information about minor errors with a narrower audience to inform management improvements. Drawing on experience with information strategies designed to improve aviation and worker safety, the institute proposed construction of two tiers of disclosure to these varied audiences, linked this system to means of reducing patterns of errors, and outlined the use of computers and the Internet that would make it work. Like the systems aimed at reducing toxic risks and chronic diseases, however, this optimistic federal plan met with political obstacles that altered its character, blocked efforts to provide patients with information needed to make informed choices, and reduced chances of effectiveness.

A concluding chapter draws together the experience of these three systems to suggest answers to puzzling questions. Can such a wide variety of separately conceived requirements be considered a cohesive policy innovation? New forms of government action are rare in the United States. Bureaucratic resistance to change, public resistance to new exercise of authority, and the complexities of deliberation create substantial obstacles. Do these policies, which have emerged without central direction or coordination, signal an important change in governance?[41]

How could a time of regulatory retrenchment and stalemate produce such innovation? The 1980s, which began and ended with economic recessions, were conservative years in U.S. domestic policy. Elected in 1980, Ronald Reagan elevated business opposition to burdensome health, safety, and environmental regulation to a dominant theme in domestic policy. In the 1990s few new regulatory laws gained support from the Republicans and Democrats who shared control of Congress.

Even more perplexing, why would major corporations and other organizations give up large amounts of previously proprietary information about activities likely to place them in an unfavorable light? Corporate managers usually have not been eager to tell the public about their contributions to societal risks. If they opposed disclosure, what coalitions proved strong enough to counter their influence?

Finally, as information technology continues to gain power, what is the future of technopopulism? At a time when there is growing concern about the shortcomings of conventional regulation, disclosure enhanced by technology represents a domain of potential strength. It creates an opportunity to place government's enduring power to command the dissemination of information in the service of public goals that are widely shared. Congress and state legislatures have channeled prevailing currents of frustration and expediency into new forms of political action.

One can imagine a rosy future. In a few years, homebuyers might routinely rely on simple digital maps to pinpoint neighborhood sources of risks ranging from crime to toxic pollution. Websites might post real-time information about levels of lead, arsenic, and microbes in drinking water, color-coding health concerns for children, the elderly, or people suffering from AIDS. Job hunters could be armed with comparisons of hazards at factories or offices, including risks posed by indoor air pollution, which scientists consider a more serious health threat to most Americans than outdoor pollution. Shoppers might quickly compare the accident rates of toys or lawn mowers as well as their prices. People shopping online might use personalized "shopbots" to consider only items that meet their personal health, safety, or environmental criteria. In groceries, familiar barcodes could link information about benefits of new disease-fighting foods with each customer's medical profile, displaying results on handheld devices. Today's piecemeal disclosure might grow into a web of reliable information about risk.

But obstacles remain formidable. Disclosure may be distorted by efforts to protect trade secrets, personal privacy, or national security. Powerful interests may truncate its scope, targets, or metrics. Like other forms of regulation, it may attract too much attention to minor problems; fail to adapt to changing markets, science, or public priorities; be weakened by a lack of resources; or become obsolete. Cognitive distortions and manipulation of data by intermediaries may subvert its goals. Whether legislated transparency ultimately becomes an effective means of reducing risks will depend on better understanding and political will.

2 Accounting for Toxic Pollution

*The public has spoken, and it's unmistakable they will no
longer tolerate toxic emissions. Might as well get on with it.*
—RICHARD J. MAHONEY*

O n June 30, 1988, Richard J. Mahoney, head of the
giant Monsanto Corporation, sent his managers a
short memo that caused consternation among the company's executives, amazed government regulators, created
national headlines, and set in motion events that initiated a
new kind of environmental policy. The memo announced
that the company would eliminate 90 percent of its toxic
air pollution in less than five years and "[w]hen we reach
that target, we will then continue to work towards the ulti-
mate goal of zero emissions. . . . We have technology in
hand to achieve a portion of the 1992 target. The rest must
come from as yet undeveloped technologies—which we
intend to find and put into practice."[1] As the maker of the
popular Roundup herbicide and NutraSweet sweetener, a
large producer of pharmaceuticals, and a major chemical
company, Monsanto used hundreds of toxic chemicals in
its operations. Regulators had worked for more than a
decade to reduce the toxic pollution caused by companies

*Richard J. Mahoney, *Newsweek*, July 24, 1989, p. 28.

like Monsanto, through minimum standards, penalties, and enforcement actions. The idea that Monsanto's toxic air pollution could be virtually eliminated overnight was unfathomable to government officials, members of the public—and Monsanto's managers.

More surprising, Mahoney's memo was not the usual grudging compliance with federal rules. Instead, it was an astounding response to the government's use of a different kind of power—the power of information. In an obscure section of a law passed two years earlier, Congress simply required manufacturers to disclose "by computer telecommunications and other means" how many pounds of toxic chemicals they released to the air, water, or land, chemical by chemical and facility by facility.[2] Enacted with little fanfare in the aftermath of a tragic release of poisonous fumes at a Union Carbide plant in Bhopal, India, that killed 2,000 people, it was designed to tell the American people for the first time something about the toxic chemicals routinely discharged into their communities.

A few days before he sent the memo, Mahoney himself had been shocked. His staff brought him a report that showed that in 1987 Monsanto released 374 million pounds of toxic chemicals to the air, water, and land. "I was astounded by the magnitude of the numbers," Mahoney recalled later. "I called in Hal Corbet, our vice president for environment, and told him that when I released the numbers I was going to announce that toxic emissions would be reduced 90 percent by 1992. He said we didn't have a clue about how to do that and suggested 50 percent. I said no, the number has got to have a nine in front of it."[3]

The reason for Mahoney's amazement was that the numbers had never been added up before. Managers focused on production and sales figures. Data about toxic pollution subject to various government permits were collected, as required by law, but each kind of permit used a different measure and the information could not easily be combined. Now suddenly Congress had required that such waste be accounted for by chemical, facility, and company; disclosed to the public; and certified by a senior executive. When Mahoney sent out his memo, Monsanto's first report was due in Washington the next day.

Mahoney responded the way he did because public access to information about the company's toxic discharges threatened one of Monsanto's most important assets—its reputation. Publicity about toxic releases—whether justified or not—could damage the company's image. A negative reaction by employees, customers, investors, or the public could hurt business. "We don't think our emissions represent any hazard," he said at the time. "But the public has spoken, and it's unmistakable they will no longer tolerate toxic emissions. Might as well get on with it."[4] Mahoney's immediate goal was simple. As he put it later: "I wanted to get off the list."[5] He began to refer facetiously to Monsanto as "a public affairs organization that makes products on the side."[6]

Other large companies were jolted into action. Executives of IBM, AT&T, Upjohn, Union Carbide, Dow Chemical, Texaco, Hoffman LaRoche, and dozens of others also attempted to make the best of a bad situation by promising large reductions. Many held meetings with community residents and offered plant tours for the first time.[7]

When national totals were released a few months later, showing that 7 billion pounds of 328 toxic chemicals were released into the environment in 1987, the response was immediate. *USA Today* ran a three-part series that highlighted companies and counties with the largest volumes of emissions. Local papers followed with multipart series. Government officials were shocked that the numbers were so large. Members of Congress and state legislators demanded new laws to crack down on toxic pollution.

Mahoney's plan worked, however. Monsanto's toxic releases were reported in the context of his pledge. He recalled later that "I got more publicity for that than for anything else I did at Monsanto."[8] What the company gained, he believed, was a national reputation for responsibility that brought large if immeasurable benefits in improved relations with regulators, employees, and community residents. In 1992 Mahoney announced that Monsanto had met its goal—toxic air emissions were reduced to one-tenth the level reported for 1988, at a cost Mahoney estimated at $100 million. He put senior people in charge of the effort, set targets for plants, encouraged community meetings, personally tracked progress, and haggled with government officials about taking some relatively benign chemicals off the list. If targets could not be met, the company sold or shut down plants or moved some production elsewhere, an effort made easier by the fact that the company was already in the midst of an effort to diversify its business.[9]

To casual observers, the publicity that accompanied this new public access to information looked like any other exposé about industry pollution. But to those watching closely, it was clear that the role of information in public life had suddenly changed. David Sarokin, who was one of the pioneers in efforts to gather data about industry's use of toxic chemicals and who later helped lead the government's disclosure program, wrote in 1991 that information "has itself become an instrument of policy. Access to information has expanded the concept and practice of democracy by promoting greater public accountability."[10]

A decade later, the power ascribed to disclosure had reached mythic proportions. A requirement that simply granted the public access to information was called one of the most effective environmental policies ever enacted. What began as a right-to-know initiative was credited with regulatory success: reported toxic releases plummeted by 45.5 percent in eleven years.[11] Public access to information became a priority in a national environmental program in which it was once viewed as a distraction. The idea was widely copied by states and other countries. Enhanced by computers and the Internet, the new disclosure system provided customized information by factory, chemical, and county at the click of a mouse. With politicians in the United States and elsewhere calling for greater transparency in business and government and criticizing conventional regulation as costly and ineffective, it became a model for addressing intractable health and safety problems.

In fact, however, this disclosure system provided a cautionary tale. The law's provisions were cut and pasted en route to approval in ways that uncoupled them from issues of risk. Congress limited targeted companies and chemicals, allowed reporting of data that were out of date and of questionable accuracy, and failed to factor in human exposure and chemicals' relative toxicity. After more than a decade of expansive claims, it remained impossible to tell whether the requirement had contributed to public health.

A Tragic Call to Action

In the early morning hours of December 3, 1984, a deadly cloud of methyl isocyanate gas drifted over a cluster of makeshift dwellings around a pesticide plant in Bhopal, India. Some people ran into the streets, choking. Others never made it out of bed. In minutes, 25 tons of toxic gas leaking from a ruptured storage tank killed at least 2,000 people and injured 100,000 more. The media called it history's worst industrial disaster.[12]

The accident was a tragic combination of systematic problems and chance events. The factory's safety problems were well known. Unusually large storage tanks for methyl isocyanate were reportedly overfilled, despite the chemical's known danger. Employees may not have been informed about dangers or what to do in case of an accident, despite previous problems. At least four accidental releases of methyl isocyanate or phosgene, also a toxic gas, had occurred at the plant in the previous three years. Rajkumar Keswani, a local journalist, had been writing articles about the plant's dangers since 1982. A Union Carbide safety audit that year also had warned of persistent safety problems.[13]

At about 11 p.m. on December 2 an unlikely series of events occurred. As reported by Stuart Diamond of the *New York Times,* who traveled to Bhopal to piece together the details of the accident, contamination caused a chemical reaction in one of the big tanks. It produced heat and increased pressure that was not noticed until nearly the time when the tank ruptured. A refrigeration unit designed to control such heat did not work. Instruments gave unreliable readings. An alarm that sounded may not have been understood by residents as an emergency warning. Evacuation plans were not put into effect and hospitals were not told of the character of the toxic chemical. By 2:30 a.m., when the gas stopped leaking, people who lived nearby were already dead.

The human tragedy quickly became a disaster for the company and local government officials. The chief minister of the state of Madhya Pradesh, of which Bhopal was the capital, brought criminal charges against the parent company, its Indian subsidiary, the factory manager, and his assistant. Several local officials resigned. As news of the disaster spread via television, radio, and front-page headlines, major chemical companies around the world announced plans to reassess safety practices. The World Bank announced that it would start work on new hazard-prevention guidelines on projects it sponsored. The U.S. Agency for International Development launched "project aftermath" to assess plans to deal with hazards in forty countries. Eventually, Union Carbide settled claims stemming from the incident with a payment of $470 million to the government of India.

In the United States the tragedy quickly became linked to growing public fears about toxic chemicals. In the late 1970s medical research had suggested associations between exposure to chemicals in wide use and some cancers. Eight months after the events in Bhopal, an accident at a pesticide plant also owned by Union Carbide, in Institute, West Virginia, caused the release of aldicarb oxime and other toxic gases, injuring 135 people. After that, reports of chemical accidents seemed to be everywhere. The Environmental Protection Agency (EPA) assembled a partial list of recent chemical accidents in the United States that was widely publicized. They totaled 6,928 since 1980, caused 139 deaths, nearly 1,500 injuries, and evacuation of nearly 200,000 people. A chlorine cloud accidentally released from a DuPont plant reportedly resulted in 76 injuries and 1 death at a crowded football stadium a mile away. A pesticide leak injured 161 people in New Jersey. Three people were killed in a nitric acid explosion in Mississippi. A report by the Congressional Research Service estimated that 75 percent of Americans lived in metropolitan areas where plants manufactured chemicals or related products.[14] The isolated incident in a remote town in India now seemed to be part of a pattern that also threatened communities in the United States. Speaking on the Senate floor, Sen. Frank R. Lautenberg, a Democrat from New Jersey, where chemical manufacturing was a major business, framed the troubling question: "Could it happen to us?"[15]

Political Forces Converge

Publicity about a distant disaster became a powerful symbol for Americans because it tapped into currents of change already under way in science, the public's growing skepticism about conventional regulation, and the idea of a "right to know" about hidden risks in everyday life. It was these forces that gave the efforts of a few members of Congress to inform the public both strength and endurance.[16]

Chemicals Produce Growing Concerns

By the mid-1980s chemicals that were contributors to unprecedented economic growth had become a source of increasing public health concern as well. The development of thousands of new synthetic compounds during the decades following World War II improved industrial efficiency and made life easier for all Americans. Annual production of synthetic organic chemicals increased fifteen-fold in forty years. Herbicides and insecticides increased agricultural yield. Medicines improved public health. Nylon, polyester, and other synthetic fabrics made clothing less expensive. Chlorine and other disinfectants provided Americans with safe drinking water despite widespread pollution of lakes and rivers. By 1986 the U.S. chemical industry, with sales of $214 billion, dominated an increasingly competitive world market.[17] The use of new and beneficial chemicals often preceded knowledge about their effects on human health or the environment, however. In 1977 the National Academy of Sciences found that only 4 percent of chemicals with annual production of 1 million pounds or more had been fully tested for chronic toxicity; 78 percent lacked any toxicity data.[18]

Two scientific advances heightened concern. In the late 1970s new developments in analytic chemistry made it possible to identify trace amounts of toxic substances in water, air, and food. At about the same time, epidemiological studies provided evidence of links between toxic chemicals and chronic diseases. In 1975 the National Cancer Institute published a national atlas of cancer mortality, showing elevated death rates in several industrialized areas. Scientists established links between cancer and asbestos, consumption of seafood contaminated with mercury and neurotoxic effects, and polychlorinated biphenyls (PCBs) and cancer in lab animals.[19]

Growing knowledge was punctuated by dramatic events. In 1962 *Silent Spring*, a best-selling book written by biologist Rachel Carson, had alerted ordinary citizens to the circuitous paths through which chemicals could cause harm to humans and animals. DDT that was sprayed on crops to limit pests ended up in rivers, human tissue, and breast milk many years later. When toxic wastes were discovered seeping into homes built atop a chemical dump in upstate New York and residents suspected an unusual incidence of cancers and other ailments, Love Canal became a powerful symbol of toxic contamination. In 1979 an accident at the Three Mile Island nuclear power plant released radioactive material into the air. In 1984 chemical companies agreed to pay Vietnam veterans $180 million for exposure to Agent Orange, a suspected carcinogen. As Congress considered disclosure of toxic chemicals, an accident at another nuclear power plant, this one in Chernobyl in the then–Soviet Union, caused thirty-one deaths and contaminated a wide area. A troubling idea gained credence. Health risks from toxic substances could be invisible, indirect, and occasionally deadly.

National Laws Fall Short of Expectations

Fear combined with frustration. More than a decade of national efforts to limit risks associated with toxic chemicals had produced limited results. In 1976 Congress gave federal regulators broad authority to gather information about new and existing chemicals, require testing, assess risks, and ban or limit the use of chemicals as needed.[20] By the mid-1980s more than a dozen national laws regulated the use, transportation, and clean-up of pesticides and other toxic chemicals in specific circumstances.

Nonetheless, seemingly simple questions remained unanswered. Regulators collected some data as part of permitting processes for air and water pollution, but total emissions of toxic chemicals for each factory and company remained unknown. There was no consensus even about what constituted a toxic chemical. Each federal environmental law had different definitions and identified a different set of substances. In the mid-1980s the National Research Council concluded that the United States still lacked any coherent national picture of the movement of key toxic chemicals.[21]

Right to Know Becomes a Political Cause

The idea that workers and community residents had a "right to know" about hazards in everyday life had gradually gained ground. Most major environmental laws authorized regulators to gather information from companies as a basis for framing and updating appropriate pollution-control standards, issuing permits, and checking on compliance. But it was rarely returned to workers or residents. Systematic disclosure simply was not a priority.

Gradually, however, information about hazards began to be seen as a right. By 1986 at least thirty-five states, sixty-five cities, and the federal government had some form of right-to-know law. In *A Citizen's Right to Know,* Susan G. Hadden traces parallel efforts by labor unions in the mid-1970s to gain access to information about workplace hazards and by environmental groups to gain access to information about community hazards. In the 1980s those campaigns merged. Philadelphia became the first city to require disclosure of information about hazardous chemicals to the public as well as to workers. Cincinnati and several California cities followed. Maryland, Massachusetts, New Jersey, and Pennsylvania also required disclosure of information about industrial hazards. California voters approved Proposition 65, which required anyone who knowingly exposed members of the public to carcinogens or reproductive toxins to issue a clear and reasonable warning unless they could demonstrate that the risk created was not significant.[22]

In practice, however, public access to information about environmental risks remained fragmentary. Federal and state laws required release of government information unless it was vital to national security, a trade secret, or specifically exempted for other reasons. But it varied in quality, could not be easily aggregated, and had to be requested piece by piece.[23]

A Chance Combination of Events Produces Change

The 1986 law that required systematic disclosure of toxic releases was a product of these broad forces but also of serendipity. The perseverance of a group of frustrated researchers, an innovative New Jersey law, and the efforts of three senators in search of a response to the Bhopal disaster provided the ingredients for what became a new disclosure policy.

For three years preceding the Bhopal incident, a small group of researchers from Inform, Inc., an environmental research organization based in New York City, had been trying to discover what chemical companies were doing to further what they said was a priority—cutting toxic pollution by reducing the use, not just the emissions, of chemicals. They set out to learn how much of which chemicals was used annually by a sample of thirty-five chemical processing plants and what happened to the waste. When they visited companies in New Jersey, Ohio, and California, however, they were surprised to find that there was no comprehensive source of information about routine releases even after more than a decade of federal regulation. "It became an impossible exercise to put the whole picture together," recalls David Sarokin, who directed the project. "Each federal program had a different way of classifying materials and of collecting information from facilities. Water permits talked about chemical oxygen demand. Air permits listed total volatile organic compounds in pounds. That doesn't tell you anything chemical by chemical. Companies generally knew as little about their waste streams as the regulators did. They were providing data that were required by law and weren't generating any information beyond that. Their people simply were not trained to pay attention to waste."[24]

By chance, Sarokin and his colleagues heard about an industrial survey conducted by the state of New Jersey that provided the information they were looking for. State officials had ordered manufacturers to report on the use and disposal of toxic chemicals facility by facility and chemical by chemical in standardized formats.[25] The survey, conducted from 1979 to 1982, gathered results of two-page questionnaires in a computer database. Designed as a research project and made possible by small grants from the federal EPA, the survey concluded that despite national and state regulation of most of the listed chemicals, "large quantities of hazardous substances are still released into New Jersey's air, land, and water."[26] "The New Jersey program cut through the programmatic issues and painted this beautiful picture," recalls Sarokin. "Suddenly we could see which chemicals were used at a plant and what ended up in the air and the rivers."[27]

Sarokin and his colleague Warren Muir took the story of their frustrating search to Washington and proposed a national survey modeled after New Jersey's program. Among those who heard their appeal was Ronald Outen, a staff member for the Senate Committee on Environment and Public Works. Outen happened to drop in on a conference held by the Conservation Foundation and caught most of Sarokin's talk. After the Bhopal disaster, Outen asked Sarokin and Muir to brief the Senate committee staff on the need for standardized disclosure. "That was a critical meeting," Outen recalls. "After that, it was a matter of dragging the proposal through the legislative maze."[28]

A bipartisan group of congressional leaders helped channel growing concern about chemical accidents into support for a federal law that required standardized disclosure of routine, intended releases of toxic chemicals. Robert Stafford, a moderate Republican from Vermont and chairman of the Senate Committee on Environment and Public Works, took the lead in fashioning a response to Bhopal. He was joined by two Democratic senators from states with particularly high levels of toxic pollution, Frank Lautenberg of New Jersey and Lloyd Bentsen of Texas. Stafford argued on the Senate floor that the public had a right to know about "deliberate releases that occur every day as well as accidental releases." Immediate action was needed: "Public concern about toxic chemicals is at an all time high. Hardly a week passes without new revelations about the dangers of chemical substances in our daily lives."[29] Outen remembers drafting what would become a proposal requiring electronic disclosure of routine releases at his dining room table. "I was vaguely aware that a thing called a modem existed but I had never used one. I really didn't have a clue about telecommunications."[30]

The Senate sponsors hitched the new disclosure requirement to a bill that set up community mechanisms to respond to chemical accidents. That bill, in turn, was coupled to a reauthorization of the Superfund law, the national program to finance the clean-up of toxic wastes. As David Sarokin put it: "Once Bhopal got the attention of Congress, the Superfund reauthorization was a train that was moving and we were able jump on it with this right-to-know car."[31]

Conflicts Produce a Skewed Architecture of Disclosure

As the proposal made its way through the political process, however, compromises left it seriously flawed. Representatives of target companies argued successfully that disclosure should be narrowed to protect trade secrets and avoid undue reporting burdens. The result was a system that provided a partial picture of toxic pollution and did not reveal anything about risks.

Limiting Who Reports

In the political atmosphere of the mid-1980s, arguments by businesses about the cost of collecting and communicating information about toxic chemicals resonated with widely shared fears of economic recession, impatience with bureaucracy, and doubts about the data's value. After the Bhopal disaster, few companies opposed disclosure outright. Instead, they fought to minimize its effects. The Environmental Protection Agency itself considered disclosure a time-consuming distraction from the agency's regulatory mission. "It looked like a huge job," explained Linda Fisher, who was chief of staff to administrator Lee Thomas at the time and subsequently headed the agency's toxics program. "People were concerned about the paperwork burden. Also, when the EPA gathered data it was as an underpinning for the regulatory program. If we saw a problem, we regulated it. This was a lot of data that were not going to be the basis of a regulatory program. The agency's initial response was: What value is this information to us or to the public?"[32]

Senator Stafford, the Senate committee chair, worked to counter those claims: "[I]t simply cannot be very expensive [for companies] to go through the files, or talk to the plant foreman, and pull these numbers together. They probably already are consolidated at most facilities in order to assure compliance with regulatory programs; and if they aren't, they should be."[33] But arguments by companies that were the prospective targets of the law and by the agency that was expected to carry it out proved stronger.

In order to win congressional approval, the disclosure provision limited companies required to report by type, by size, and by quantity of toxic emissions. An initial proposal in the House of Representatives to require "any person" who discharged cancer-causing chemicals to disclose that fact to the public brought widespread objections that it would impose reporting burdens on farmers, gas stations, printers, dry cleaners, hospitals, and beauty parlors. Ultimately, Congress required only manufacturers to disclose their toxic releases. That meant excluding large categories of businesses—power plants and mining operations, for example—that were responsible for substantial toxic emissions. It also meant excluding federal and state government facilities from public scrutiny. In addition, only manufacturers that had ten or more full-time employees and that produced or used large amounts of chemicals (firms that annually used 10,000 pounds or manufactured 25,000 pounds of a listed chemical) were required to report. Senator Stafford assured his colleagues that "in response to concerns that have been raised" the final bill had been reduced to "apply to fewer facilities and require less reporting" and required no additional testing or monitoring.[34]

After the law was passed, government reports acknowledged that the disclosure system missed much of the public health problem. By excluding neighborhood businesses, as well as toxic pollution from cars and trucks, Congress left out sources whose toxic emissions could have disproportionately large effects on human health because they were located in densely populated areas. An early report told the public that excluded "warehouses, dry cleaners, and mining operations may be substantial sources of chemical releases."[35] Regulators estimated that restricting disclosure to firms with ten or more employees excluded 48 percent of manufacturing facilities.[36] A later report by the EPA estimated that neighborhood businesses and other small polluters accounted for 35 percent of air toxics, and cars, trucks, and other mobile sources accounted for 41 percent.[37]

Limiting Chemicals Reported

To secure quick approval, disclosure was also limited to a partial list of toxic chemicals. Senator Lautenberg introduced an amendment that limited reporting to a group of 329 chemicals or chemical categories that had been assembled from lists produced in New Jersey and Maryland for state-specific purposes. The lists were based partly on toxicity but also on such factors as the amount produced or used in the state and the chemicals' regulatory status. The bill's sponsors were reluctant to leave the listing of chemicals to regulators. The Environmental Protection Agency had been slow to identify toxic chemicals under existing legislation. Gaining agreement on a new national list would have been time consuming and perhaps impossible.

Selecting chemicals for disclosure was a potentially explosive political issue because companies feared incurring increased costs for collecting and processing information, being faced with the possibility of public pressure to reduce emissions that did not violate any law, and giving valuable information to competitors. Scientific uncertainty made the task harder. Toxicity was a complex scientific concept and most chemicals in broad use had not been completely tested. The Chemical Manufacturers Association, the American Petroleum Institute, and the Reagan administration supported a bill that would have excluded from disclosure all chemicals that did not cause immediate health effects, including dioxin, asbestos, and PCBs, toxins that were associated with long-term developmental problems, neurological damage, and cancer.[38] Once the law was passed, environmental officials were candid in telling the public that chemicals on the combined list "vary widely in toxicity" and that "the list of chemicals currently covered does not include all toxic chemicals of concern."[39]

Limiting Events Reported

In the name of protecting trade secrets, the Chemical Manufacturers Association and other lobbyists for industry also persuaded members of Congress to limit disclosure to end-of-the-pipe releases. In 1986 both Republicans and Democrats were working to reorient national policy toward pollution prevention rather than emission control. Pollution prevention emphasized changing raw materials, industrial processes, or technologies to reduce not only immediate toxic pollution but also overall use of such chemicals.[40]

The Senate committee's bill initially reflected this new approach.[41] But industry lobbyists persuaded the bill's sponsors that disclosure of chemical use might reveal formulas and production processes that were trade secrets, despite state experience to the contrary.[42] Congress therefore narrowed the right-to-know requirement to toxic "releases" and directed the National Research Council to evaluate the value and feasibility of reporting chemical use.[43] The council ultimately recommended a pilot study "to test the feasibility of the national collection of mass accounting information."[44]

Limiting Accuracy and Timeliness of Information

Ironically, the law that was supposed to provide instant access to information produced results that were always out of date, that were often based on estimates arrived at in different ways, and that did not include data needed to assess risks to public health or the environment.

Congress locked in timetables. The law explicitly provided that companies submit their annual reports on toxic releases to the EPA "on July 1" for "releases during the preceding year."[45] Typically, it has taken the EPA nearly another year to process data and issue a national report. The law also allowed companies to base disclosure on estimates rather than the monitoring of toxic chemical releases.[46] Estimates introduced a wildcard. Companies could choose from a variety of techniques that did not have to be consistent from chemical to chemical, company to company, or year to year. Estimates could be based on calculating waste from known inputs and outputs, common ratios for emissions, engineering judgment, or other indicators. Two years after manufacturers submitted their first reports, the National Research Council noted that "Congress was aware that the toxic chemical release estimates reported . . . might not accurately reflect the amounts actually released."[47]

Most important, limiting reporting to pounds of releases of each chemical, with no accounting for their relative toxicity or variations in exposure, uncoupled it from broader goals of reducing risks to human health and the environment. A determination of risk would have required adjusting for relative toxicity, factoring in a dose-response assessment, and developing an understanding of who was exposed, how often, for what length of time, and to how much of the toxin.[48]

Compromise Creates Complexity

By the time it was approved, a simple impulse to provide the public with better information had produced an exceedingly complicated system. The new law required manufacturers to report annually their routine and accidental releases of toxic chemicals to land, water, or air to state officials and the EPA. Releases had to be reported chemical by chemical and facility by facility. Owners or operators of facilities completed a standardized form for each listed chemical if 10,000 pounds or more were used or 25,000 pounds were manufactured or processed during the calendar year starting in 1987.[49] The requirement applied only to facilities that had ten or more full-time employees and were included in Standard Industrial Classification codes 20 through 39. The first reports were to be submitted to the EPA by July 1, 1988.[50]

The EPA, in turn, created the Toxics Release Inventory (TRI), a national database that included the maximum amounts present at each facility during the year, the waste treatment or disposal methods employed, an estimate of treatment efficiency achieved, and the annual amount of the chemical released to the air, water, or land; the EPA made these data "accessible by computer telecommunication and other means to any person on a cost reimbursable basis."[51] The reports were intended to serve multiple purposes: to inform the public, including citizens of communities surrounding facilities; to provide information to federal, state, and local governments; to assist researchers and other persons in data gathering; and to aid in the development of appropriate regulations.[52]

A complex compromise protected trade secrets. Manufacturers were permitted to withhold a chemical identity and replace it with the chemical's generic name if they claimed that the chemical was a trade secret and could document that claim. They had to show that the company had not disclosed the information to any other person except employees or other persons bound by confidentiality; that the company had taken reasonable measures to protect confidentiality and intended to continue to take such measures; that the information was not required to be disclosed under any other federal or state law; that disclosure was likely to cause substantial harm to the firm's competitive position; and that the chemical identity was not readily discoverable through reverse engineering.[53]

The law provided meaningful penalties. Violators could be fined up to $25,000 per violation per day. Firms that made frivolous claims of trade secrets could also be fined $25,000 for each violation. Anyone convicted of knowingly revealing a trade secret could be subject to criminal penalties. Citizens could sue firms for failing to submit reports or the EPA for failing to carry out its provisions.[54]

Translating Law into Practice

Legislative approval was the beginning, not the end, of creating the new disclosure system. In approving the law, Congress handed to an overworked, underfunded EPA, whose leaders were already skeptical of the requirement's usefulness, an unprecedented array of regulatory issues that had to be resolved quickly. It gave the agency legal authority to correct or at least minimize some of the law's shortcomings. As a practical matter, though, choices made in the twenty-one months between the time the law was signed and the first industry reports were due were limited by time, resources, and politics.

Despite the specificity of legislators' directions, the EPA could add or remove chemicals from the disclosure list, broaden or narrow the industries required to report, and raise or lower the amount of annual releases that required reporting. It could require federal agencies that were big users of toxic chemicals, such as the Department of Defense or the Department of Energy, to report their releases.

A Race against the Clock Constrains Choices

The magnitude of the job and practical limitations restricted the EPA's options. The agency's assigned task was to construct a disclosure program for information that had never been gathered before, extract data from companies unaccustomed to preparing such reports, compile this material into a database that did not yet exist, and make this information available by electronic communication, which was still in its infancy—and to do all this quickly at a time when other priorities seemed more pressing.

Legislated timetables ruled out many choices. Congress had required the EPA to create a reporting form and basic program guidelines within seven and a half months after the law was signed and to be ready to receive thousands of reports in less than twenty-one months. With its budget cut substantially during the Reagan administration and senior positions vacant, the agency had fallen far behind in issuing and enforcing national pollution control standards—its primary mission—and had been repeatedly criticized by Congress for missing deadlines. Public disclosure appeared to be a distraction from these responsibilities, not a new means of furthering them. "It is pretty speculative at this point as to whether it pays off as something positive. It could be something negative in the sense it is just a lot of paper work," Lee M. Thomas, EPA's new administrator, told Philip Shabecoff of the *New York Times*.[55] Charles Elkins, who was assigned to run the program, recalled later that "there was tremendous cynicism within the agency because the data was so shallow in terms of what they were used to dealing with. In their eyes, TRI data is an inch deep and a mile wide. It doesn't give enough information on why the releases occurred, for example, or what's behind the numbers."[56]

Nonetheless, regulators went about their tasks in a businesslike manner, consulting with a broad range of interested groups, making basic decisions, and getting the job done. From the start, they treated construction of the disclosure system as a major action that required public participation in the design of detailed rules. They convened two public meetings; consulted with state, company, and public interest group representatives; surveyed user needs; estimated costs to government and industry; and considered how information should be made available to the public electronically. The EPA estimated federal costs at between $4.0 million and $13.8 million a year and industry costs at $400–500 million in the first year (based on 165,100 reports on an average of four chemicals and one mixture per facility).[57] Six months after the law was enacted, the agency published proposed reporting rules and invited public comment. It issued a final rule in February 1988, four and a half months before companies were required to report for the first time.[58]

However, practical constraints led the EPA to make three decisions that carried forward limitations in the law. First, the EPA declined to use the authority granted it by Congress to provide the public with a more complete picture of toxic pollution by including more sources, despite pressure from industry, states, public interest groups, and academics to do so.[59] Second, program managers made an early decision not to accompany reported data with interpretation. Citizen groups pressed the agency to provide information about the significance of releases due to toxicity, the likelihood of human exposure, and environmental effects. Industry representatives urged regulators to provide a context for the billions of pounds of toxic releases reported in order to assuage the public's fears. "Some of these numbers are going to sound absolutely frightening," warned Charles J. DiBona, president of the American Petroleum Institute.[60] But the agency lacked the time, money, and data to provide meaningful interpretation. Susan Hazen, the program manager at the time, recalls that "there was a very conscious decision made the first year that our job was to get the data in and get the data out."[61] Government reports simply stated facilities' toxic releases in pounds per chemical and added them up. Interpretive material was limited to descriptions of the geographical distribution of releases and of decreases and increases over time. Third, the agency did not develop a national enforcement strategy. Enforcement was delegated to regional offices that used varying inspection approaches. Initially, reporting rates were low. The General Accounting Office (GAO), an investigative arm of Congress, estimated in 1991 that an average of 35.7 percent of facilities did not report, as high as 83 percent in some states, mostly due to lack of awareness of the program, and that the agency had been slow to take action due to a shortage of resources.[62]

Electronic Disclosure Raises Novel Issues

What appeared to be a simple if unusual provision that releases be made accessible electronically created new political coalitions and changed the roles of public officials and private groups. Initial decisions isolated the new reports from other agency data, made them available more than a year after releases took place, and limited their accessibility in practice. EPA officials negotiated an agreement with the National Library of Medicine, an arm of the National Institutes of Health, to provide the new information as part of its Toxicology Data Network (TOXNET). That decision was influenced by time and resource constraints but also reflected the agency's view that the information was not central to its mission. According to the director of the agency's Information Resources Management Office, "Our position was, we are not in the retail information business, and we could not be."[63] To translate facility reports into a national database, EPA's master tape was used to create a data file for public release through TOXNET; this, in turn, was used to create CD-ROMs, microfiche, paper copies, and computer disks.[64]

The process was time consuming. "Almost every field of information became a bone of contention for somebody," recalls David Sarokin. "Even facility identification was a mess for the first few years. Facilities gave different names at different times and companies were being bought and sold."[65] A time lag of eighteen to twenty-four months between releases and public reports persisted during the 1990s.

When the accessibility of the new data proved limited in practice, right-to-know groups, employee safety and health organizations, community activists, and pollution control advocates banded together to improve it. Despite their different agendas and constituencies, these groups had a common interest in electronic disclosure that included such features as menus and mapping capability. The Working Group on Community Right-to-Know, formed in 1988 by the Friends of the Earth, other environmental groups, and OMB Watch, a group advocating improved public access to information and citizen involvement in government, became a permanent coalition that worked for broader access to information. It set out to educate nonprofit groups about electronic access and set up its own database for toxic releases, RTK Net, which later became a cooperative effort between the Working Group and the EPA.[66] These struggles to create a workable system received little public attention, but the first company reports made national news. An obscure information requirement suddenly became seen as an agent of corporate change.

Disclosure Creates Headlines

Richard J. Mahoney's dramatic commitment on June 30, 1988, to cut Monsanto's toxic air releases by 90 percent created headlines for two reasons. First, it revealed a surprising threat. Mahoney told the public what he and many other chief executives had learned only days earlier—that large quantities of harmful chemicals were being dispersed into the air and water and disposed of on land despite a long-standing national commitment to protect the public from such toxins. Second, it suggested bold action. Releases were not an inevitable by-product of unprecedented prosperity. They could be nearly eliminated immediately. Mahoney told the public that at least one large corporation was suddenly willing to virtually stop releasing toxins into the air without any legal requirement to do so.

The politics of reputation led giant corporations, which had for years countered government efforts to regulate toxic chemicals, to suddenly take preemptive action. Commitments by Monsanto and other large corporations preceded government disclosure by nearly a year. The first national report, which would show a release of 6.2 billion pounds of listed chemicals, would not be distributed until May 1989, after nine months of processing by the EPA. But industry leaders saw what was coming. "The public is going to see this as a new health threat," warned American Petroleum Institute president DiBona.[67]

Their predictions were correct. Nearly a year later, when the first full-scale national report was released to the public in May 1989, toxic chemicals created headlines across the country. For the first time, journalists, environmental groups, and the public had access to systematic information about the release of such chemicals by state, by community, by factory, and by substance. Flaws in the data that rendered conclusions suspect were overlooked. Intermediaries became powerful interpreters of the new information. Public interest groups and journalists translated the report's opaque numbers into simpler formats that ranked companies and communities by amounts of toxic pollution. Within a few weeks of the first reports, the National Wildlife Federation, the nation's largest conservation group, published *The Toxic 500*, a report ranking communities with the most toxic pollution, declaring that the results "speak to a nation at risk."[68] National, state, and local groups followed with scores of reports about polluters in individual counties, cities, and towns, with titles like "The Good, the Bad, and the Toxic" (about California's largest polluters) and "Out of Control" (about Michigan's polluters). Citizen Action produced annual reports listing the worst polluters nationally and by state, based on aggregate total releases per plant.[69]

In its three-part series, the national newspaper *USA Today* told readers that "a whopping 7 billion pounds of toxic chemicals—a veritable witches' brew of poisons—were pumped into the air, land and water by 19,278 factories." The newspaper, which had purchased the full magnetic tape of the data, ranked companies, factories, and the 500 counties with the highest volumes of reported releases. Highest ranked companies were identified as the leading polluters: "Amax Magnesium in Rowley, Utah, is the biggest air polluter; Aluminum Co. of America (ALCOA) in Point Comfort, Texas, dumps the most on land; Agrico Chemical in Under Sam, La., is the leading water polluter." It reported that "more than half the toxic chemicals released to water were dumped into the 2,348-mile-long Mississippi."[70]

Easy access to factory-by-factory and chemical-by-chemical information brought local stories to life. In Connecticut, news reports revealed that tetrachloroethylene, or "perc," a probable human carcinogen used to clean greasy surfaces, was a common air pollutant. United Technologies Corp. released 1.4 million pounds of perc into the air above plants in East Hartford, North Haven, and two other areas. In Casper, Wyoming, an Amoco plant released large quantities of the carcinogen benzene into the air.[71] High-tech companies did not escape the heat of publicity. An environmental group called the Silicon Valley Toxics Coalition called a press conference to accuse semiconductor firms of using the skies between San Jose and San Francisco as an open sewer for the disposal of 12 million pounds of toxic chemicals. An industry spokesman countered that emissions were dispersed in low concentrations that did not cause health problems.[72]

Manufacturers launched unprecedented public relations campaigns, dubbed by *Business Week* "the swarm to inform," to explain their environmental performance to community groups. In Port Arthur, Texas, Texaco Inc. representatives briefed media and local officials about the annual release of 76,000 pounds of benzene, explaining that emissions were legal and the concentrations were not threatening. Dow Chemical USA set up computers in public places where it had plants so that citizens could review information about toxics. Monsanto trained plant managers in risk communication and established community advisory panels at some plants. Theresa Pugh, environmental quality director of the National Association of Manufacturers, observed that "many companies have never explained their manufacturing processes to the public before."[73]

Industry groups championed better management of toxic substances and better community relations. The Chemical Manufacturers Association created a Responsible Care Program and asked members to adopt management codes and respond to community concerns. The American Petroleum Institute, the National Electrical Manufacturers Association, and other trade associations established management principles for chemical waste. Some companies also cried foul. Alcoa complained that totals were exaggerated because the 1987 list contained aluminum oxide, a chemical of low toxicity that was widely used in aluminum manufacturing.

Under attack by environmental groups, local plants made their own commitments. The manager of the B. F. Goodrich chemical plant in Akron, Ohio, pledged to cut toxic emissions 70 percent after environmentalists publicized the plant's report to the government. After Armco Steel in Middletown, Ohio, which made flat-rolled steel used by automakers, topped its county's list, the manager promised to spend $4 million to reduce benzene emissions by 97 percent in two years. A company spokesman said that it had never added up toxic emissions before and had found ways to cut emissions by increasing efficiency.

Caught in a web of publicity, industry officials even joined members of Congress in calling for new legislation. A spokesman for the Chemical Manufacturers Association argued that the numbers could be misleading but acknowledged that the industry would support new legislation because it is "becoming apparent that the current approach to air toxics isn't doing the job."[74] Senior EPA officials said that the Reagan administration would support amendments to the Clean Air Act to regulate toxic chemicals more strictly.

Unrelated events increased the requirement's impact. In February 1988 California businesses starting warning customers about products and pollutants that could cause cancer or birth defects under the terms of Proposition 65, the state ballot initiative approved in 1986. Oil companies posted thousands of signs at the state's gas stations announcing that "detectable amounts" of such chemicals "may be found" on the premises.[75] In June 1988 W. R. Grace pleaded guilty to charges that it lied to the EPA about toxic chemicals used at its Woburn, Massachusetts, facility, which was being blamed for eight leukemia deaths and later became the subject of a best-selling book, *Civil Action*.[76] In 1989 the long-debated issue of the cancer risk associated with daminozidea (sold under the name Alar), a ripening agent sprayed on apples, came to a head when the television program *60 Minutes* reported that this chemical was suspected of causing cancer. Millions of customers stopped buying apples, and Alar was hastily withdrawn from the market.[77] Accidents continued to make news. In February 1988, shortly before companies submitted their first reports, 6,000 people were evacuated overnight when a tank at a Chevron U.S.A. refinery leaked crude oil containing hydrogen sulfide and sent eighty-four people to emergency rooms.[78]

High numbers were equated with high risk even though disclosed data did not support the linkage. Government officials and journalists created unintentional distortions when they made choices about how to prioritize and summarize the data. Caveats were included, but they were often buried beneath shocking revelations. Few readers would have understood that facilities releasing large amounts of low-toxicity chemicals could be a source of less risk than facilities releasing small amounts of highly toxic substances. Charles L. Elkins, director of the EPA's Office of Toxic Substances, wrote in the *New York Times* that "many, although not all, of the chemicals have been linked to cancer, neurological and reproductive disorders, and other chronic human health problems." Only at the end of his article did he note that "[t]oxic chemicals do not always pose a risk to public health; many chemicals may dissipate or be neutralized before humans, animals or ecosystems are exposed to them."[79] *USA Today* identified companies with the highest totals as the biggest polluters but acknowledged in the sixteenth paragraph of the story that "determining the health impact is difficult without knowing whether people were exposed, in what concentrations or volumes, and over what length of time."[80]

Disclosure derived its power not from sudden increases in toxic releases or evidence of a new threat to public health but from the simple fact that numbers were added up for the first time and linked to identified sources. Rep. Henry A. Waxman (D-Calif.) recalled that when he estimated in 1985 that 80 million pounds of toxic chemicals were released into the air each year "industry went haywire. They denounced the figure as environmental paranoia." Industry's first reports under the next law showed releases of air toxins totaling 2.7 billion pounds.[81]

Releases of Listed Chemicals Plummet

The next astonishing news was that the reported releases of listed chemicals declined dramatically after companies began disclosing their levels to the public. By 1989, after only two years of reporting, total releases and transfers of listed chemicals had decreased 19 percent.[82] From 1988 to 1999, according to the government, facilities reduced total releases by 45.5 percent, from 3.2 billion pounds to 1.5 billion pounds, for chemicals reported in all years. Companies reduced air emissions by 60 percent and surface water emissions by 66 percent.[83]

This apparent drop was not limited to a few large companies or to states known for their environmental vigilance. A GAO survey in 1991 found that half of the facilities had made operational changes to reduce releases.[84] Louisiana, a state that ranked second in releases of listed chemicals in 1988 and was not known for environmental initiatives, experienced a reduction of 38 percent in one year. Shocked by the initial totals, legislators in that state also passed a law that required a list of 100 toxic air pollutants to be cut in half between 1987 and the end of 1994.[85]

While previous trends were unknown, data quality was uncertain, and the effects of disclosure were hard to disentangle from other forces at work, virtually everyone assumed the law had caused a major reduction in toxic pollution. No other environmental law had been associated with such dramatic results. The unexpected lesson that would ultimately reverberate throughout government, particularly as information technology created new possibilities for communication, was that the systematic disclosure of standardized information concerning private sector performance could be a powerful inducement for companies to improve environmental practices.

Government, industry, and environmental groups used the data to construct a towering structure of further policies. Regulators used the data to pressure companies to reduce emissions further. Industry used them to identify and measure improvement, while environmental groups used them to build a case for more stringent regulation. Total pounds of toxic releases, regardless of toxicity and the exposure or relative safety of disposal, became an accepted metric for environmental progress.

Success Brings Expansion

Perceived success created pressures to expand disclosure but did not correct its fundamental flaws. In 1990 Congress broadened the system to include reporting of total toxic waste and recycling as part of a law that officially adopted pollution prevention as a national policy.[86] Once again, however, legislators considered and rejected the notion of requiring reporting of industry *use* of toxic chemicals, a more basic change that would have brought the disclosure system in line with that newly proclaimed policy. With industry arguing that such a requirement would reveal trade secrets, a stalemate on that issue continued through the 1990s.

Early in 1991 William K. Reilly, President George H. W. Bush's EPA administrator, launched a program to create pressure for further voluntary reductions.[87] He sent letters to 600 chief executive officers of large manufacturing companies asking that they reduce their releases of seventeen particularly toxic and widely used chemicals by one-third by the end of 1992 and by half by the end of 1995. Those letters were followed by appeals to another 5,000 companies later in the year. Reilly announced that the 33/50 program, as the effort was known, was getting "reductions faster and more cost-effectively than under any regulatory program I administer."[88]

In August 1993 newly elected president Bill Clinton broadened the disclosure system again by requiring federal facilities to report their toxic releases and reduce them by 50 percent by 1999.[89] Two years later he ordered companies seeking federal contracts of $100,000 or more to certify that they were reporting toxic releases to the public, regardless of whether the law required it.[90] In 1997 the EPA required mining operations, power plants that burned coal or oil, hazardous waste treatment and disposal facilities, wholesale distributors of chemicals, and petroleum bulk plants and terminals to report, and the agency doubled the number of chemicals to be disclosed.[91] In October 1999 the EPA drastically lowered reporting thresholds for dioxin and eight other toxic chemicals that accumulate in human tissue.[92] However, the requirement still excluded discharges from vehicles, small businesses, most pesticides, volatile organic compounds, fertilizers, and other nonindustrial sources.

Programs initiated by states, industry, and other countries also accepted the system's legitimacy. By 1991 EPA administrator Reilly reported that an increasing number of states were basing their environmental accounting on the federal disclosure program. New Jersey required disclosure of information on chemical use by manufacturers located in the state in 1987. Massachusetts required reporting of most uses of toxins and also required some services, such as dry cleaners and beauty shops, to report.[93] Minnesota and Maine adopted disclosure requirements that were broader than national rules. California required that companies warn employees and consumers about products that contain any substance "known to the State of California" that causes "cancer, birth defects or reproductive harm," unless the company could show that the risk of exposure was not significant, as determined by the state.[94] Reilly reported that Canada had initiated a program of disclosure of toxic chemicals and that the EPA was helping Mexico, Europe, Scandinavia, and Japan design such programs.[95]

Then, on Earth Day 1997, President Clinton capped the trend. He hailed the program as a "very powerful early warning system . . . the most powerful tool in a democracy: knowledge."[96] In its annual report of toxic releases for that year, the EPA expanded on the theme: "[A]ccording to many, the TRI program is one of the most effective environmental programs ever legislated by Congress and administered by EPA."[97] What began as a right-to-know initiative was now applauded as a particularly successful regulatory measure.

Structural Flaws Exposed

In practice, however, structural flaws became increasingly apparent. Information that was always more than a year out of date when given to the public might be useful for tracking trends, but it told consumers, employees, investors, and community residents nothing about current toxic pollution. Data for calendar year 1989 were not assembled in a national report until September 1991—twenty months after the end of the year in which the reported toxic chemicals were released into the environment. A decade later, the pattern remained much the same: 1998 data were not made available in a national report until June 2000—eighteen months after the end of the year in which chemicals had been released. Time lags were particularly significant, since releases "can change dramatically from one year to the next."[98]

Continuing inaccuracy plagued the system. Different companies used different estimating techniques. In 1991 a startling example of the limits of estimation was provided by an unusual government-industry study. The EPA and the Amoco Corporation launched a joint project to explore in detail what pollution was actually emitted at the company's thirty-five-year-old refinery at Yorktown, Virginia. The often-cited results showed that the actual amounts of toxic chemicals discharged were two and a half times higher than had been estimated in disclosures to the public, mostly because monitoring revealed significant sources of toxic pollution not previously known or reported, including emissions from blowdown stacks and barge-loading operations.[99]

Paper changes also became a growing concern. In 1994 the GAO concluded that company estimates of toxic waste were not reliable because "annual variations . . . may likely reflect changes in the companies' methods of estimating waste or in economic conditions, rather than reflecting improved environmental performance." The GAO noted that

companies "often do not have data systems sophisticated enough to provide reliable estimates of production and related waste."[100] Environmentalists also questioned whether reductions resulted from changes in
accounting for wastes rather than actual decreases in toxic pollution.
Three years earlier the National Wildlife Federation had published *Phan-
tom Reductions: Tracking Toxic Trends,* an analysis of twenty-nine companies, which concluded that reductions in releases were usually due to
changes in measurement techniques, reductions in production, or changes
in interpretation of the law's terms. In its own study that year to determine what accounted for the decline in facility releases, the EPA concluded that paper changes were a factor and that fluctuations in production accounted for the largest absolute change.[101] A detailed survey by
Thomas E. Natan Jr. and Catherine G. Miller of the Hampshire Research
Institute of eighty facilities that reported large decreases in releases from
1991 to 1994 found that "just one type of paper change, redefining on-
site recycling activities as in-process recovery, which does not have to be
reported, accounted for more than half of these facilities' 1991–1994
reported reductions" listed as waste.[102]

As more programs relied on the data, accuracy problems spread. As
previously noted, one such program launched by the EPA administrator
in 1991 encouraged companies to reduce reported releases by 50 percent.
However, announcement of success was marred by a GAO report that
found more than one-quarter of the decreases were "paper reductions"
and many took place before the program began. The GAO noted that the
EPA officials were "concerned about their ability to accurately measure
progress."[103]

To its credit, the government called attention to these issues. National
reports cautioned that dramatic reductions in releases reflected a mix of
changes in production quantities and methods, one-time events, and
changes in definition, estimation, or thresholds. Reporting 1989 data, the
agency noted that "improved emissions estimates, changes in accounting
procedures, and a better understanding of the TRI requirements account
for at least some of these decreases."[104] Officials were careful to note that
releases represented "only a portion of all toxic chemical releases nation-
wide."[105] In 1998 Congress asked the General Accounting Office to
review the accuracy of disclosed information. The GAO noted that, while

the EPA continued to work on improving data management, it had not developed standards to assess data accuracy or find and correct errors.[106]

Uncertainties about how disclosure information related to risks remained the most important flaw in the system. Chemicals that varied greatly in acute and chronic toxicity were treated alike. Despite official claims that disclosure could reduce risks, agency officials often were more candid. Charles Elkins, director of the EPA's Office of Toxic Substances, acknowledged that "there is not enough information in the forms to know whether you should be scared or not." The information "means very little in terms of human health" because of the lack of exposure and toxicity data. For the first few years, Elkins said, data would be limited to helping the EPA identify "hot spots" with high levels of toxic emissions.[107] Defenders of the system argued that it was a pollution reduction program rather than a risk reduction program. But the purpose of government programs to reduce pollution was to reduce risks.[108]

By the mid-1990s the system was under attack from respected oversight organizations. In April 1995 the National Academy of Public Administration formally criticized it for failing to link chemical reports to risk information. The academy pointed out that only such linkage would create incentives for firms to reduce the most harmful emissions first.[109] The GAO issued a candid appraisal in 1998 pointing out the obvious— that local communities needed information about toxicity and exposure to understand risks.[110] Persistent overselling may also have discouraged reform efforts. Congress showed no interest in improving a disclosure system that was widely credited with causing corporate executives to make drastic cuts in toxic pollution.

The Impact of Information

Recognizing the peculiarities inherent in disclosure, researchers have nonetheless attempted to discern whether and how it influenced firms' environmental performance. Once the requirement was credited with creating incentives for pollution reduction, empirical evidence of its impact on company practices became of central importance. Research efforts began to build a knowledge base about the economic and political pathways through which disclosure might produce corporate change. They suggested that it sometimes created perceived threats to reputation and that companies' responses were influenced by such factors as their size or national prominence. However, empirical research also indicated that responses may have emphasized quick fixes more than basic changes in processes or products and that pressures created by disclosure could be trumped by other economic or political forces. Apparent declines in toxic releases were heavily influenced by industry-specific, media-specific, state-specific, and facility-specific factors.[111]

Responses may have varied with firm size, amount of releases, or consumer contact. Shameek Konar and Mark A. Cohen of Vanderbilt University examined responses of firms from 1989 to 1992 and concluded that large firms with reputational capital to lose were more likely than smaller or little-known ones to reduce disclosed toxic emissions. Controlling for firm size, they found that the larger the initial level of emissions, the larger the reductions.[112] Examining voluntary commitments by large firms to make reductions, Seema Arora and Timothy N. Cason found that large firms with high levels of releases were more likely to participate than smaller firms with fewer releases.[113]

Responses by facilities also were linked to the character of the communities surrounding them. Examining air emissions of carcinogens and using data on expected cancer cases, individual lifetime cancer risk, and the percentage of registered voters who voted in the 1988 presidential election (as a surrogate for collective action), economist James T. Hamilton of Duke University concluded that facilities in areas with higher expected death rates associated with releases of carcinogens had higher reductions of releases between 1988 and 1991, as did facilities in neighborhoods with more collective action among citizens (as indicated by higher voter turnout).[114] A survey by the *National Law Journal* in 1993 of more than 200 corporate counsels found that pressure from community activists affected the decisions of more than half of the firms contacted, sometimes forcing pollution reductions.[115]

Hamilton also found that investors and journalists responded to high levels of reported releases. He examined the effect of the disclosure of data in 1989 on stock prices of publicly trade companies and found an average loss of $4.1 million in stock value on the day the information was released. (Three-quarters of reported releases were from publicly traded companies.) Losses were less for firms where investors had previous information about pollution patterns. He suggested that investors may have used the new data to update their expectations of liabilities, compliance costs, or the loss of goodwill. In addition, the higher a facility's releases, the more likely the company was to receive attention from print journalists.[116] Konar and Cohen found that firms whose stock price declined significantly cut toxic releases more than their industry peers, even if their peers had higher levels of releases to begin with.[117]

Behind the often-cited precipitous drop in releases lies a complex story of media-specific, industry-specific, and state-specific trends.[118] Overall, the data suggest a core of positive developments. Reported toxic releases into the environment have declined by almost half, releases of some chemicals that may be particularly harmful to human health have declined at a faster rate than total releases, and recycling has increased—all in the context of a rapidly growing economy. As shown in figure 2-1, reported releases declined by 46 percent from 1988 to 1999 for a core group of chemicals reported in all years. Air releases declined by 61 percent, and water releases declined by 66 percent.[119]

However, factors such as recycling costs, changing demand for products, and legislative or enforcement actions have been linked to enormous variation in results from year to year. Air releases, for example, have declined at a fairly steady pace, while on-site land disposal increased by 24 percent from 1993 to 1998 and off-site land disposal increased by 53 percent as prices of recycling fluctuated. Of the three carcinogens with the largest releases in 1999, dichloromethane decreased by 40 percent since 1995, while styrene and formaldehyde increased by 26 and 22 percent, respectively. While toxic releases decreased overall by 46 percent from 1988 to 1999, releases in the food and beverage industry increased 62 percent and releases of metals and their compounds (about two-thirds of which were from the primary metals sector) increased 32 percent.

Despite the usual emphasis on national trends, the states of Texas, Ohio, and Indiana have accounted for nearly 20 percent of national releases, and three counties (Gila, Arizona; Tooele, Utah; and Lewis and Clark, Montana) accounted for about 2.5 percent of national releases in 1999. Fifty of almost 21,000 manufacturing facilities that reported toxic releases accounted for 31 percent of all releases in 1999.

Figure 2-1. *Toxic Releases, 1988–99*[a]

Millions of pounds

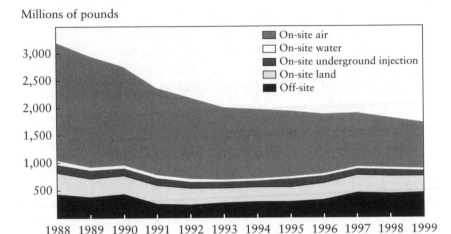

Source: U.S. Environmental Protection Agency, TRI Public Data Release Report (April 2001). On-site release data from section 5 of TRI Form R. Off-site release data from section 6 of TRI Form R.

a. Does not include chemicals deleted from or added to the TRI list since 1988, aluminum oxide, ammonia, hydrochloric acid, and sulfuric acid. Data from industries first reporting to TRI for 1998 are not included. Off-site releases include metals and metal compounds transferred off-site for disposal, solidification/stabilization, and wastewater treatment.

Data also suggest that the impact of disclosure may have varied over time. Most of the often-cited decreases in toxic releases occurred in the first five years of reporting. From 1988 to 1993 total releases decreased 37 percent, with reductions averaging 7 percent a year. From 1993 to 1998 total releases decreased 10 percent, with reductions averaging 2 percent a year. Two reasons may account for the slowed decline. First, some manufacturers were able to make relatively inexpensive and rapid changes in the early years. Second, in the booming economy of the mid-1990s, increased production may have made absolute reductions more difficult.

Results also indicated an apparent preference among firms for quick fixes. According to their 1999 reports, less than 25 percent of manufacturing facilities reduced waste through source reduction, the preferred environmental approach under current national policy. More firms substituted chemicals, repaired leaks, or altered maintenance routines.

Some trends remain particularly troubling. From 1995, when the EPA required reporting for nearly 300 new chemicals, to 1999, on-site land disposal of listed chemicals increased 14 percent, off-site land disposal increased 46 percent, and surface water discharges increased 32 percent. These increases are important because many of the added chemicals were carcinogens or reproductive and developmental toxins. Also, despite a decade of reductions, releases of listed chemicals into the environment remain substantial. In 1999 manufacturers reported that 1.7 billion pounds of toxic substances were released into the air and water or disposed of on land. Annual generation of toxic waste, most of it recycled or treated, increased by 5 percent during the 1990s, to 23.1 billion pounds.

What the data do not reveal is also noteworthy. Causation remained uncertain. Reporting was not constructed in a way that made it possible to disentangle the impact of disclosure from that of other economic or political forces. Plant closings or shifts in production could cause releases to plummet, just as decisions to lower toxic emissions could. In some states, particularly in the Northeast, disclosure coincided with a dramatic loss of manufacturing jobs. Also, long before Congress required disclosure, companies were under regulatory pressure to reduce risks from toxic chemicals. At least seven major federal laws enacted since 1970 had included such regulation as a priority. In addition, the Montreal Protocol, signed September 16, 1987, initially froze use of certain ozone-depleting chemicals at 1986 levels and later called for their phase-out in industrial countries by the mid-1990s. Phase-out had a substantial impact on releases between 1991 and 1994.[120] Whether reductions in releases represented a new trend could not be discerned. Some indicators suggested that levels of toxins in the environment had been decreasing rapidly before the disclosure system was created. Average levels of lead in the blood of humans decreased 78 percent between 1976–80 and 1988–91. The level of PCBs in Lake Michigan trout declined rapidly from 1974 to 1990. Mercury production peaked in 1964 and has been declining since.[121] A more nuanced understanding of the combined effects of disclosure, economic forces, regulatory actions, and management choices remained elusive.

Technopopulism Creates New Possibilities and Conflicts

Even in its early years, the Internet has altered the political fundamentals of disclosure. It has broken the immutable law of communication that in-depth information can be conveyed only to a narrow audience. It has lowered information-processing costs for users and made it possible for users to customize information to their particular needs. Suddenly, government agencies, businesses, and consumer groups have found it economically and technically feasible to provide rich and nuanced portraits of environmental problems using data from a variety of sources. Users could search for specific information about their communities, illnesses, or fears. At the same time, though, technology has increased concerns about accuracy and renewed resistance to disclosure by groups that stand to lose by revelations. The Internet has also introduced new issues of fairness, reawakened industry efforts to broaden protection of trade secrets, and created concerns about the impact of disclosure on national security.

Broadening Participation in the Design of Disclosure

In the late 1990s officials at the EPA moved aggressively to place new technological capabilities in the service of improved communication about environmental risks. They combined data about toxic releases with data about toxicity and exposure and made results available on the Internet. One early project attempted to estimate cumulative exposures to toxic chemicals in the air, in food, and in drinking water; identify the most serious exposures and the most affected communities; and estimate health risks.[122] A second attempted to estimate the relative risk of the toxic chemicals disclosed to the public based on amounts released, toxicity, and exposure, thus allowing comparisons by chemical, geographical area, and facility.[123] A third, known as the Sector Facility Indexing Project, consolidated and placed on the Internet permits, compliance records, releases, and accident data involving 600 facilities in five major industries, with the idea that risk information could be added later. These initiatives responded to years of pressure from industry and consumer groups to calibrate disclosure of toxic chemicals to reflect risks. They also responded to a specific directive by President Clinton in 1995 calling on the agency to "reinvent" environmental regulation and improve "risk-based" enforcement.[124]

Opposition was swift and powerful. The plan to compare cumulative exposure to toxic chemicals among communities drew protests from big-city mayors, who feared for their cities' reputations. Consolidation of information about industrial facilities drew protests from the industry representatives, who argued that the information was misleading and target companies should be involved in the project's design. The EPA agreed to postpone the posting toxicity information for chemicals pending further review.

As controversy over electronic disclosure intensified, opposing groups forged new coalitions. Trade associations representing major industrial sectors formed a Coalition for Effective Environmental Information in 1996. Members included the Chemical Manufacturers Association, the American Petroleum Institute, and the Automobile Manufacturers Association. The coalition hired Mark Greenwood, formerly director of the EPA's toxics program, to represent their interests. State environmental officials, who had formed their own organization in the mid-1990s to represent their interests before the EPA and Congress, made data accuracy a top priority. Right-to-know, labor, and environmental groups also strengthened their efforts to fight for rapid dissemination of information on the Internet.

Industry attacks shifted from complaints about reporting burdens to more powerful arguments about basic fairness. If government was going to give the public composite portraits of companies' environmental performance that could affect their reputations in new ways, manufacturers wanted a stronger voice in how information was integrated and what was made public.[125]

When the EPA proposed in 1997 to combine information about toxic releases, permits, and compliance records for specific facilities to construct hazard rankings, for example, a coalition of environmental groups pressed for rapid launching of the project on the web. But the new industry coalition enlisted members of Congress to demand an opportunity to help shape the way data were presented and interpreted. Senate Majority Leader Trent Lott and several other senators wrote the agency, voicing concern about the lack of opportunity for comment on the proposal. The organization of state environmental commissioners approved a resolution complaining that they had not been consulted about the project's design. Both industry and state representatives expressed concerns that hazard rankings could be misleading without more extensive analysis of interactions between chemical releases, toxicity, weather patterns, chemical dispersion properties, and populations. They demanded a review of methodology by the agency's science advisory board and sought an injunction in federal court to stop the public release of information. The injunction was denied, but pressure was sufficient to cause the agency to give up the idea of hazard rankings. Although industry representatives had argued for a decade that disclosure of toxic releases should be placed in the broader context of risks to the public, forging agreement on how such risks should be characterized proved an insurmountable obstacle.

Broadening Protection of Trade Secrets

Industry groups also sought to broaden protection of trade secrets. The ease and low cost with which fragmentary information could be assembled on the web led to fears that competitors could easily construct a "mosaic" pattern of secrets. In 1998 the Chemical Manufacturers Association produced a detailed report charging that the government did not give business an adequate opportunity to claim confidentiality for fragments of information that could be pieced together by competitors in this way.[126] Contributing to industry fears was the growing professionalization of corporate spying. The shadowy practices of industrial espionage were replaced in the 1990s with a growing profession of "competitive intelligence," in which competitors used legal methods to obtain information about production costs, new product introductions, market share, manufacturing processes, and expansion plans—often from public sources.[127] Another industry study found that the EPA's website could be used to assemble information about a plant's physical layout, chemical reaction sequences, product and by-product streams, and production capabilities. The study also warned that broader disclosure of chemical uses, still an agency goal, could provide foreign competitors with information about manufacturing costs, efficiency, probable technical advances, specific chemicals used, and probable expansion plans.[128]

Counterarguments cast doubt on the relative importance of disclosed information in the construction of such electronically derived mosaics. A 1998 survey by security specialists concluded that the greatest risk of losing proprietary information came from persons with a trusted relationship within the company. Environmental officials in New Jersey and Massachusetts reported that fewer than 2 percent of facilities made confidentiality claims on their state's broad requirements that company use of toxic chemicals be disclosed to the public.[129] The new political pressures had consequences, however. In the late 1990s, the EPA gave up, once again, the controversial idea of requiring disclosure to include toxic chemicals used in production or embedded in products.

Protecting National Security

The Internet also changed the politics of information by raising new concerns that disclosure of toxic releases could threaten national security. The issue focused on worst-case scenarios in chemical accidents rather than routine releases.[130] Congress had ordered companies to disclose the size and direction of toxic plumes and other possible effects as part of risk-management plans in order to aid responses to accidents. When the EPA issued regulations to carry out the law in 1996, the agency announced that scenarios would be posted on the Internet beginning in June 1999.

Industry representatives argued that even though much of the information in question was already available to the public, often provided voluntarily by companies, Internet access could make it easy for terrorists to maximize destruction in communities. An EPA study concluded that such risks were very small but were perhaps twice as high if data were posted on the Internet because of the efficiency with which plants around the country could be scanned.[131] Defenders of disclosure countered that an appropriate response to vulnerability would be to reduce hazards rather than to reduce access to information.[132] But under pressure from members of Congress, representatives of the Federal Bureau of Investigation, and members of the National Safety Council, the EPA decided in November 1998 not to post worst-case scenarios on the web. When right-to-know groups then suggested that they would obtain such data under the Freedom of Information Act and post it themselves, Congress took the extraordinary step of enacting legislation to remove public access to worst-case scenarios. It allowed government officials and researchers to obtain such information but made it a crime for them to disclose it. It

required companies to hold public meetings to summarize such information and directed the government to issue regulations governing such
public disclosure before the provision expired in one year. Right-to-know
groups quickly found a way around the prohibition, however. Since the
law did not prohibit companies from releasing information directly to
the public, one group responded by revealing 14,000 such scenarios on its
website. Eventually, the EPA posted risk management plans on the web,
without information about possible consequences to neighboring communities. In the aftermath of September 11, the agency removed the plans
from the web altogether. Henceforth, they would be available to the public only in federal reading rooms, roughly one per state.[133]

The Increasing Power of the Navigator

As electronic access became routine, entrepreneurs who designed software
to provide the public with information emerged as influential intermediaries. These navigators gave whomever they worked for—citizen groups,
industry, or the government—new means of promoting their perspectives.

Environmental Defense, a leading advocacy group, in the spring of
1998 launched a website that demonstrated the power of the navigator.
Their Scorecard website merged routinely disclosed facts about toxic pollution with environmental information from other public databases to
create a new picture of risks. Users who typed in their zip code could find
industrial sources of toxic chemicals in their county, compare the importance of toxic pollution from industrial sources with such pollution from
vehicles and small businesses, investigate the toxicity of specific chemicals, learn what was known about exposure, and send prewritten faxes or
e-mails to a company president, the administrator of the EPA, or a member of Congress.

The site was created by Bill Pease, a former community organizer who
was trained in toxicology, at an initial cost of about $1.5 million. Work-
ing at the School of Public Health at the University of California at Berke-
ley in the early 1990s, Pease was deluged with requests from people to
explain government data on toxic releases. Later, as a senior environmental health scientist at Environmental Defense, he appealed to the
Clarence E. Heller Charitable Foundation in San Francisco to back his

idea of explaining toxic releases on the Internet. Teaming up with two computer experts, Philip Greenspun, a graduate student in computer science at the Massachusetts Institute of Technology, and David Abercromby, an expert in complex data systems, Pease began working on Scorecard in January 1996 and launched it in April 1998. Frederick Webber, president of the Chemical Manufacturers Association, immediately issued a statement warning his members that the Internet site would create pressure for further cuts in toxic releases. A new source of political power had emerged.[134]

It was easy for users to search information in new ways that created multiple lists of polluters. With a few clicks, they could rank sources of toxic pollution nationally, by state, or by county and show chemicals with high volume and low toxicity or low volume and high toxicity—tasks that had previously taken enterprising reporters or advocates months of work. Data could be characterized in forty different ways. Chemicals were ranked by an inevitably controversial risk-scoring system, reflecting a combination of toxicity and exposure. In 2001 the website added data on toxic releases in Canada.

By 2002 an array of websites designed by environmental groups, government, and industry brought consumers, employees, investors, and community residents information about toxic chemicals that was increasingly user friendly. RTK Net, the first effort to bring ordinary citizens usable information about toxic pollution, also allowed users to search toxic releases by geographical area, facility, industry, and company and provided information about chemical accidents and compliance with federal laws. The site let users choose low, medium, or high levels of detail.[135] EPA's Envirofacts website added new features. In addition to searches by facility, chemical, and geographical area, it provided separate searches for general and technical users and increasingly sophisticated maps that showed sources of pollution.[136] The EPA continued to improve TRI Explorer to promote its perspective on toxic pollution. The Chemical Manufacturers Association (now the American Chemistry Council) launched a website that highlighted the jobs plants provided, the taxes they paid, and the products they made, as well as their improving environmental and safety performance.[137]

One issue provided an early indication of next steps in the politics of technopopulism. By posting information about more than two-thirds of high-production chemicals that lacked basic toxicity data, Scorecard increased pressure on chemical companies to undertake such testing. The site highlighted the magnitude and consequences not only of what was known but also of what was not known about toxic pollution and human health. Publicity placed new pressure on companies by highlighting the common practice of introducing chemicals into wide use before their health effects were determined. Karen Florini and David Roe, senior attorneys at Environmental Defense, began negotiating individual agreements with companies to test common chemicals, and national politicians took up the cause. On Earth Day, April 22, 1998, Vice President Al Gore announced a "chemical right-to-know initiative" aimed at speeding up collection and dissemination of toxicity data for widely used chemicals. The chemical industry agreed to an extensive testing program, at a cost of $26 million a year.[138]

A Work in Progress

As information technology continues its exponential advances, one can imagine that accurate and timely indicators of risk could help people make informed choices about products, services, jobs, investments, and political action. Actions by consumers, investors, workers, and voters could put constructive pressure on companies to minimize threats to public health and the environment. A lively information marketplace could improve data quality, encourage research, and define dimensions of uncertainty. Over time, a backdrop of reliable knowledge could reduce scares from isolated incidents, improve trust in business and government, and promote constructive public participation in government decisions about reducing risks. Because the flow of information is not circumscribed by national boundaries, international transparency ultimately could help improve health, safety, and environmental protection in many countries.

Government officials continued to proclaim that disclosure of toxic chemicals represented a significant step along this path. It was renowned for its success in reducing releases of listed chemicals by nearly half in a decade. An array of federal programs was based on its results and assumed their reliability. State governments and other countries copied and extended it. Created as a right-to-know requirement, it had become a symbol of the power of information to produce social change.

Less heralded were its precautionary lessons. Political rhetoric masked systematic flaws. The system's architecture—the who, what, when, and how of disclosure—limited its potential to improve public health and the environment. Conflicts over protecting trade secrets and minimizing regulatory burdens truncated its scope. Flawed metrics treated events with widely varying health consequences alike, did not reveal sources of most toxic pollution, and compromised timeliness and accuracy. Information technology created opportunities to correct some of these problems but also introduced new conflicts. Persistent gaps between claims made for disclosure and its limitations raised the specter of perverse effects: misdirecting public attention and industry resources, discouraging constructive midcourse corrections, and undermining public trust in business and government.

3 Food Labeling to Reduce Disease

The Tower of Babel in food labels has come down, and American consumers are the winners.

—LOUIS W. SULLIVAN*

On November 30, 1992, two cabinet secretaries charged with overseeing the nation's food policies requested an urgent meeting with President George H. W. Bush. Louis W. Sullivan, secretary of health and human services, and Edward Madigan, secretary of agriculture, asked the president to decide issues so difficult that months of staff meetings, their own negotiations, and intervention by the Office of Management and Budget had failed to resolve them.

The controversy they brought to the president was not about a giant recall of contaminated food or the future of genetic engineering, however. It was about what the public should be told about fat. They could not agree on how to show high or low amounts on packages of processed foods, whether recommended daily levels should be based on a

---

*Louis W. Sullivan, quoted in Marian Burros, "U.S., Ending Dispute, Decides What Food Labels Must Tell," *New York Times*, December 3, 1992, p. A1.

2,000-calorie-a-day diet or a 2,500-calorie-a-day diet, and what the term *light* on labels should mean. And they were at odds about whether restaurants should be required to conform their menus to government definitions. Groups like the National Cattlemen's Beef Association and the Salt Institute were battling over these issues because a new law required government-designed labels on cereal boxes, soup cans, candy bars, and thousands of other processed foods. As they waited outside the Oval Office, Vice President Dan Quayle told the two cabinet officers that he could not believe these questions were being placed before the president.[1]

This unlikely meeting illustrates both the high stakes and minutiae involved in employing public disclosure to produce social change. Two years earlier, Congress had approved a new law aimed at reducing more than 1.5 million deaths a year from heart disease, cancer, and other chronic diseases. The Nutrition Labeling and Education Act did not call for strict standards and harsh penalties, however. Instead, it simply required manufacturers to tell the public what was in processed foods and adopt government-mandated definitions for terms like *light* and *low fat*. For public health groups and consumer organizations, the new law represented a victory. They hoped it would improve informed choices by consumers and force companies to create healthier products. But for producers of foods that were relatively high in fat and other nutrients linked to health problems, it represented a potential threat to lucrative markets.

As the president prepared to meet with his cabinet officers, two decades of planning hung in the balance. Efforts to introduce nutritional labeling had begun in the 1970s, as evidence of links between diet and disease became increasingly persuasive. Except for a very limited category of products, the issue had remained stalled until Congress acted in 1990. Now the remaining regulatory issues had caused the Bush administration to miss a November 8 deadline for final rules. And in the presidential election on November 2, President Bush, a Republican, had been defeated by Democrat Bill Clinton. If a new administration had to revisit the issues, it could mean more years of delay.

The Food and Drug Administration (FDA), part of Dr. Sullivan's department, had worked out many of the remaining technical problems, and the Department of Agriculture (USDA), which regulated labeling of processed foods containing meat and poultry, had agreed in principle to adopt conforming rules. But Secretary Sullivan insisted that labels be based on a 2,000-calorie diet and that fat content be shown in the context of recommended daily consumption. He had brought along placemats from McDonald's that listed nutrients using a 2,000-calorie diet. They remained scattered on tables and sofas as the meeting continued for more than an hour. He also told the president that consideration of a 2,500-calorie diet would mean more delay while comments were solicited. Secretary Madigan countered that a 2,000-calorie diet would make the fat content appear larger than appropriate. For many men and physically active women, 2,500 calories made sense. FDA commissioner David Kessler wrote later in *A Question of Intent,* "What USDA preferred, to my surprise, was as little information as possible on the label . . . the concern about labeling revolved around one word—fat. . . . Once the meat industry realized that our proposed label would make it far simpler for a shopper to gauge fat intake, it vigorously lobbied the USDA to follow a different course."[2]

Virtually every can of soup, box of cereal, and package of hot dogs sold in the United States now displays the compromise that President Bush handed down a few days later. Food labels would be based on a 2,000-calorie diet and amounts of nutrients would be related to recommended daily consumption, as the FDA had proposed, but percentages of nutrients based on a 2,500-calorie diet would be shown also, in a footnote. Companies would have to conform to strict definitions of terms like *low fat* and *fat free.* But *light* or *lite* could denote a low salt content as well as a low fat content, as the industry proposed, and restaurants did not have to conform to the strict definitions required for labels. Finally, companies were given the extra year they wanted to change labels. The new requirements would not take effect until May 1994. Once the decision was made, both cabinet officers applauded it. Secretary Sullivan declared that "the Tower of Babel in food labels has come down, and American consumers are the winners."[3]

This compromise cleared the way for a new national approach to a serious public health problem. In 1988 the surgeon general of the United States had delivered a stark warning: "For the two out of three adult Americans who do not smoke and do not drink excessively, one personal choice seems to influence long-term health prospects more than any other: what we eat."[4] After use of tobacco, overconsumption of fat and other nutrients was the largest contributor to preventable deaths. It was linked to heart disease and cancer, the nation's two leading causes of death, as well as to diabetes, stroke, and other serious ailments.[5] Even small changes in diet could produce large health benefits.

For the most part, though, Americans had had no way of knowing what they were eating. For more than twenty years, scientists and policy-makers had agreed about the need for nutritional labeling but disagreed about how to do it. In the 1980s better informed consumers showed growing interest in healthy products, and some companies revealed a few nutrients voluntarily. However, limited labeling required for products with added nutrients or nutritional claims did not include amounts of cholesterol, saturated fat, and fiber, nutrients that scientists believed had the greatest impact on health. More than half of packaged foods lacked any nutritional information.

Curiously, it was a few words of fine print on the label of one brand of cereal that finally produced national action. In 1984 the Kellogg Company revised the label of its All-Bran cereal to suggest that fiber might reduce risks of some cancers. That seemingly small change triggered scores of health claims from other companies, a crackdown by state officials on such claims, and, six years later, a national system of nutritional labeling.

Although the risks addressed were different, conflicts associated with nutritional labeling were strikingly similar to those involved in creating toxic chemical disclosure four years earlier. Both pitted the public's interest in understanding risks to public health against companies' interests in protecting proprietary information. Both featured clashes between the importance of complete and accurate disclosure and the importance of minimizing regulatory burdens. Both also created tension between the need to convey complicated information about unique practices and products and the need to standardize and simplify. And both were characterized by battles between entrepreneurial politicians and public interest groups, who sought to broaden disclosure, and companies executives, who sought to narrow it.

By mandating nutritional labeling, Congress and the FDA achieved something remarkable. They placed a large body of closely guarded information concerning health risks permanently in the public domain.

But the compromises outlined in the 1990 law and elaborated in further legislation in 1994 and 1997 also created confusion and limited potential benefits. If labels could change the competitive position of products or companies, then the who, what, and how of disclosure was worth a fight. The new laws excluded restaurants, fast-food operations, and grocery delicatessens from labeling requirements at a time when Americans spent nearly half their food dollar away from home. They bowed to pressure from health food stores and the supplement industry to allow the marketing of herbal remedies without the usual safety reviews. The new laws required careful premarket review of claims that nutrients prevented disease but no review at all of claims that they improved circulation or strengthened bones. Congress also barred states from setting stricter standards for disclosure, favoring national consistency over state priorities.

These compromises did not destroy the system, but they created new trouble by limiting its reach, impairing communication, and perpetuating bureaucratic anomalies. Disclosure intended to inform the public about diet and disease left out risks and benefits of little-tested supplements and left shoppers unprepared to assess the new generation of disease-fighting foods that began to appear on grocery shelves.

A Cacophony of Health Claims Sparks National Action

Surprisingly, nutritional labeling, which called upon some of the largest and most powerful companies in the world to reveal to the public detailed information about their products, gained approval during a period of regulatory retrenchment. In the late 1980s cutting back on the burdens of federal regulation remained a prevailing national theme. Budget cuts left regulators without resources to carry out even existing mandates to protect the safety of the food supply. There was a broad consensus that the risks of heart disease, cancer, diabetes, and other chronic diseases could be greatly reduced by improvements in the American diet. But that understanding was not new in 1990, and consumers, while showing increasing interest in healthy eating, were not clamoring for data about grams of protein, carbohydrates, and fat in their breakfast cereal.

Why, then, was the issue catapulted to the top of the national agenda after twenty years of stalemate? A single action by one cereal maker provided the political force that led to the sudden prominence of nutritional labeling. In October 1984 the Kellogg Company launched a new campaign to promote the healthy qualities of its All-Bran cereal. The centerpiece of the campaign was a new message on the box: high-fiber foods "may reduce your risk of some kinds of cancer."[6] In linking fiber to reduction of cancer risks, Kellogg knowingly crossed a line that had been drawn with painstaking care by Congress, patrolled by government regulators for fifty years, and legitimized by the courts. To protect the public from unscrupulous marketers who peddled their products as cures for every ailment, federal policy had long held that only products sold as drugs could make claims to prevent or cure diseases. Each such product had to be tested for safety and effectiveness and approved by the government before it could be sold. Companies that attempted to market foods with disease claims were told to pull them from grocery shelves until their safety and effectiveness were proven in clinical trials, a process that often took many years and could cost millions of dollars.[7]

The government had been under increasing pressure to alter this legal boundary, however. In the 1970s and 1980s researchers began to discover that some nutrients did indeed reduce risks of heart disease, cancer, or other ailments. A number of studies established a link between overconsumption of cholesterol (found in animal fat) or saturated fats (found in vegetable oils as well) and an increased risk of heart disease. By the mid-1980s many medical experts also agreed that a diet that was high in fiber could reduce the risk of some kinds of cancer, in particular colon and rectal cancers. Public and private health organizations began encouraging Americans to include more fiber in their diets. Other research suggested that overconsumption of sodium could contribute to hypertension. But despite advances in science, labeling rules remained the same.

Kellogg's new campaign drove a wedge between the research and regulatory arms of the federal government. In the company's view, regulators were blocking a legitimate marketing opportunity because they were not paying attention to the latest science. Kellogg asked the National Cancer Institute (NCI), a division of the federal government's National

Institutes of Health, for an endorsement for its new message about bran. The NCI agreed.[8]

The new label stymied regulators at the FDA. Taking action against the claim meant countering the advice of the government's own medical authorities. Ignoring it meant encouraging other manufacturers to suggest that their products could fight all kinds of diseases. A heated debate within the executive branch ensued. President Ronald Reagan had promised to reduce burdensome regulation, and the Office of Management and Budget, which had been charged by the president to act as a gatekeeper for new agency actions, opposed a crackdown. The FDA's Center for Food Safety and Applied Nutrition wanted to stop Kellogg's campaign and enforce the government's traditional policy. The Federal Trade Commission (FTC), regulator of food advertising, favored letting companies make health claims so long as they had a reasonable basis for their statements. Faced with this dilemma, the administration sought middle ground. The FDA took no action against Kellogg but on August 4, 1987, proposed a new rule that would let companies label foods as "effective in the prevention, cure, mitigation, or treatment of any disease" if the agency approved them as "supported by valid, reliable . . . scientific evidence."[9]

Other food processors had been quick to exploit what they perceived as a new marketing opportunity that might disappear if new rules were finalized. By 1989 nearly one-third of all advertising for packaged foods included some kind of health claim, creating a bonanza for some companies. Sales of cereals containing oat bran increased more than 70 percent by volume.[10] Even well-known brands touted small amounts of beneficial nutrients for their disease-preventing or health-enhancing properties without alerting customers to the presence of large amounts of fat or other nutrients linked to chronic disease. Safeway donuts were labeled as containing "new oatbran—reduces cholesterol," despite 10 grams of fat. Muffins and potato chips emphasized that they contained oat bran, even if in tiny amounts. Cookies were labeled cholesterol-free when they were high in saturated fat and calories. Bertolli and Filippo Berio sold "light" olive oils that were light only in color, and Sara Lee Corp. launched "light classics desserts" that were lighter in texture but not in calories. Sometimes companies lowered fat or salt per serving by reducing listed serving sizes rather than fat. Soup cans servings per can increased from 2 to 2.5. Soft drinks servings were reduced from 12 to 6 ounces. Ralston-Purina labeled Bran News as a "high-fiber cereal" when it had only 3 grams of fiber per 1 ounce serving. Kellogg advertised that Cracklin' Oat Bran could reduce some kinds of cancer but withdrew the claim after consumer advocates took out newspaper ads pointing out that it contained 4 grams of fat. In a settlement with the New York state attorney general, Kellogg also withdrew a claim that Rice Krispies had more "energy-releasing B vitamins" for a "pick me up" after scientists pointed out that the American diet was not deficient in B-vitamins and the cereal's nutrients could not provide a "pick-me-up." Manufacturers also touted the benefits of unproven supplements like Honeybee Pollen Nuggets or Supernatural Fish Oil Concentrate that claimed to prevent or treat breast cancer, diabetes, heart disease, asthma, and other diseases.[11]

The most immediate consequence was confusion. Shoppers had no way to weigh benefits and risks of different products, and regulators did not have the resources to enforce the law, even if they had wanted to. As David Kessler, who would soon head the FDA, put it, the agency "was under-funded, understaffed, and demoralized."[12] Even food companies protested. They had no way to distinguish their healthy soups or cereals from those that made sham claims. A vice president of marketing for Borden's dairy division told *Business Week:* "This is such a charade, it is unbelievable." Robert J. Gillespie, president of Best Foods agreed. "Without guidelines, we almost run the risk of going back to the snake-oil era." In a cover story chronicling the new claims, the magazine concluded that "the supermarket food aisles look like a modern medicine show."[13]

Echoes of Early Policies

References to the era of snake-oil and medicine shows recalled the commercial excesses a hundred years earlier that first led Congress to limit claims that products could cure dread diseases. At the beginning of the twentieth century, remarkable advances in food science and technology created national markets and improved nutrition, but they also produced unsafe practices, deceptive health claims, and public pressure for government regulation. This pattern of technological progress, commercial overreaching, and government action would be repeated several times, as food policies lurched forward roughly once a generation, finally leading to nutritional labeling.

At the beginning of the century, President Theodore Roosevelt championed the first use of food labeling to reduce risks. The Pure Food and Drug Act of 1906 outlawed adulteration of food and mislabeling of bulk containers shipped in interstate commerce. It responded to reports that food companies were using inedible substances like wood chips in bread and claiming that patent medicines could cure baldness or cancer. In 1906 Upton Sinclair, a committed socialist who worked his way through college writing dime novels, published *The Jungle,* a stomach-turning tale of meat processing at the Chicago stockyards. These practices represented the dark side of remarkable advances in technology that were transforming food marketing at the turn of the century. Families accustomed to purchasing flour, eggs, and produce from the bins and baskets of neighborhood merchants and farmers instead bought packaged cereals, crackers, and meats made by Quaker Oats, H. J. Heinz, and Campbell's. Processed foods were brought to their communities via a national network of railroads to be sold at the A&P and other grocery chains.[14]

A generation later Congress responded to deceptive health claims and new understanding of links between nutritional deficiencies and diseases with the stricter rules that would govern food labeling for the next fifty years. The Food, Drug, and Cosmetic Act of 1938 and its regulations required companies to label processed foods with their names, quantities, and ingredients, as well as the manufacturer's name and address, and forbade false or misleading statements, including claims that left out material facts.[15]

By 1941 nutrition had become a national security issue as well. Mobilization of troops highlighted the poor health of many recruits and the need for better diets to fortify them against infectious diseases like pneumonia, scarlet fever, influenza, and dysentery. Acting on a report by the National Defense Advisory Commission in 1940, President Franklin D. Roosevelt convened a National Nutrition Conference in 1941, which led to the first government recommendations of daily allowances for nutrients. After the war, national policy continued to emphasize the need to eat enough of essential nutrients. The federal government became the meal planner for increasing numbers of Americans by financing school breakfast and lunch programs and offering food stamps to families in poverty. In 1958 Congress also responded to new concerns about cancer-causing additives by requiring testing and premarket approval and banning those known to cause cancer in humans or animals.[16]

Consumers Demand Both Hamburger Helper and Healthy Choice

At the same time, evidence accumulated that overconsumption as well as underconsumption of basic nutrients could create serious health risks. As early as 1961 the American Heart Association recommended low-fat diets to help prevent heart disease. In 1979 the National Cancer Institute issued dietary guidelines to lower cancer risk. In 1988 *The Surgeon General's Report on Nutrition and Health* recommended nutritional labeling to reduce risks of chronic disease and stop misleading marketing. It concluded that overconsumption of fat and other nutrients played a prominent role in five of the ten leading causes of death for Americans—coronary heart disease, cancer, stroke, diabetes, and arteriosclerosis—and warned against deception: "Today, the traveling patent medicine man has been largely replaced by the highly skilled and organized use of electronic means to promote fraudulent marketing—computers, customized mailing lists, national advertisements. . . . The medium and the details have changed, but the message and the goals remain. It is difficult for consumers to evaluate the validity of health claims perpetrated by quacks and faddists."[17] A year later the National Research Council echoed these concerns. It found strong evidence that the risk of heart disease could be reduced by limiting consumption of foods high in saturated fat and cholesterol. Risks of colon, prostate, and breast cancers could be reduced by limiting consumption of total fat.[18]

Americans were eating more convenience foods that were high in fat and sugar, but they were also looking for healthier products. The American Heart Association reported increases in obesity from 25 percent of the population between 1976 and 1980 to 33 percent between 1988 and 1991. Americans consumed an average of 37 percent of their calories in fat, one-third of it in saturated fat. Fewer people ate breakfast and 20 percent of calories came from snacking. More people were dieting, but people were also more sedentary, working behind counters and desks instead of in fields and factories. Grocery stores carried more snacks and prepackaged meals, and more shoppers could afford them. Food spending as a portion of disposable income continued to decline—from 14 percent in 1970 to 11 percent in 1996. When General Mills introduced Hamburger Helper in 1971 it was such an immediate success that the company could not meet demand. By the late 1980s only 28 percent of families had someone at home all the time, and people were spending as little as fifteen minutes a meal on food preparation. The number of families with microwave ovens skyrocketed from 10 percent in 1978 to more than 70 percent in 1990. Families also ate more fast food and restaurant meals. By 1990 meals eaten away from home accounted for 43 percent of the American food budget, compared to 34 percent in 1970.[19]

At the same time, better informed shoppers looked for healthier products. Fifty-five percent of respondents to government surveys in 1989 knew that eating high-fat foods could increase the risk of heart disease, up from 29 percent in 1979. Twenty-five percent knew that fats could cause cancer. More than 30 percent knew that fats and sodium were causes of high blood pressure, compared to 6 percent ten years earlier. From 1976 on, people ate less beef, fewer eggs, and less butter and drank less whole milk than in earlier years. Annual consumption of beef dropped from 78.8 pounds per person in 1985 to 67.8 pounds in 1990. Between 1980 and 1990 annual egg consumption dropped from 272.4 per person to 235.7, butter consumption decreased 4 percent, and daily salt consumption dropped by nearly 25 percent. Industry research showed that as many as two-thirds of consumers were making changes in their eating to reduce fat, cholesterol, or oils. When Conagra Inc. launched a Healthy Choice line of frozen dinners with low fat, sodium, and cholesterol in 1989, they captured 22 percent of the frozen dinner market within a few months in portions of the country where they were introduced. The same year, Kraft introduced Breyer's light ice milk as well as low-calorie cream cheese, mayonnaise, and sour cream. More than half of the 800 dairy products launched in 1988 were nonfat or low fat. Surveys indicated that nutrition ranked with taste, convenience, price, and product safety as consumer priorities.[20]

Food companies responded to shoppers' conflicting demands by trying to satisfy all of them. They introduced more convenience foods, launched more lines of healthy products, and engaged in aggressive marketing of both. Streamlined supermarkets carried more items, including ethnic, organic, and diet foods. Competition for shelf space increased and products had to prove themselves quickly. As government officials began to view labeling as an important means of protecting public health, companies viewed labeling as an increasingly important means of promoting products.

Nutritional Labeling Remains Stalled

Americans who wanted to reduce their risks of heart disease and cancer by eating healthier foods lacked the information to do so. Limited labeling requirements adopted in 1973 were an important advance, but their main goal was to ensure that people consumed enough vitamins, minerals, and proteins. They did not require disclosure of saturated fats, cholesterol, fiber, or other nutrients linked to heart disease and cancer, and they applied only when manufacturers added calcium, vitamins, or other nutrients or made nutritional claims. They did not standardize serving sizes so that products' nutritional content could be compared. The government had not updated recommended daily allowances since 1972. The Institute of Medicine warned that the "information that nutrition labeling does provide is incomplete and misfocused."[21]

Efforts to revise labeling to reflect links between diet and disease were characterized by two decades of false starts. In 1979, after a series of public meetings, the FDA, the Department of Agriculture, and the FTC jointly suggested changes in labels and disease-prevention claims. But that proposal was never finalized.[22] In 1985 the FDA added sodium to the list of nutrients that had to be disclosed when manufacturers added nutrients, but in 1986, when the agency proposed adding cholesterol, no final rule was issued.[23]

Political Forces Converge

Ironically, the Reagan administration's antiregulatory stance helped provide the momentum for broader labeling. The FDA's failure to pull boxes of All-Bran cereal from grocery shelves set off a chain reaction. Federal inaction triggered state action, congressional initiatives, and a campaign by public health organizations and consumer groups to require broader labeling. State action, in turn, caused beleaguered food companies to rethink their stand. The prospect of a single national system of regulation began to look preferable to scores of different state rules. With the controversy making headlines across the country, Congress took up the cause.

State Governments Respond to Sudden New Health Claims

When well-known companies like Kellogg and Sara Lee suddenly peppered labels with claims that products could help prevent disease and federal regulators looked the other way, a number of enterprising state attorneys general moved in to defend the regulatory barrier between foods and drugs that the FDA had abandoned by inaction. Multistate task forces of state prosecutors accused national companies of fraudulent labeling for marketing their foods with disease-prevention claims. By the late 1980s at least sixty-five labeling bills were introduced in twenty-two states. Nine attorneys general and the Federal Trade Commission were investigating claims. Prosecutors moved against major fast-food companies, signing a settlement with McDonald's, Burger King, Jack in the Box, Kentucky Fried Chicken, and Wendy's to list product nutrients prominently at all their outlets.[24]

Consumer Groups Promote Labeling as a Public Health Issue

Federal inaction and the wilderness of exaggerated health claims also galvanized consumer groups and public health organizations. They began to promote nutritional labeling as a public health issue rather than simply a "right-to-know" effort. The American Heart Association, the American Cancer Society, the American Dietetic Association (representing 58,000 nutritionists), and the American Association of Retired Persons joined with the Center for Science in the Public Interest and other consumer groups to convince Congress to act. They marshaled evidence that current labeling caused confusion, they worked to obtain media coverage, and they supported legislation.[25]

Congressional Democrats and a New Administration Seize the Moment

Leading Democrats in Congress channeled these diverse pressures into legislative action. In the House, the cause was taken up by Henry Waxman (D-Calif.), the powerful chairman of the Health and Environment Subcommittee of the Energy and Commerce Committee. He specialized in ushering complex changes in health and environmental policy through the political process. In 1989, when he was also at work on a complicated reform of the nation's framework for controlling air pollution, Waxman tried to forge a majority to back comprehensive nutritional labeling. He was supported by John Dingell (D-Mich.), the committee's chairman, and by other members who felt that the Reagan White House had unfairly blocked labeling initiatives. Once it gained prominence, the labeling proposal moved through the House in steps that would have made it a model civics lesson. It was the subject of more than half a dozen hearings over two years and extensive negotiations with the food industry and consumer groups.[26]

In the Senate, nutritional labeling was taken up by Howard Metzenbaum (D-Ohio), a veteran member of the Environment and Public Works Committee. He had a track record of leading campaigns on controversial measures to improve consumer protection. Introducing the bill, Metzenbaum noted that "for far too long, we Americans have been shopping in the dark. . . . We're here to shine a little light on the food that lines our supermarket aisles . . . because what you don't know can hurt you. . . . Consumers are fed up with food labels that are at best confusing—at worst, downright deceptive."[27] Important support also came from the new administration. When George H. W. Bush replaced Ronald Reagan as president in January 1988, chances for approval suddenly increased. The Bush administration endorsed nutritional labeling and proposed new regulations to require it.[28]

The Food Industry Supports Congressional Action

Surprisingly, it was the food industry itself that provided the most important support for the new system of transparency. Companies with national markets faced the prospect of having to comply with dozens of new state labeling rules. They also faced lawsuits by state prosecutors that threatened their reputations with customers. By 1990 the Grocery Manufacturers Association, the National Food Processors Association, and other large trade associations that represented the formidable $400 billion industry threw their weight behind national labeling rules. Senator Metzenbaum explained: "One thing that concerns the industry is 50 states having 50 different labeling laws—which would be worse than a Federal law."[29]

Large processors concluded that national regulation might improve their competitive position as well. By 1990 the chorus of questionable health claims on cereal boxes and soup cans made it hard for companies that had designed products authentically low in saturated fat or high in bran to gain profits from their efforts. Even if consumers were willing to pay more for cereals rich in bran or soups with minimal salt, they lacked information to distinguish them from less healthy products. In an increasingly competitive industry, government-required labeling might also produce an advantage for the giant companies over smaller competitors. Kellogg, Campbell's, Heinz, and other big companies had resources to invest in new labels, compliance personnel, and reformulated products. It would be harder for small companies to finance improvements to meet changing consumer tastes. The large companies needed national action.[30]

On the specifics of labeling, however, broad support quickly splintered into contests to preserve market niches. Processors of meat, dairy products, fats, salt, sugar, and beverages lobbied for definitions and formats that would place their products in a favorable light. They also launched new advertising campaigns to counter evidence of health risks. The beef industry advertised beef as "real food for real people" and as food that "gives strength." Egg producers advertised the "edible, incredible egg," and the sugar industry reminded consumers that their product was "100 percent pure, natural." Even manufacturers of palm oil, high in the saturated fats that were linked to heart disease, took out full-page ads in *USA Today* advertising it as "a healthy and nutritious vegetable oil." Not all producers bought into the calculus of national labeling. While major trade associations supported federal rules, groups representing specific interests, like chocolate and sugar manufacturers, ultimately opposed it.[31]

Congress Narrows Disclosure

It is hard to imagine a more difficult regulatory task than the one that confronted congressional proponents of nutritional labeling in the fall of 1989. Their goal was to use the power of information to reduce the more than 1 million deaths each year from heart disease, cancer, and other chronic diseases by designing a standardized system of disclosure for key nutrients that would let shoppers compare tens of thousands of products, from tomato soup to tortillas, and encourage companies to develop healthier products. They had to find a way to alert shoppers to the relationship between specific amounts of nutrients and risks of a variety of diseases when much of the science remained uncertain. All that information had to be made comprehensible to millions of Americans with varying amounts of time, interest, and understanding and with varying dietary needs and preferences. They knew that many people would spend only a few seconds looking at a label. And the new information had to fit on every package of cheese and bar of candy. Never before had Congress attempted to construct such a sophisticated information strategy to protect public health. In approaching this task, congressional leaders resolved contentious issues in ways that gave the disclosure system some particular strengths, but they also made compromises that impaired effective communication and limited the products to be labeled. A decade after a new labeling system was painstakingly constructed, these features created new confusion.

The Battle over Structure

Clashes among competing values dominated debate about the structure of nutritional labeling. The most difficult issue, the conflict between national uniformity and state discretion, was resolved in favor of uniformity, a decision that ultimately strengthened the new system. But conflict between offering reliable information and preserving companies' freedom to promote their products was resolved with a confusing compromise that provided strict review of disease claims but provided no review of claims that nutrients strengthened bones, circulation, or brain function. The clash between providing simple signals and presenting nutritional information in its full quantitative complexity was resolved by discarding the idea of simple signals. Since most shoppers lacked basic nutritional education and often gave labels only a cursory glance, that decision limited the potential for communicating with large portions of the public.

NATIONAL UNIFORMITY VERSUS STATE DISCRETION. Ironically, consumer groups and federal officials argued for preserving states' rights, while the food industry argued for stronger federal regulation. National uniformity in labeling rules became food companies' top priority. Instead of simply constructing a national floor for nutrition labeling, they wanted Congress to outlaw state requirements that were more stringent or differed from the national system. The industry would find it difficult "to maintain its efficient distribution system if the states are free to impose food safety and labeling requirements different from those of the federal government," John R. Cady, president of the National Food Processors Association, told Congress.[32]

Sixteen food organizations sent a letter to the White House warning that state discretion would hurt the industry and weaken its ability to compete internationally. Consumer groups and advocates for states pointed out that Congress rarely preempted state law and that residents of different jurisdictions should be able to set their own priorities. The Bush administration, which campaigned on a promise to return power to the states, joined consumer groups in opposing preemption. A compromise gave industry most of what it wanted. Congressional leaders were persuaded that national companies would have difficulty complying with conflicting and inconsistent laws. As finally approved, the new system required uniformity in nutritional labeling and health claims but allowed states to add further warnings and petition for exemptions.[33]

STRUCTURED DISCLOSURE VERSUS FREEDOM TO COMMUNICATE. Paradoxically, policies that required new access to information also restricted its free flow. Congress proposed to specify the content and format of labels and to allow only scientifically supported health claims. That interfered with companies' ability to use labels to describe the benefits of their products in any way they chose. In determining whether regulatory restrictions on such commercial speech were legitimate, courts traditionally considered whether a government interest was substantial, whether regulation directly advanced that interest, and whether the fit between government ends and means was reasonable. Twelve years after nutritional labeling was approved, the boundary between these two values was still being debated in the courts.[34]

In Congress, the degree of scientific certainty became the focal point of the debate about limiting label claims. A subcommittee of the House Committee on Government Operations argued that no disease claims should be allowed on food labels.[35] Industry representatives argued for broad discretion. In the end, congressional sponsors made an unfortunate compromise. They regulated some health claims but not others. The law provided that claims concerning specific diseases would be allowed only if the FDA determined, "based on a totality of publicly available scientific evidence, that there is a significant scientific agreement, among experts qualified by scientific training and experience to evaluate such claims, that the claim is supported by such evidence." However, health claims concerning stronger bones, better circulation, or other improvements in body structure or function required no review at all. The distinction may have made sense to regulators but proved unfathomable to the public.[36]

SIMPLE RISK SIGNALS VERSUS PRECISE INFORMATION. Consumer groups argued for simple signaling to supplement detailed factual information. They pointed out that most members of the public did not have a sophisticated understanding of nutrition and were unlikely to devote much time to reading labels. Linking amounts of nutrients to recommended daily values was not enough. Quantitative information did not tell shoppers anything about nutrients' relationship to diseases. Simple symbols could provide a quick reference. Stoplight colors, stars, pie charts, or terms describing amounts of fat and other nutrients as "high" or "low" could attract consumers' attention and provide them with enough information to improve purchases.[37] Food companies resisted simple signals. They argued that it was the total diet, not single servings, that mattered. Nutritionists and experts at the FDA concurred. Their studies suggested a conundrum: people wanted labels with detailed factual information even though simpler formats promoted better understanding.[38] The FDA also pointed out that each person's dietary needs were different. It would be a mistake to designate individual foods as good or bad. Especially in the face of uncertain science, it was better to keep broad value judgments out of the labeling system.[39]

Ultimately, the industry prevailed. Nutritional labels did not identify health risks or suggest what actions should be taken to reduce them. Labels proved to be useful mainly to people who already understood links between diet and disease; were educated about the meaning and importance of fats, cholesterol, proteins, and carbohydrates; and already had dietary goals. They generally did not create *new* consumer interest in nutritional issues.[40]

Narrowing the Targets and Scope of Disclosure

Congress also substantially narrowed the range of companies, products, and substances that would be subject to labeling, disconnecting the disclosure system from the dimensions of the risks it addressed. A variety of political pressures led to the exclusion of foods that totaled nearly half of the public's food purchases, placing little-tested dietary supplements on a separate track and designing a more lenient regulatory regime for the meats, which included some of the foods in the American diet with the highest fat content. The benefits of disclosure were pitted against competing values, especially the regulatory burdens involved in measuring nutrients and developing new labels. But it was effective lobbying that decided the issues. The result was a law that claimed to equip consumers to make informed choices about diet and disease but failed to provide them with much of the information needed to do so.

INCLUSIVE LABELING VERSUS MINIMIZING REPORTING BURDENS. One compromise excluded from labeling the sources of meals on which Americans spent most of their food dollars. It allowed restaurants, fast-food outlets, grocery delicatessens, and small processors and retailers to avoid telling customers anything about the nutritional value of their products.[41] By 1990 Americans spent nearly half their food budget on meals eaten away from home, a portion that was increasing. Even when they ate at home, they often ate pizza, fast food, or carry-out meals from restaurants. Fast-food outlets, where more than 45 million people ate every day, supplied one-third of meals consumed away from home.[42]

Proponents of more inclusive labeling, including the prestigious Institute of Medicine, argued that it was important not only to foster informed choices but also to provide incentives for businesses to develop healthier products. Fast food and restaurant foods were often particularly high in fat and sodium. Fast-food labeling would be relatively inexpensive because products were standardized and limited in number. Restaurants could provide nutritional information on request. Both restaurants and small businesses could minimize costs by relying on computer programs to provide nutritional profiles of standard food items.

The Restaurant Association and representatives of fast-food outlets and convenience stores countered that revealing nutrients would be impractical and costly. In many restaurants, menus changed frequently. Convenience stores and delis sold some items that were not standardized and they would not have resources needed to analyze their nutrients. Printing nutritional information on fast-food wrappers and cups also would be costly. Aiming to gain quick approval of a compromise bill, neither Congress nor the FDA was willing to press these issues.[43]

CONSUMER PROTECTION VERSUS BUREAUCRATIC INERTIA AND ENTRENCHED INTERESTS. Congress also made labeling voluntary for fresh meats, poultry, and seafood, even though meats were some of the most significant sources of cholesterol and fats linked to heart disease and cancer, and it made labeling voluntary for fruits and vegetables, even though they were sources of some of the most beneficial nutrients for reducing risks of those diseases. It also placed herbal remedies and other dietary supplements on a separate, and ultimately less restrictive, track, even though little was known about their benefits and risks.

Legislators chose not to disturb a historic division of responsibility between the Department of Agriculture, which regulated meats, poultry, and produce, and the FDA, which regulated most processed foods. This administrative chasm was echoed in the divided jurisdiction of congressional committees. The Department of Agriculture and agricultural committees had a reputation for being industry friendly and created more informal monitoring systems. The FDA and committees with jurisdiction over public health had a reputation for being consumer friendly and created more systematic monitoring. In this respect, the new law perpetuated a system that made sense to legislators and regulators but did not serve the interests of the public.[44]

At the last minute, Congress also separated dietary supplements from the new preapproval requirement for health claims for foods. It was a small amendment that, together with future legislative and regulatory action, would have huge consequences. It hitched together well-under-stood and beneficial vitamins and minerals with herbal remedies and amino acids whose safety and effectiveness were unknown and set them off on a different regulatory path from other nutrients.

Senators Metzenbaum and Orrin Hatch (R-Utah) added a floor amendment requiring the FDA to establish a system for evaluating health claims for "vitamins, minerals, herbs, or other similar nutritional sub-stances" but allowing flexibility in what that procedure would be.[45] Both senators suggested that a different system was needed to take account of rapid advances in supplements and their unique marketing and use. Sen-ator Hatch emphasized "the essential right of our citizens to have access to . . . supplements without fear of their being branded unlawful drugs."[46]

At the time, these remedies represented a fringe market of less than $1 billion in annual sales. It was a small part of a growing social move-ment that favored "natural" foods and alternative health approaches and was of little interest to the food industry or regulators. Ten years later, after further congressional action, a $12 billion market of 29,000 sup-plements in pills, foods, and drinks featured extravagant claims that yucca could fight arthritis, shark cartilage could reduce cancerous tumors, and parsley could eliminate small kidney stones. Not only were these claims misleading, researchers also began to uncover damaging interactions of supplements with prescription medications, adulteration with toxic chemicals, and widespread mislabeling. Consumers also had to guess about the safety and effectiveness of thousands of products that combined foods with supplements. The modern medicine show was back in business.

A New Disclosure System Emerges

The law that was signed by President Bush on November 8, 1990, was appropriately heralded as the most important change in national food policy in fifty years.[47] The House Report declared that it reflected a "bipartisan agreement about the need for mandatory nutritional labeling and about the need for consistent, enforceable rules" about health claims.[48] Instead of setting minimum standards or trying to influence markets with taxes or subsidies, legislators employed the government's power to command the disclosure of information in an innovative way to tackle a major public health problem. Manufacturers were required to tell the public in standardized formats the amounts of total fat, saturated fat, cholesterol, sodium, total carbohydrates, complex carbohydrates, sugars, dietary fiber, and total protein in each serving in the context of daily diet. They were required to list total calories and calories from fat in each serving. Serving sizes were standardized to conform to amounts customarily consumed. Products that were not labeled accurately and completely could be deemed misbranded by the FDA and removed from the market. States also could bring enforcement actions in federal court after providing the FDA with notice and an opportunity to act. While most disclosure systems start with primitive and disputable measures, here experience and scientific consensus produced a sophisticated set of metrics and risk-signaling mechanisms that gave credibility to nutritional labeling from the start. For the first time, interested shoppers could discern the nutrients in virtually every can, bottle, or package of processed food and compare quantities to recommended daily consumption.[49]

Some of the most contentious issues were forwarded to the FDA for resolution. The law required standard definitions for terms like *lite, low fat,* or *low salt* but did not say what those definitions should be. The FDA also had to decide which health claims deserved initial approval and how to coordinate its efforts with other agencies that controlled labeling of fresh meat and regulated advertising.[50] Paradoxically, the effort to create flexible incentives to reduce disease risks involved federal officials in dictating the minutiae of label design. The law told the agency to specify the exact format and appearance of nutritional panels. Regulators could require companies to highlight information by placing it in larger type, bold type, or contrasting color in order to "assist consumers in maintaining healthy dietary practices."[51] In regulations, the FDA directed that the nutritional label had to be to the right of the main display panel in letters no less than one-sixteenth of an inch high. Information had to be presented in specified order, starting with serving size, servings per container, total calories, calories from fat, and so on. It had to be presented in a box, set out in two columns, printed in one color on a neutral background and headed "Nutrition Facts." A "low-fat" product could derive no more than 30 percent of its calories from fat. A "high-fiber" product had to contain at least 20 percent of the recommended daily amount of fiber.[52] Congress also required that companies convey information "in a manner which enables the public to readily observe and comprehend such information and to understand its relative significance in the context of a total daily diet."[53] The FDA took up that challenge with a display of entrepreneurial spirit, seeking consumer views, testing different formats, and designing the label that has become familiar to millions of shoppers.

Nutritional Labeling in Practice

New labels were launched successfully. Something like 17,000 U.S. food manufacturers redesigned 257,000 product labels to meet the new requirements. For small firms, relabeling could be costly. The FDA estimated that only 20 percent of firms had conducted nutritional analyses in the past and that new analyses would cost about $1,785 for each product. Market leaders were 1.5 times more likely to have already introduced nutritional labeling than were other firms. Nonetheless, three years after new labels were required, an FDA survey found that 96.5 percent of products regulated by the agency displayed the Nutrition Facts label.[54]

Large food companies responded to consumer interest in healthier products and to new label requirements by adding rather than replacing products. They continued to sell soups, snacks and packaged meals that were high in fat and salt but also developed healthier variations. Research by the FDA in 1996 found dramatically increased market share for fat-modified products. Reduced-fat cookies increased from virtually 0 to 15 percent of the market from 1991 to 1995, with nearly 300 products introduced. Sales of fat-modified cheeses increased from 4 to 10 percent of the market, and the number of such products on the market tripled. Similar patterns were found for corn chips, peanut butter, and crackers.[55] An empirical study by Christine Moorman, a professor of business administration at Duke University, found a statistically significant increase in brand extensions with lower levels of sodium, fat, cholesterol, and other negative nutrients after the law took effect. The National Food Processors Association stepped up its support for companies' consumer education efforts and some retailers gave employees special training so that they would be better able to answer customers' questions. Firms with resources and skills to design and market new products made more changes toward healthier products and made them more quickly than firms with fewer such capabilities. Critics suggested that the law may have limited production flexibility and increased the cost of introducing new products, especially for small companies, since each change required a new label.[56]

Shoppers showed interest in using the new information. Surveys before and after the law took effect in 1994 indicated increases in the frequency with which consumers consulted nutritional labels. While results varied, as many as half of consumers reported using the labels often by 1995, an increase of 10 percent or more from previous years. Consumers reported that they used the information to determine how much of specific nutrients the product contained, judge overall nutrient content, and compare products.[57]

Regulation of Health Claims Triggers New Confusion

Some aspects of new health claims rules confused rather than enlightened, however. For the first time, companies were permitted to promote products with label statements linking specific nutrients to the reduction of risks of specific diseases. As has been previously noted, claims that nutrients reduced risks of specific diseases were meticulously reviewed and preapproved by regulators, while claims that they improved circulation, memory, or other bodily functions received no review for accuracy. Because health claims could serve as powerful marketing tools, the result of this system was that companies began labeling products with a wide variety of unreviewed claims that did not necessarily reflect sound science.

Congress allowed health claims that characterized the relationship between a nutrient and "a disease or health-related condition" only if regulators agreed that the claim reflected significant scientific agreement.[58] From the outset, it was clear to everyone that these would be relatively few in number. Initially the FDA approved seven disease claims about which there was broad scientific consensus. Companies were allowed to say that calcium reduced risks of osteoporosis; high-fat diets increased risks of cancer; saturated fat and cholesterol helped reduce risks

Table 3-1. *FDA-Authorized Health Claims*

Nutrient and dietary property	Health claim
Calcium	Helps maintain healthy bones and may reduce risk of osteoporosis
Low sodium content	May reduce risk of high blood pressure
Low fat content	May reduce risk of some cancers
Low saturated fat or cholesterol levels	May reduce risk of heart disease
Fiber in fruits, vegetables, and grains	May reduce risk of heart disease and some cancers
Fruits and vegetables	May reduce risk of some cancers
Folic acid	May reduce risk of brain and spinal cord birth defects
Dietary sugar alcohols	May reduce risk of tooth decay
Soluble fiber from whole oats or psyllium husk	May reduce risk of heart disease
Soy protein	May reduce risk of heart disease
Plant sterol or stanol esters	May reduce risk of heart disease
Whole grain foods	May reduce risk of heart disease and some cancers
Potassium	May reduce risk of high blood pressure and stroke

Source: U.S. Food and Drug Administration, A Food Labeling Guide (www.cfsan. fda.gov [June 1, 2002]).

of heart diseases; fiber reduced risks of cancer; fruits, vegetables, and grains with fiber reduced risks of heart disease; high-sodium diets increased risks of hypertension; and fruits and vegetables reduced risks of cancer. By 2002 the agency had approved six more. These claims are summarized in table 3-1.[59]

At the same time, Congress placed no such restrictions on claims that characterized a relationship between a nutrient and improved bodily functions. The consequences were peculiar. Claims that a nutrient supported the immune system did not need to be backed by significant scientific agreement while claims that it supported the body's antiviral capabilities did. Claims of relief from occasional sleeplessness were not reviewed while claims of reducing difficulty in falling asleep were. Claims that products helped maintain cholesterol levels did not require review but those that suggested they lowered cholesterol did.[60]

To companies and consumers, this was a distinction without a difference. Claims that products improved circulation or strengthened bones had as much market power as those that targeted specific diseases. Surveys suggested that shoppers were increasingly confused and frustrated about healthy eating. Government-organized focus groups indicated that consumers viewed all health claims as disease claims and therefore might buy products to fight diseases that had no such capabilities. Pauline Ippolito, a senior economist at the FTC and a leading analyst of consumer responses to food labeling and advertising, found "no evidence suggesting that this is a meaningful distinction to consumers."[61]

Bureaucratic entanglement contributed to consumer confusion. By leaving three agencies in charge of regulating health claims under separate laws, Congress placed public protection at the mercy of patchwork agreements. In addition to the FDA, which made rules for labels of most processed foods, the Department of Agriculture regulated labeling for frozen pizza and other processed foods that contained more than 2 percent cooked or 3 percent uncooked meat, and the Federal Trade Commission made rules for health claims in food advertising. Despite efforts at coordination, agency approaches differed. Whereas the FDA authorized disease claims based on significant scientific agreement, the USDA reviewed them on a case-by-case basis, and the FTC judged claims in advertising based on whether they were unfair, deceptive, or misleading in a material respect. These differences sometimes led to practical absurdities. Frozen pizza with less than 2 ounces of pepperoni had to conform to FDA rules, while pizza with more than 2 ounces followed the USDA rules. Processors could not always predict if they would be allowed to promote innovative products. In 2000 companies using stanol esters in foods or supplements to lower cholesterol could make that claim in advertising under FTC rules but not on labels under FDA rules.[62]

A New Compromise Further Complicates the System

In 1997 Congress added a third category of claims to a system that was already confusing. In an effort to provide more timely information, an amendment to the labeling law allowed firms to make disease claims *before* there was scientific agreement if they were based on current, published, authoritative statements by federal research agencies or the

National Academy of Sciences and if firms notified the FDA 120 days before marketing.[63] Congress responded to arguments by food processors that the standard of significant scientific agreement deprived the public of valuable information, that people were capable of weighing uncertainties, and that the FDA had been slow in approving disease claims based on new science. They pointed to a four-year delay between an important finding in 1992 by the Centers for Disease Control that foods with folic acid helped prevent neural tube defects and the FDA's approval that companies could assert that link on labels. The change addressed a serious issue for risk-disclosure programs: how to inform the public about possible benefits or risks when science remained uncertain. The result was that labels might feature disease claims that had been rigorously reviewed by the government to be certain that they reflected significant scientific agreement, claims about improved circulation and stronger bones that had not been reviewed at all, *or* disease claims that did not necessarily reflect significant scientific agreement but were based on authoritative statements by a public health agency.[64]

Some companies also took their arguments to court, contending that restrictions on disease claims violated the First Amendment's protection of commercial speech. An important decision by the U.S. Court of Appeals for the District of Columbia in 1999 required the FDA to reconsider four disease claims at issue, explain more fully the reasons for rejecting them, and determine if less restrictive rules were feasible.[65]

Soups to Fight Depression? Cereals to Improve Memory?

However, it was the exception Congress had carved out for dietary supplements that created the greatest confusion in labeling and exposed the public to significant new risks. Responding to a groundswell of demands by supplement manufacturers, health food retailers, and individuals who relied on alternative medicines, Congress approved new legislation in 1994 to wall off supplements from the usual safety rules for food and drugs. Instead of requiring proof of safety before marketing, the new law allowed herbal remedies, vitamins, minerals, and amino acids to be sold unless the government showed them to be unsafe. Companies only had to notify the government of evidence of safety seventy-five days before marketing. Manufacturers could make expansive claims that supplements improved memory or reduced depression so long as statements were accompanied by disclaimers that told shoppers that the supplement was not FDA-approved or intended to treat disease. If health risks arose, the burden of proof was on the government to show that a supplement had been marketed without "reasonable assurance" that it did not present "significant or unreasonable risk of illness or injury."[66]

This law demonstrated the political power of the supplement industry and its customers. When the FDA proposed in 1993 to subject supplements to the same framework of standardized disclosure that governed foods, advocates of alternative medicines joined conservative opponents of government regulation and industry representatives in an unprecedented campaign. Supplement manufacturers formed a Nutritional Health Alliance and produced handouts for health food stores that told shoppers to "write to Congress today or kiss your supplements goodbye!" Owners of health food stores and groups that promoted alternative medicines orchestrated petitions, TV spots, appeals to shoppers, and hundreds of thousands of letters to members of Congress. One television ad featured a SWAT team crashing into actor Mel Gibson's house to seize his vitamins. Sen. Barbara Boxer (D-Calif.) said she received 35,000 letters on dietary supplements in 1993, twice as many as she received on education.[67] In the House, opponents of tougher labeling prevailed over John D. Dingell, chairman of the Energy and Commerce Committee, and Henry Waxman, chairman of the subcommittee that crafted rules for nutritional labeling. In the Senate, Edward M. Kennedy (D-Mass.), chairman of the Labor and Human Resources Committee, was also outvoted.

Six years after the law was approved, supermarkets featured Kava Kava Corn Chips to "promote relaxation," Ginkgo Biloba Rings to "increase memory and alertness," and Chunky Tomato Soup with St. John's Wort to "give your mood a natural lift." Herb-enhanced drinks had become the fastest growing segment of the beverage industry, with Snapple drinks promising to "enlighten your senses"; Celestial Seasonings marketing a Tension Tamer tea laced with kava, a sedative; Pepsi producing Wisdom, Karma, and Adrenaline Rush drinks containing herbs like St. John's Wort, which is used to improve mood, and guarana, a stimulant; and Coke test-marketing Elations, a drink containing glucosamine, as "joy for joints." Supplements grew from a $1 billion market in 1990 to a $16 billion market in 1999, with many snacks and cookies marketed to children and adolescents.[68]

Benefits were uncertain. Nutritional experts cautioned consumers that there was no direct evidence that snack foods containing echinacea would support the immune system or that soups with herbal additives such as St. John's Wort would ease depression. Risks, however, could be serious. Initial research indicated that St. John's Wort might activate an enzyme that interfered with other medication or cause nerve damage under some circumstances. Ginkgo and ginseng, a popular combination taken to improve memory and cognitive functioning, might affect the secretion of insulin and reduce blood sugar, making them potentially dangerous for people with diabetes. Ginkgo acted as a blood thinner, increasing risks of internal bleeding when taken in combination with other drugs.[69] By the close of the decade, the FDA attributed 134 serious illnesses to a supplement called ephedra, which was being taken for weight loss or increased energy, and nine deaths to a weight-loss product called Formula One. One investigation in California concluded that nearly one-third of herbal supplements imported from Asia either contained drugs that were not listed as ingredients or contained lead, arsenic, or mercury. Testing by consumerlab.com found that half of ginseng products contained high levels of toxic pesticides and one-third contained less of the herb than claimed. *Consumer Reports* concluded in December 2000 that "nobody really knows how much these foods contain. There's no standard, validated testing method to analyze foods and beverages for the presence and concentration of herbs."[70]

By 2001 indications of risks were serious enough to prompt calls to revise labeling requirements. The FDA warned companies against adding untested supplements to foods or drinks. Consumer groups and nutrition professionals called for a single safety standard for foods and supplements, as they had a decade earlier. Even major processors joined the appeal. An industry group representing Cargil, General Nutrition, Monsanto, Novartis, and other large food and supplement manufacturers declared that "there is no scientific reason to support different standards for safety for foods and dietary supplements."[71]

A New Generation of Disease-Fighting Foods Defies Regulatory Categories

It was the remarkable advance of food technology rather than the politics of exotic supplements, however, that provided the greatest long-term challenge to the new system of disclosure. Just as the 1990 labeling law was taking effect, food companies began to bring to market products specifically designed to reduce risks of disease. These were the first tentative steps into a new generation of disease-fighting foods made possible by advances in biotechnology. Products defied the traditional regulatory distinction between foods and drugs. The nation's system of informing the public about diet and disease proved ill equipped to communicate their risks and benefits.[72]

For giant drug and food companies, the vision of the future was one of profitable foods sold as preventive medicines. The completed mapping of the human genome in 2000 created the practical possibility that propensities for heart disease, cancer, diabetes, and other chronic ailments could be predicted. At the same time, advancing technology created the possibility of engineering familiar foods to reduce specific risks of disease and creating edible vaccines to protect whole populations against hepatitis, tetanus, or cholera.[73] The first of this new generation of products, introduced in the late 1990s, included unusual substances that appeared to have specific disease-fighting properties. A division of Johnson & Johnson began marketing Benecol, a margarine aimed at lowering cholesterol that contained stanol esters from pine trees; Lipton launched a similar margarine called Take Control; and Kellogg marketed an Ensemble line of products also aimed at lowering cholesterol. Giant food and drug companies initiated joint ventures to develop new products. Novartis, the Swiss pharmaceutical firm, joined with Quaker Oats, and General Mills joined with DuPont to create foods with health benefits. Sales of such "functional foods" were projected to reach $49 billion by 2010, as shown in figure 3-1.[74]

The disclosure system that was intended to inform the public about links between diet and disease did not provide clarity on the risks and benefits of these new products for either shoppers or manufacturers. Outdated

Figure 3-1. *Historical and Expected Growth in Sales of Functional Foods in the United States, 1995 to 2010*

Billions of dollars

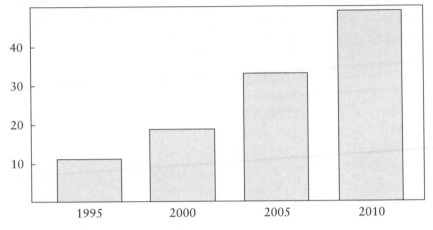

Source: U.S. General Accounting Office, *Food Safety: Improvements Needed in Overseeing the Safety of Dietary Supplements and "Functional Foods,"* GAO/RCED-00-156 (2000), p. 7.

regulatory categories allowed companies to go forum shopping for the fastest way to bring products to market. New substances could be introduced as generally recognized as safe, a regulatory category meaning no review or disclosure of safety or effectiveness was needed, or as supplements, meaning little regulation of statements was required.[75]

The Limits of Labeling—The Controversy about Genetically Modified Foods

Controversy about the safety and environmental implications of foods made with genetically modified organisms (GMOs) in the late 1990s produced broad support for labels but also raised doubts about whether they could tell consumers anything useful about risks and benefits. As concern about genetically modified foods spread from Europe to the United States, opponents demonstrated at the World Trade Organization meeting in Seattle in 1999, marched outside Kellogg's headquarters in Battle Creek, Michigan, and hacked down fields of genetically modified corn.

Incidents increased public anxiety. Polls that year showed that 75 percent of Americans favored labeling and more than fifty environmental and public interest groups endorsed the idea. As the issue gained momentum, both Al Gore, the Democratic nominee for president in 2000, and Ralph Nader, an independent candidate, added their support. Incidents increased concern. In 2000 more than 300 products were recalled from grocery shelves because they contained genetically modified Starlink corn, which had been approved only for animal feed. In 2001, tests by independent labs of foods that companies voluntarily labeled "non-GMO" found as much as 40 percent of DNA came from genetically modified plants. One sampling by the *Wall Street Journal* found that sixteen of twenty "non-GMO" products tested contained evidence of genetic material used to modify plants.[76]

Interestingly, the issue arose after more than 70 million acres of transgenic crops were under cultivation in the United States and after farmers had become accustomed to mixing them with conventional crops. By 2000 more than half of the nation's processed foods included genetically engineered ingredients, and GMO and non-GMO crops were often stored, transported, and processed together. Separating them would be costly and difficult.

But the more fundamental problem was that labeling products as "GMO" or "non-GMO" could mislead shoppers instead of telling them anything significant about benefits and risks. GMO referred to a wide variety of processes, ingredients, and possible consequences. The National Research Council emphasized the importance of assessing each product individually rather than attempting to generalize about effects on health or the environment. Some crops produced with GMOs were chemically identical to conventional ones. Others contained proteins from other organisms that raised potential issues for the 2 percent of American adults and 8 percent of children with food allergies. Instead of informing, GMO labels could mislead.[77]

As the issue grew more contentious, the FDA attempted to craft a compromise. It rejected the idea of mandatory labeling but agreed to set guidelines for the voluntary use of "non-GMO" labels and proposed that companies give four months' notice before planting genetically modified crops and provide assurances of their safety.[78]

Public Education Shortchanged

The use of disclosure as a public health measure placed problems of effective communication at center stage. Ultimately, the important question was not what labels said but what shoppers understood, how they changed their buying and eating habits, and whether those changes led companies to market healthier products. Over time the most important limitations of labeling proved to be limitations of effective communication.

First signs were promising. Congress funded a $1.5 million campaign that used creative ideas to let the public know about the existence of the new labels. In May 1994, as they began appearing in grocery stores, electronic scoreboards at Yankee Stadium and nine other major league parks flashed messages that announced "a new food label: check it out." Goodyear blimps and a running news tape in Times Square carried similar messages. Boston Red Sox pitcher Roger Clemens literally pitched for the new label by throwing to Donna Shalala, secretary of health and human services, in a public service announcement that aired on television stations. Curious George, a monkey in a series of children's books, explained the label to children in television spots.[79]

But legislative and educational efforts produced mismatched results. Congress and the FDA decreed a labeling system that relied on complex factual information for use by consumers who lacked the sophisticated knowledge to understand associations between heart disease and saturated versus unsaturated fats or links between high-salt foods and hypertension. As the new labeling law worked its way through Congress, virtually everyone had emphasized the importance of consumer education. In its influential report in 1989, the Institute of Medicine recommended "a comprehensive effort to inform the public about the likelihood of certain risks and the possible benefits of dietary modification."[80] But Congress never allotted sufficient resources for such an effort. After the government's initial label-awareness campaign, education relied heavily on efforts by public health groups and existing government programs, such as the Dietary Guidelines and Food Pyramid that gave consumers general advice but little specific knowledge about diet and disease.

Even if extensive education had been funded, cognitive problems might have made the task of improving understanding particularly difficult. A generation of research by economists and psychologists suggested that consumers were less likely to be concerned about risks that were relatively familiar, explainable, voluntary, and incremental rather than catastrophic. They assigned disproportionate importance to risks of events that were easily brought to mind, ignored evidence that contradicted current beliefs, and tuned out when confronted with information overload. They also tended to be more influenced by negative than positive information and to assign higher value to loss than to gain. In addition, several steps had to precede and follow searches for information in order to produce changes in behavior. Motivation, belief that change was possible, informed choice, attention to the total diet, and sustained efforts mattered.[81]

The absence of a continuing education effort was of particular significance because advice changed frequently and became increasingly complex. A 1995 survey by the Food Marketing Institute found that 40 percent of consumers interviewed considered it very likely that experts would change their views within five years about which foods were healthy. They were right. New research results from the NCI in 2000 cast doubt on whether consumption of bran and other fiber helped to reduce risks of some kinds of cancer. Experts warned that some people might be consuming too much rather than too little calcium.[82] After years of delivering to the public the relatively simple message that fat should not exceed 30 percent of calories, the American Heart Association and other public health organizations announced in 2001 that a healthy diet could include 35 to 40 percent of calories from fat, but people should eat less trans fats and saturated fats (no more than 10 percent of calories) and more omega-3 fats, which are found in some fish, nuts, tofu, and canola oil.[83]

Anachronistic Responses by Consumers

Over time, the limits of nutritional labeling were reflected in the anachronistic responses of consumers. People with more education and higher income consumed nutrients linked to chronic disease at higher rates than people with less of both. Specific knowledge about nutrition improved with education and income, as one might expect. But consumption of fat, saturated fat, and cholesterol also increased. Similarly, people reduced fiber consumption as education and income increased, despite better understanding of evidence that it reduced risks of some kinds of cancer.[84] In a report summarizing these trends, Lorna Aldrich of the Department of Agriculture's Economic Research Service suggested that, as incomes and education rose, people ate more meals away from home, which tended to contain more fat and for which nutritional information was usually lacking. By 1998 Americans spent an average of 47 percent of their food budget away from home, up from 43 percent in 1990.[85] "Overall," the report concluded, "it appears that the forces of rising incomes and convenience are outweighing nutrition and health information."[86]

People over age sixty or with less education were more likely to find the nutritional information hard to understand. Virtually all surveys indicated that the new labels were an improvement over the past. More shoppers noticed them and more used them to obtain product-specific information, such as amounts of fat or calories. But label use by consumers over sixty did not increase. For the 40 million Americans over the age of sixteen with significant literacy needs and for recent immigrants, for whom language often compounded problems of limited education, the quantitative format and complex terminology may have remained a significant barrier to use. Research also suggested that people were skeptical of health claims and had difficulty understanding them. Most consumers did not understand the meaning of "percent daily value," could be misled by "fat-free" or "cholesterol-free" claims, remained unaware of how the government regulated label claims, and did not use them to make product choices. In 2001 FDA economists concluded that "government regulation of label claims was an aspect of the new food label that was poorly communicated to American consumers."[87]

On the important question of the degree to which new food labels influenced consumers' product choices, most surveys did not find significant effects. More than 30 percent of shoppers in 1995 and 1996 said they had stopped buying a product within the last month or six months because of information on food labels, according to surveys by the industry's Food Marketing Institute. But that was about the same portion as pre-1994, when comprehensive labels were introduced. In 1997 that portion decreased to 28 percent, while those who started buying a product because of label information increased a little to 25 percent.[88]

Changes in eating habits also showed anachronistic results. Between 1989–91 and 1994–95 per capita consumption of whole milk and eggs continued a long decline, while consumption of ice cream and soft drinks increased rapidly. Average daily intake of total fat fell during the 1980s but increased steadily after 1990. Per capita consumption of sugars increased by more than 25 percent in fifteen years. Calories consumed per person and the portion of the American population considered obese continued to increase, as they had for two decades. No sudden changes in the mid-1990s suggested a notable impact of nutritional information on labels.[89]

By the end of the decade, sales of low-fat foods appeared to be leveling off or declining. Surveys showed a 12 percent decline from 1999 to 2000 in how often customers purchased fat-free products. Sales declined 33 percent for fat free potato chips, 22 percent for fat-free ice cream, and 12 percent for fat-free cookies and margarine in one year. Surveys found that consumers of fat-free foods were disappointed with the taste of these products and discouraged about their contribution to weight loss.[90] From 1996 to 1999 the portion of consumers who said they sought out low-fat, low-cholesterol, or low-salt foods declined substantially, according to surveys by the industry's Food Marketing Institute.[91] People had more information from increasing sources about diet and disease but were often frustrated about how to use it. The American Dietetic Association concluded that "[t]he public is weary of conflicting and negative nutritional messages. . . . Between 37% and 70% of consumers believe they need to eliminate their favorite foods to achieve a healthful diet."[92] By 1997 annual surveys showed that only about 25 percent of Americans continued to pay close attention to the labels. A Department of Agriculture report concluded in 1999 that it was not yet clear whether there would be substantial consumer gains from nutrition labeling. As government officials met in July 2000 at a national summit on nutrition to consider next steps, President Clinton summarized discouraging trends: "The vast majority of Americans still don't have healthy diets. We are eating more fast food because of our hectic schedules, and we're less physically active because of our growing reliance on modern conveniences. As a result, more and more Americans are overweight or obese, including 1 in 10 children."[93]

Economic and cultural trends contributed to these changes, of course. Food costs continued their century-long decline as a portion of household budgets, making overconsumption cheaper and larger portions common. Instead of laboring in jobs that required physical exertion, increasing numbers of workers sat at desks or served customers behind counters. Children spent more time watching television, doing homework, or using computers.

Practical Problems Proliferate

Revelations about unlisted allergens, continuing delays in reflecting new science on labels, and confusion concerning supplement labeling highlighted the importance of improving the accuracy, adaptability, and consistency of disclosure. In a two-year investigation, the FDA and state inspectors found that one-quarter of food plants visited failed to list all allergens on labels and that only half of manufacturers checked products for accurate labeling of ingredients. Even the trace amounts of eggs, nuts, shellfish, or other allergens that were permitted under federal rules could trigger dangerous reactions in some people. Faced with the prospect of more stringent labeling rules, Kraft, Hershey, General Mills, and other large companies adopted voluntary guidelines that called for better testing and disclosing even small quantities.[94]

The labeling system also proved slow to convey to the public an important revision in scientific understanding. Researchers estimated that trans fatty acids in convenience foods like chips, cookies, and fast food contributed to tens of thousands of premature deaths each year. These trans fats, which were liquid vegetable oils that had been partially hydrogenated to turn them into solids, were widely used in margarines, baked goods, and fast foods. Scientists found that they lowered beneficial cholesterol and raised harmful cholesterol. Walter Willett of Harvard's School of Public Health, who pioneered some of the groundbreaking research concerning trans fats, told *U.S. News and World Report* in January 2001: "The introduction of trans fats into the diet was the biggest food-processing disaster in U.S. history." Nonetheless, opposition from the Institute of Shortening and Edible Oils, representing most of the industry, and manufacturers of products high in such fats, as well as debate about a threshold amount above which labeling would be required delayed even the proposal of a change in labeling until 1999. Three years later no final action had been taken.[95]

The shortcomings of the labeling rules for health-enhancing foods and supplements produced problems so extreme that they prompted a stern warning by the GAO: "Consumers face health risks because current federal laws and agencies' efforts do not effectively and consistently ensure that [supplements or health-enhancing foods] are safe."[96] Nor did they receive information about benefits needed to make informed choices. People could not tell the difference between health claims that were government-approved for accuracy and those that were not, and they could not decipher different standards applied by the FDA, the USDA, and the FTC: "Consumers are faced with a confusing array of claims—some that require rigorous scientific support and others that can be made with less evidence—with no clear way to distinguish between them. . . . As a result, consumers may make inappropriate dietary choices and rely on ineffective products to treat their health problems."[97]

Labels Leap from Soup Cans to the Web

By 2001 the product-bound information of nutritional labels had begun to migrate to the World Wide Web, creating the potential for empowering consumers with more accessible information. An array of Internet-based resources added new dimensions to label information and showed how shoppers might make quicker and better informed judgments about the benefits and risks of the soups and cereals they purchased every week. The supermarket chain Stop & Shop experimented with a website called smartmouth.com, where customers could list what they had bought recently and specify "less sodium" or "more fiber" to generate a list of alternative products.[98] Unilever offered dieting tips online and let purchasers of its SlimFast shakes and bars track weight loss and chat with other dieters.[99] ConsumerLab.com, the company that had tested popular supplements and found that many did not contain what they purported to, posted new reports that most health bars misstated health claims and amounts of nutrients, causing manufacturers to hurriedly prepare new labels.[100] Health food chain GNC installed computer terminals to provide summaries of scientific evidence about supplements, rating findings by their degree of reliability. The American Dietetic Association proposed an Internet-based surveillance system to provide quick public alerts about emerging safety problems with supplements in order to reduce health threats.[101] Websites such as naturaldatabase.com and thedietarysupplement.com made it easier to access emerging scientific evidence about little-tested herbs and amino acids. There was even a site to evaluate nutritional websites. Tufts University launched an overarching Nutritional Navigator to rank the accuracy and depth of information on other nutrition-oriented sites.[102] On the horizon were personal software agents, or "shopbots," that would allow online shoppers to consider only those products that met their predetermined criteria.

The ubiquitous bar code became the leading contender to become the new "label" for processed foods in an age of digital shopping. Introduced into grocery stores in 1974, bar codes contain simple product information that can be read electronically. They reduce labor costs by speeding checkouts and cut operating costs by quickly updating inventories. In the late 1990s cell phones, pocket organizers, and pagers began to be equipped with scanners that could link expanded bar codes on product packages to websites where customers could get quick answers to questions about diet and disease.[103]

How far this migration to the web might go was uncertain. Food purchasing (along with travel and clothing) was among the fastest growing categories of online retailing. Half of consumers were expected to spend some part of their food budget online between 2000 and 2005, according to a report by the Boston Consulting Group.[104] Information technology had the potential to improve communication of complex information about diet and disease by integrating data from many sources, layering it, allowing shoppers to customize it to their needs, and providing two-way communication between them and the supermarkets and companies that sold and manufactured their food. However, in 2002 marketing executives still viewed the web as a resource mainly for consumers who were already interested in specific product characteristics.[105]

Technology also could not overcome political limitations. So long as government rules did not require public access to nutritional information for food purchased in restaurants, fast-food outlets, or as carry-out meals, no amount of technology could reduce risks of disease stemming from overconsumption of fat and other nutrients in those meals. So long as laws perpetuated categories of claims that made no sense to consumers and applied less strict disclosure rules to little-tested supplements than to common foods, no amount of technology could reveal their risks and benefits. And so long as several agencies regulated the information available to the public, no amount of technology could produce consistent ground rules.[106]

In the end, information technology was simply a tool. It could promote understanding. It could also spread misinformation and create mountains of data that no one used. What it could not do was expand reliable information beyond existing political limits, eliminate outdated disclosure rules, or resolve bureaucratic confusion.

Disclosure as Public Policy

In the 1990s enterprising members of Congress placed permanently in the public domain a vast amount of previously proprietary information about the risks and benefits of processed foods by means of an intricate system of compromises. Their work resolved conflicts among values and interests and broke a stalemate of nearly two decades, but it created a system with serious limitations.

Political imperatives truncated the scope, targets, and mechanics of disclosure. Food processors supported national labeling but opposed state initiatives. Makers of snacks and meat products that were relatively high in fat or salt sought labeling criteria that minimized attention to those nutrients and avoided simple signals to shoppers. Restaurants and fast-food operations lobbied successfully to exclude their meals from a new disclosure regime. Makers of herbal supplements and vitamins won a battle to exclude their products from restrictive disclosure rules. And government officials protected the existing structure of fragmented authority.

Unprecedented trends raised the stakes in these conflicts. A better educated public created new markets for products that claimed to improve health. Busier families searched for convenience foods, ate out more often, and relied on the media for quick, practical information about nutrition. The line between foods and medicines blurred as pharmaceutical companies combined with food processors to create new products with specific health benefits.

A first decade of experience suggested that disclosure systems could mimic problems endemic to more conventional forms of regulation and that effective communication of complex risks remained an extremely difficult undertaking. Compromises excluded from labeling products that amounted to nearly half of the average family's food budget. Failure to revise a historical distinction between foods and drugs left consumers confused and frustrated when a new generation of disease-fighting spreads, soups, and frozen meals appeared on the market. Division of responsibility among several agencies created inconsistencies in ground rules. When science and markets changed rapidly, labeling changed slowly. Unintended consequences led to new public health problems. Disclosure proved to be a useful variation on regulation but not an escape from its challenges.

Less familiar were the cognitive obstacles to communicating complex information about health risks to a broad audience. When the government set standards or created taxes or subsidies to reduce risks, communicating with the public about the character and degree of risk was usually a secondary consideration. But when the government used disclosure to reduce risks, communication itself became a regulatory mechanism. Barriers to effective communication included cognitive shortcuts that led people to underrate risks that were familiar and controllable and overrate risks that were unusual or had rare but catastrophic consequences. Cognitive distortions could be minimized with carefully designed signaling about unhealthy products and diet-disease links. But political obstacles limited the feasibility of using icons, color-coding, or simple graphics.

Added to early experience with disclosure of toxic chemicals, nutritional labeling provided the outlines of an emerging populist trend in public policy, enhanced by technology: it provided public access to standardized factual information about corporate practices and products as a means of reducing risks. In some ways, the two systems were polar opposites. Nutritional labeling addressed valued product characteristics rather than waste from industrial processes. Its influence on companies and consumers was carried out mainly through market mechanisms rather than political processes. Information was accessible on a company-created label with each purchase instead of in a once-a-year government report. Its metrics were relatively mature and included links to expected risks.

However, they also had remarkable elements in common. Both were products of expediency and frustration. Both represented oblique responses to a single episode—in this instance, a sudden proliferation of misleading health claims on labels of products Americans bought every day. Both granted the public access to corporate information previously viewed as private. Both increasingly relied on information technology to empower the public to understand and use that information. Both focused on practices or product characteristics that created risks but usually did not violate any law. Both featured mandatory disclosure of factual information, identification of companies or products that were sources of risk, disclosure to a broad audience, and a regulatory purpose. Both were supported in principle by target companies but substantially narrowed due to effective lobbying, so that they addressed only a portion of the risk at issue, as we have seen. Taken together, these differences and similarities began to establish the potential breadth and power of disclosure as a policy instrument and provide early warnings about difficulties inherent in its use.

4 An Epidemic of Medical Errors

If errors were a disease, we would call it an epidemic.

— John M. Eisenberg*

etsy A. Lehman, an award-winning health columnist for the *Boston Globe* newspaper, died December 3, 1994, from an accidental overdose of chemotherapy drugs at the Dana-Farber Cancer Institute, one of the nation's most respected cancer hospitals. Ms. Lehman, who was being treated for breast cancer, was the wife of a scientist who worked at the hospital and the mother of two young children. She was reportedly given four times the standard dose of two drugs on each of four days. The mistake was not discovered until months after her death. A similar overdose by the same medical team left another breast cancer patient with permanent heart damage.[1]

The chemotherapy overdose that led to Betsy Lehman's death was perhaps the most widely publicized medical mistake of the 1990s. But other tragic errors also made news.

---

*John M. Eisenberg, director of the Agency for Healthcare Research and Quality, testimony at hearing on medical errors, Senate Committee on Health, Education, Labor, and Pensions, February 16, 2000.

The mistaken amputation of the wrong leg of a diabetic patient at a hospital in Tampa, Florida, drew national attention in 1995. The same year, a seven-year-old boy died when doctors administered a lethal dose of topical adrenaline instead of a routine anesthetic during a surgical procedure. In 1997 Karl Shipman, a physician, fell from a ladder and broke his wrist. Shipman reportedly died when an infection related to the fracture spread to his spine and was misdiagnosed at the Denver hospital where he had practiced medicine for thirty-five years. When these mistakes occurred, they appeared to be bizarre and unrelated events.[2]

On November 29, 1999, William C. Richardson, chairman of a panel of the prestigious Institute of Medicine (IOM), called a press conference to inform the American public that such deaths and injuries were not isolated incidents. They were extreme examples of a serious and previously unrecognized pattern of health risks. Between 44,000 and 98,000 patients died in the United States annually as a result of medical errors in hospitals.[3] That was more than the 43,458 people who died in 1998 in motor vehicle accidents, the 42,297 who died from breast cancer, and the 16,516 who died from AIDS. In addition, as many as 938,000 hospital patients were injured each year as a result of such errors. "These stunningly high rates of medical errors," Richardson argued, "are simply unacceptable in a medical system that promises first to 'do no harm.'"[4]

The institute, the branch of the National Academy of Sciences that was chartered by Congress to advise policymakers on health care issues, reported that serious errors were also common at good hospitals and among well-trained doctors and nurses. They were often caused by lack of information or miscommunication rather than carelessness. Medical errors occurred because the delivery of health care was fragmented and complex and because the medical profession created a culture of perfection that made it hard to recognize and learn from past mistakes. Hospital licensing and accreditation processes had paid only limited attention to patient safety. Big companies, government Medicare administrators, and other group purchasers had made few demands that errors be reduced. The additional toll of errors in doctors' offices and clinics remained unknown. High rates of error were costly not only in deaths and injuries but also in the loss of trust by patients in the health care system, loss of morale by health care professionals, loss of productivity by workers, and in many other ways. In economic terms alone, estimated national costs of preventable errors resulting in injury or death totaled between $17 billion and $29 billion a year.[5]

The institute issued an urgent call for national action: "Given current knowledge about the magnitude of the problem, the committee believes it would be irresponsible to expect anything less than a 50 percent reduction in errors over five years." To reach this goal, it did not recommend strict new regulation of hospitals or health maintenance organizations (HMOs) or stiff penalties for doctors. Instead, it called on government to construct a two-tier information strategy. To hold providers accountable for serious errors, create incentives to reduce them, and respond to the public's right to know, the institute called on Congress to see that every state required standardized public disclosure by health care organizations of incidents where medical treatment resulted in death or serious injury. To create a knowledge base that would translate such incentives into corrective actions by hospital managers, the institute recommended that Congress encourage voluntary, confidential reporting by doctors, nurses, and other health care workers of less serious errors and near misses.[6]

Response was immediate. President Bill Clinton announced that he favored national action to reduce medical errors by 50 percent in five years, including the creation of a new national office of patient safety, as the institute's panel had recommended. He promised that hospitals that were operated by the military or the Veterans Administration or that received funds from the federal Medicare program would take immediate steps to promote patient safety. Leading Democrats and Republicans introduced at least seven bills to carry out the institute's recommendations, and Congress appropriated $50 million for fiscal 2001 for a federal office of patient safety and for new research. Fifteen state legislatures also took up proposals aimed at reducing errors.

The issue received national media attention for weeks after the report was released. A poll taken by the Kaiser Family Foundation two weeks after the report was made public found that an astonishing 51 percent of respondents were aware of the report. The private Joint Commission on Accreditation of Healthcare Organizations (JCAHO), which had been criticized for conducting only planned visits to hospitals, announced that its representatives would start making random inspections in January

2000. Aetna, one of the nation's largest health insurers, committed an additional $1 million to patient safety research. The American Hospital Association (AHA), a trade association, began a project to reduce medication errors, and many hospitals launched their own investigations of how serious errors were handled. Executives of several large companies, including General Motors and General Electric, redoubled their efforts to use information about errors to guide employees to the safest health care providers. A national campaign to improve patient safety, considered long overdue by many experts, appeared to be under way.[7]

Two years later, however, this call for disclosure of medical errors had splintered into conflicts among groups representing doctors and hospitals, public health groups, consumer advocates, and representatives of trial lawyers over the design of reporting systems. The American Medical Association (AMA) and the AHA opposed the kind of hospital-by-hospital disclosure of serious errors that would be meaningful to consumers. They clashed with the American Nurses Association and a variety of consumer groups that supported such transparency. Organizations representing health care providers also argued that information about errors should have broad protection from discovery in lawsuits. On that issue they clashed with the American Trial Lawyers Association, which sought to narrow such confidentiality. A new federal office of patient safety and a promising public-private coalition, the National Quality Forum, attempted to encourage research and grapple with the issue administratively, as did several oversight groups and selected hospitals. But a consensus for congressional action remained elusive.[8]

Issues of public disclosure versus confidential reporting and national uniformity of information versus state autonomy divided congressional leaders. In an effort to produce a workable compromise, the Senate Health, Education, Labor, and Pensions Committee circulated draft bills that narrowed the focus to emphasize confidential reporting and excluded any provision for informing the public about serious errors. But representatives of doctors and hospitals, oversight groups, and trial lawyers could not agree on the scope of confidentiality. Two years after leaders of both parties told the public that there was an urgent need for national action, no plan to establish reporting systems for either serious egregious errors or even minor errors had emerged.

These events demonstrated both the growing importance of disclosure as a strategy for reducing risks and some formidable barriers to its effective use. Democratic and Republican administrations, leading members of Congress, state officials, executives of large corporations, oversight groups, and the medical community forcefully promoted the idea that information, combined with improved understanding, better system design, updated training, and cultural change in the medical profession, could reduce a serious risk to public health. A web of reliable data would itself produce economic forces to improve management and political forces to improve accountability.

Conventional wisdom about patient safety was transformed. New research on the causes of errors and lessons from experience in aviation, manufacturing, and nuclear power created an updated perception that many errors were the result of recurring system failures rather than one-time mistakes by individuals. Mistakes could be reduced by structured reporting and analysis of information to reveal those failures. The idea that reporting of a broad category of errors to a narrow audience could improve hospital management, while reporting of a narrow category of errors to a broad audience could improve public accountability, demonstrated that tiers of disclosure could help mediate among conflicting values. A new federal office of patient safety, substantial funds for research, and plans to make better use of existing information created possibilities for progress.

However, at least in the short term, conflicting values, political interests, and resource shortages blocked efforts to place much of this new knowledge in the service of reducing risks. Information strategies proved controversial and often costly. The idea that the public needed to be informed about serious medical errors quickly receded from the national agenda. The notion that hospital managers needed confidential, voluntary reporting of less serious errors to improve practices remained entangled in a congressional debate about the boundaries of confidentiality. Physicians' concerns about liability countered efforts to improve reporting. State officials' concerns about federal control hindered efforts to standardize information. Hospital administrators' concerns about financial stability slowed adoption of systems to uncover, analyze, and correct errors. A rare alignment of new understanding, promising approaches, and national attention created an opportunity to save lives and reduce injuries. A familiar combination of practical obstacles blocked efforts to take advantage of it. Pockets of innovation reduced errors at some hospitals but also highlighted gaps between promise and practice. For the public at large, little changed.

A Disease of Medical Progress

The frequency of medical errors was news to most of the American public in 1999, when the IOM released its report. But to a smaller circle of physicians, hospital administrators, and medical organizations the report was no surprise. They had been gathering evidence for more than a decade showing that such errors created serious health risks. They had worked to bring about a new understanding of systematic causes and to suggest management changes to minimize them. This foundation of understanding, elementary though it still was, supported the two propositions that prepared the way for public action. The first was that medical errors were common even at good hospitals and created serious health risks. The second was that such errors could be substantially reduced by using disclosure to create pressures for the redesign of hospital care.[9]

Howard H. Hiatt, dean of the Harvard School of Public Health in the early 1980s, believed that health care could be improved by applying evidence-based, interdisciplinary approaches to complex problems. With the size of malpractice awards and the cost of malpractice insurance both increasing rapidly in the early 1980s, Hiatt enlisted the support of James Vorenberg, dean of Harvard Law School, and David Axelrod, New York State's commissioner of health, to launch a broad analysis of deaths and injuries caused by medical treatment. Hiatt assembled a team of physicians, economists, and lawyers to examine the frequency with which treatment caused harm, the degree to which harm was preventable, its costs, and its relationship to negligence and malpractice litigation. New York State supported the research with a $3.5 million appropriation. Governor Mario Cuomo considered the study a good investment: the state's doctors paid nearly $1 billion annually in malpractice premiums. Soon after the study began, Lucian L. Leape, a pediatric surgeon who would become one of the leaders in a national effort to improve patient safety, joined the team.[10]

The results of what became known as the Harvard Medical Practice Study astounded Hiatt, Leape, and their colleagues. Nearly 4 percent of patients, almost 1 million people a year, suffered serious health problems as a result of treatment in hospitals, and about two-thirds of those injuries were judged to be preventable; half were caused by negligence, and few patients who received negligent care were compensated. Most adverse events resulted in minor health problems and recovery within a month, but 13.7 percent led to longer disabilities and 13.6 percent resulted in death.[11] Other studies corroborated the seriousness of the problem. An analysis of 15,000 discharges from a representative sample of hospitals in Colorado and Utah in 1992 found that 2.9 percent of patients in each state experienced adverse events, of which 53 percent were judged preventable. Clearly, neither medical safeguards designed to ensure patient safety nor legal safeguards designed to ensure accountability were working.[12]

Looking for steps that might improve patient safety, Leape found a rich body of research on why systematic flaws occurred in complex systems even when those systems were fortified with elaborate safeguards. Driven partly by the development of atomic energy, aerospace advances, and the increased use of complex technology during and after World War II, human factor specialists and cognitive psychologists had explored the interrelationship between behavior and technology. British psychologist James Reason had applied this work to accidents, such as the escape of radioactive material at the Three Mile Island nuclear power plant in 1979 and the explosion of the *Challenger* space shuttle in 1986. He concluded that most errors were caused by mismatches between the design of complex technology and the ways in which humans processed information. On occasion, systematic problems combined with chance events to produce disastrous results, as shown in figure 4-1. Errors could be minimized by learning from past mistakes to organize tasks better and discourage cognitive distortions.[13] Manufacturing firms had already demonstrated that errors could be significantly reduced by improving systems, in what they called a quest for Six Sigma quality.[14]

Leape realized that these ideas could provide an underpinning for a new approach to patient safety. He argued that successful accident pre-

Figure 4-1. *The Dynamics of Accident Causation*

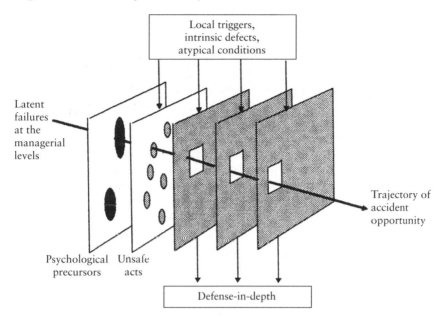

Source: James Reason, *Human Error* (Cambridge University Press, 1990), p. 208. Reprinted with permission.

vention had to focus on root causes: system errors in design and implementation. Hospitals would need to reduce reliance on memory, improve information access, error proof critical tasks, and standardize processes. His views suddenly gained prominence when Betsy Lehman died.[15]

Efforts to reduce particular categories of errors showed how this might be done. In the last decade errors associated with anesthesia had been reduced substantially (see box, "Reducing Errors in Anesthesia"). Studies by David W. Bates and his colleagues conducted at Massachusetts General and Brigham and Women's Hospitals in Boston demonstrated that many of the common errors in administering drugs were traceable to clusters of procedural problems. At Brigham and Women's Hospital, introduction of computerized systems for ordering medications reduced medication errors by more than 50 percent.[16] That was particularly significant since about 20 percent of medical errors were mistakes in medication,

Reducing Errors in Anesthesia

Some pioneers in patient safety had already demonstrated that a systems approach could reduce specific errors dramatically. In 1954 Ellison Pierce, then a resident at the University of Pennsylvania Hospital, saw that as many as one patient a week was suffering cardiac arrest due to anesthesia. Vital signs were being monitored simply by observation. Anesthesiologists watched breathing and took the patient's pulse periodically. Six years later, as vice chairman for anesthesia at Peter Bent Brigham Hospital in Boston, Pierce began collecting information on mishaps involving anesthetics and became convinced that there were many unnecessary deaths.

With malpractice suits increasing, and anesthesiologists concerned about the profession's reputation, Pierce, who went on to become vice president of the American Society of Anesthesiologists, lobbied successfully for adoption of uniform standards for equipment. State laws followed. In 1988, for example, New Jersey required that deaths and injuries from anesthesia be reported to state authorities. Doctors who failed to report could lose their licenses. Deaths from anesthesia mistakes decreased dramatically, from an estimated 1 in 10,000 cases in the early 1980s to 1 in 200,000 by 1990.[1]

1. Jan Ziegler, "A Medical Specialty Blazes a Trail," in *Reducing Medical Errors and Improving Patient Safety* (National Coalition on Health Care and Institute for Healthcare Improvement, 2000), pp. 26–31. Institute of Medicine, *To Err Is Human: Building a Safer Health System* (National Academy Press, 1999), p. 27.

and they appeared to be increasing as new drugs were introduced at a faster pace than in the past and more patients took combinations of medications to treat multiple chronic ailments. Leape called such errors "a disease of medical progress."[17]

Medical Leaders Examine Errors

This combination of shocking incidents and emerging new approaches brought leading researchers and medical professionals together in the mid-1990s to consider how to improve safety at hospitals. In 1996 the American Association for the Advancement of Science, the American Medical Association, and the Joint Commission on Accreditation of Healthcare Organizations convened a conference on patient safety at the Annenberg Center for Health Sciences in Rancho Mirage, California. The AMA established a National Patient Safety Foundation in 1997 as an independent, nonprofit organization to further research, new approaches, and better communication about errors.[18]

In confidential sessions convened by Harvard's John F. Kennedy School of Government in an effort to change the views of opinion leaders about medical errors, Paul O'Neill, then CEO of Alcoa Corp., told several major providers of care about his approach to safety: "Fix it and don't tell me how much it costs." Then, in 1998, the National Round-table on Health Care Quality, a group of leaders meeting since 1996 under the auspices of the Institute of Medicine, emphasized that medical errors were one of the most serious quality of care issues in the United States and called for urgent action "to overhaul how we deliver health care services, educate and train clinicians, and assess and improve quality."[19] The same year, an advisory commission appointed by President Clinton and chaired by Secretary of Health and Human Services Donna Shalala and Secretary of Labor Alexis Herman concluded that the prevention of medical errors should be a national priority and called for the use of information strategies to reduce their incidence. Their recommendations were part of a federal initiative to improve quality of care (see box, "Information Strategies and Quality of Care"). When none of these efforts produced a popular mandate, the IOM decided to lead a call to action to alert Americans to this persistent source of needless deaths and injuries and frame an approach to reducing them.[20]

Existing Accountability Systems Fail to Protect Patients

Frustration with traditional measures intended to protect patient safety also drove change. Federal and state rules, oversight standards of professional groups, and hospital procedures had failed to provide effective incentives to prevent medical errors. They produced the rhetoric and sometimes a regulatory shell, but they did not protect patients.

Information Strategies and Quality of Care

Efforts to improve patient safety coincided with a growing emphasis on information strategies to address a broader problem: quality of care. Both Democratic and Republican reform proposals in the early 1990s had called for disclosure systems to improve quality of care. When President Bill Clinton submitted his plan to Congress in 1993, he proposed report cards for health care providers to allow consumers to shop for the least costly and highest quality care.[1] Proposals by Sen. Robert Dole (R-Kan.) and Sen. George Mitchell (D-Maine) also included report card provisions.[2]

Major public health organizations called for granting patients routine access to their medical records as a means of improving treatment. Technology made it possible to store patient records on wallet-sized cards and to make copies of x-rays and other images on CD-ROMs. Treatment of chronic diseases required a more collaborative approach to medicine than did acute care. The Institute of Medicine concluded that "transfer of information . . . is a key form of care."[3]

1. The Health Security Act, H.R. 3600, 103d Cong., 1st sess. (1993). The administration bill called for quality measurement to be set by a new national council, appointed by the president and including providers, academic experts, and representatives of public health organizations. Performance measures would be selected based on their significance, reliability, validity, links to outcomes, and relationship to public health goals and updated annually. In addition to data gathered from providers, information was to be collected from standardized consumer surveys administered by the government.

2. For a careful analysis of the use of report cards in health care reform (concluding that limitations in measurement and understanding of the ways consumers process such information prevent report cards from assuring quality), see Jason Ross Penzer, "Grading the Report Card: Lessons from Cognitive Psychology, Marketing, and the Law of Information Disclosure for Quality Assessment in Health Care Reform," *Yale Journal on Regulation* (Winter 1995), p. 207.

3. Institute of Medicine, *Crossing the Quality Chasm* (National Academy Press, 2001), p. 72.

A patchwork of federal rules was not designed to identify and correct medical errors. As the nation's largest purchaser of health care, the federal government set scores of standards and provided 40 percent of the funding for private hospitals. As the nation's largest provider of care, the government ran 500 hospitals and clinics for 8 million members of the military and their families and 172 medical centers for veterans. As the purchaser of care for its employees, the government negotiated directly with 300 health plans.[21] However, the magnitude of the regulatory task and a persistent shortage of resources limited accountability in practice. In principle, the federal government ensured quality of care at hospitals participating in the Medicare system. But in practice, national oversight was limited. A federal requirement that participating hospitals report mortality levels each year was discarded when medical groups questioned whether it adequately reflected variations in patient populations. A peer-review system that provided for confidential investigation of some errors allowed doctors to veto disclosure of findings to patients. Federal regulators delegated to states and the Joint Commission for the Accreditation of Healthcare Organizations (JCAHO) the responsibility to respond to complaints and medical errors. By 1999 forty-five states relied on accreditation by the commission as a basis for licensing hospitals. JCAHO, a private organization funded mainly from hospital fees, which totaled an estimated $35.5 million in 2000, increasingly relied on health care providers themselves to maintain systems of accountability.[22]

The federal Food and Drug Administration (FDA) received reports about adverse events associated with prescription medications, perhaps one-third of which were a result of medical errors. But the agency received reports on only 1 to 10 percent of adverse events, mostly from manufacturers, and the system was not designed to provide information about the frequency or character of errors. Recent efforts to introduce electronic reporting, streamline databases, and harmonize standards with other countries were aimed mainly at identifying side effects or drug interactions that premarket clinical trials did not reveal.[23]

Most states did not require that hospitals report medical errors to public authorities. That meant that the magnitude of the problem and the seriousness of risks to patients simply were not known. In the fifteen states that mandated some reporting of errors and other adverse events, purposes were limited, resources were lacking, and the portion of events reported was small. In 2001 the National Academy of State Health Policy, an independent research group, cautioned that there was danger in "creating systems that lead the public to believe that a problem is being addressed when, in fact, it may be worsened unless sufficient resources are provided and effective strategies developed to detect underreporting and prevent abuses."[24]

In New York, a state with one of the most sophisticated patient safety efforts, reporting was sparse and communication flawed. According to an investigation by the *New York Times* in 2001, managers of different hospitals often did not tell each other about doctors who had been disciplined, patients were not notified, and hospitals knowingly hired doctors who had made repeated mistakes. Physicians' malpractice records often were available only in the courthouse where each suit was filed. Antonia C. Novello, the state health commissioner, told reporters Jennifer Steinhauer and Ford Fessenden: "Patients are left hanging and totally at risk. You have to ask yourself here, why was the public good not served?"[25]

Patient suits for malpractice, a traditional mechanism for providing accountability, were also limited in practice. Malpractice fears were often cited as one reason why medical personnel were reluctant to report errors, and insurance rates had risen more than twenty-fold since 1960, after adjusting for inflation. Rates for some specialties totaled $150,000 a year by 1990. "Nothing has soured the practice of medicine and robbed it of its joy as much as the climate of malpractice litigation," observed Lucian Leape and his coauthors in 1991. At the same time, the Harvard Medical Practice Study found that very few patients injured by negligent errors received compensation. A small portion of patients injured by negligence (1 out of 7.5) filed suits, only about half of such suits resulted in compensation, and few cases where patients were compensated featured persuasive evidence of negligence (1 out of 6). Patients often were not informed when errors occurred in their treatment. Leape and his colleagues concluded: "It is fair to say that all parties agree that the tort system in America is failing to meet either of its objectives: it neither fairly compensates victims of injury nor effectively deters injury from occurring."[26]

Other medical groups encouraged voluntary reporting of medical errors, but results remained sparse. The AMA's Code of Ethics made it clear that physicians were "ethically required to inform the patient of all the facts necessary to ensure understanding" when errors occurred.[27] In August 1998 U.S. Pharmacopeia launched MedMARx, a voluntary, Internet-based system for reporting medication errors aimed at giving hospitals better data for corrective actions. In hospitals that chose to participate, employees could report medication errors anonymously via the Internet in standardized form and hospitals received back aggregate data for their own facility and comparative information for other hospitals (which were not identified). The Foundation for Accountability, founded by Paul Ellwood in 1995 and based in Portland, Oregon, also worked to develop performance measures for the public.[28]

Hospital managers themselves traditionally responded to serious errors by disciplining responsible individuals but not necessarily by correcting systemic problems. They usually had no financial incentive to reduce errors. Perversely, many mistakes increased doctors' fees and hospital revenues by increasing in-patient days and treatments. Most hospitals launched risk-management programs as malpractice costs escalated in the 1970s and 1980s, but such programs focused mainly on financial risks to the institution itself rather than on the risks to patients. Nonetheless, some hospitals and health plans did adopt more effective systems. The LDS Hospital in Salt Lake City used computerized medical records to monitor many practices, including medical errors. The system alerted health care workers to situations that might cause errors—sudden changes in doses, abnormalities in laboratory tests, and possible drug interactions, for example. David Classen reported in 1991 that automated detection resulted in a sixty-fold increase in detection of adverse events due to medication.[29]

A New Roadmap for Improving Patient Safety

The catalyst that ignited this combination of growing understanding and growing frustration to finally produce national attention was a remarkable report by nineteen experts on patient safety. Meeting for two years under the auspices of the Institute of Medicine, this group marshaled evidence of shocking numbers of serious errors and forged an agenda for action. Physicians Lucian Leape, Mark R. Chassin, and Donald M. Berwick, who had done early work on reducing medical errors, were joined by Charles R. Buck, Cris Bisgard, and Gail L. Warden, who represented General Electric, Delta Airlines, and the Henry Ford Health

System. William C. Richardson, president of the W. K. Kellogg Foundation, known for innovative approaches to health care, led the committee, which also included representatives of professional and consumer groups. The IOM chose Janet Corrigan, who had directed the Clinton administration's commission on quality of care, as project director.

This diverse group captured national attention with two declarations. First, they told the American public in stark terms that medical errors were a leading cause of deaths and injuries. Second, they cast a wide net, drawing in evidence from aviation safety, quality control in manufacturing, and workplace safety, to demonstrate that this human toll was unnecessary. It could be quickly reduced by seemingly simple actions by government officials and health care providers, especially collecting, sharing, and learning from information. Medical errors created an immense burden of patient injury, suffering, and death and, whether or not they led to injuries, "just shouldn't happen."[30]

This call to action solved seemingly impossible puzzles. One concerned the character of the problem. Researchers had known for years that medical errors caused serious risks, but no one knew for sure how many occurred each year or what they were. State statistics and media reports provided clues about their pervasiveness, but most errors were not reported to anyone. There was not even agreement about how medical errors should be defined. How could the nation act on a problem when its dimensions remained largely unknown? The committee members solved this puzzle by introducing evidence from the Harvard Medical Practice Study and other respected sources to create national estimates of the number of people killed or injured by medical mistakes each year. They illustrated their points with information about errors in medications, the one type of incident for which substantial evidence existed, and they emphasized that their estimates were conservative, since little was known about errors outside hospitals.

A second puzzle concerned the character of the solution. Reporting systems could create conflicting incentives. In principle, public disclosure of serious errors was essential for accountability, but in practice it might drive reporting of errors underground. Fearing lawsuits or disciplinary actions, doctors and nurses might be less inclined to acknowledge mistakes when they occurred. More requirements for transparency might

Table 4-1. *Information Strategies to Reduce Medical Errors*

Public reporting for accountability	Confidential reporting for management change
Mandatory	Voluntary
Errors involving death or serious injury	Errors involving near misses or minor injuries
Reporting by organizations	Reporting by organizations and practitioners
Information released to the public	Information shared among hospitals and clinicians

Source: Adapted from Institute of Medicine, *To Err Is Human,* p. 87.

produce less knowledge. The panel solved this problem by demonstrating that disclosure versus confidentiality, often viewed as an all-or-nothing proposition, in fact represented a continuum of choices. Tiers of disclosure could be tailored to serve particular purposes (see table 4-1). One tier, not emphasized by the committee but widely favored by leaders in the medical community, could provide reporting to individual patients and their families when errors occurred, as a moral obligation. A second tier could provide reporting of minor errors and near misses to a limited audience of clinical leaders, managers, and oversight groups, for the purpose of learning about causes and improving care processes. A third tier could provide reporting of errors that caused deaths or serious injuries to the public at large, for the purpose of providing accountability. In short, ethical concerns called for reporting of single events to individual patients. Improved management called for reporting of a broad class of events to a narrow audience. Accountability called for reporting of a narrow class of events to a broad audience.

Foreshadowing the political struggle that was to follow, the panel noted that these goals were conceptually compatible but "in reality, they can prove difficult to satisfy simultaneously."[31] Donald M. Berwick, a panel member and long-time expert on improving quality of care, explained the conflict at a Senate hearing: "We find widespread distrust by the public in the lack of transparency of the health care system today. The public thinks we are hiding our flaws from them, and, in some ways, we are. We know that our recommendation for mandatory reporting is controversial. If we overdo it, then a severe mandatory system could chill the development of the more important voluntary systems. On the other hand, we do not think that a voluntary system, alone, is sufficiently responsive to the patient's concerns about accountability. We need to find the right balance between a system for learning which has to be voluntary and a system for public accountability which has to have mandatory elements."[32]

The committee assembled evidence for the feasibility of tiers of disclosure. Two decades of experience in reducing errors in commercial aviation provided a powerful precedent. Airline mistakes that resulted in death or serious injury were reported to the National Transportation Safety Board, which reported on causes to the Federal Aviation Administration and to the public. These reports were used to determine penalties, require corrective actions, assess liability, and enable passengers to compare airlines. Near misses and minor incidents were reported confidentially to the National Aeronautics and Space Administration through an entirely separate Aviation Safety Reporting System. These reports were used to determine systematic problems and provide a basis for safety alerts.[33] The federal Occupational Safety and Health Act required employers to keep records of workplace hazards that caused injury or illness, to track trends and determine areas of concern. A separate National Institute for Occupational Safety and Health (NIOSH) assessed causes of hazards, funded research, and recommended actions by employers to improve health and safety. In both programs, disclosure for accountability from information collection was institutionally separate from disclosure for systems improvement.[34]

Public reporting was essential to "ensure a response to specific reports of serious injury, hold . . . providers accountable for maintaining safety, respond to the public's right to know, and provide incentives to health care organizations to implement internal safety systems that reduce the likelihood of such events occurring."[35] In this context, the panel declared, "[r]equests by providers for confidentiality and protection from liability seem inappropriate."[36] Disclosure would "create sufficient pressure to make errors so costly in terms of ability to conduct business in the marketplace, market share and reputation that the organization *must* take action. . . . Such external pressures are virtually absent in health care today."[37] Confidential reporting of minor errors was equally important to allow hospital managers to analyze system flaws and devise corrective actions. Such reporting would "provide rich information to health care organizations in support of their quality improvement efforts."[38]

The panel emphasized costs and public-private complexities. Using disclosure to help minimize medical errors was inevitably costly and labor-intensive because it involved determining root causes and introducing system changes. Federal, state, and private roles were intertwined, with federal agencies providing core definitions, funding, and legal assurances of confidentiality; states establishing basic mechanisms for disclosure; and health care providers supervising reporting, assessing causes, and instituting corrective measures.[39]

Medical Errors Suddenly Gain a Place on the National Agenda

In December 1999 medical errors, seldom discussed publicly by hospital administrators or government officials in the past, suddenly became national news. The institute's report drew attention to serious risks and means to reducing them. Donald M. Berwick, head of the Institute for Healthcare Improvement, defined the moment: "I have never before seen such a tremendous opportunity for improvement as we now have due to public attention to the issue of patient safety. If we act promptly and with courage, millions of future patients will be saved the pain and risk of injury from errors in their care."[40]

President Clinton echoed the report's call for reducing medical errors by 50 percent in five years and promised that 6,000 hospitals that participated in the Medicare program would be required to initiate programs to reduce errors, Veterans Administration hospitals would computerize medication orders within a year, and military hospitals and clinics would also require reporting of errors.[41] Bipartisan support in Congress quickly produced high-profile hearings, funding approval for further research, and proposed legislation. Congress quickly appropriated $50 million for fiscal 2001 for an interim office of patient safety within the Department of Health and Human Services and for new research on medical errors.[42]

Three months later, eleven federal health agencies echoed the call to action in an interagency report: "Federal and state governments have the responsibility to ensure, through mandatory public reporting, that the Nation can determine whether health care institutions have met an adequate standard of patient safety." All states should have mandatory reporting systems for serious errors within three years.[43]

State and local officials, medical organizations, and large purchasers of care also responded quickly. At least fifteen legislatures took up proposals aimed at reducing errors. In New York, new legislation authorized the creation of a state center for patient safety charged with improving public access to health care information, reducing medical crrors, and tightening requirements that hospitals quickly investigate incidents.[44] A Pittsburgh Regional Healthcare Initiative mobilized government and private groups to reduce medication errors and hospital infections by sharing data.[45] The American Medical Association, representing doctors, endorsed the use of information strategies to improve patient safety. The AMA's Foundation for Patient Safety had led efforts to introduce such approaches for years. Dennis O'Leary, president of the Joint Commission on Accreditation of Healthcare Organizations, the private group that accredited most of the nation's hospitals, told members of Congress in February 2000: "Medical error reduction is fundamentally an information problem. The solution . . . resides in developing mechanisms for collecting, analyzing, and applying existing information."[46]

Within weeks, General Motors, General Electric, and six other major corporations announced that their coalition, the Leapfrog Group, would use purchasing power to reduce risks to employees. Some large public purchasers of health care, including the states of Maine, Massachusetts, and Washington, joined with these private purchasers to encourage hospitals to take specific steps to reduce errors.[47]

Conflicts Produce Political Stalemate

The appearance of consensus was short-lived, however. In February 2000, when President Clinton announced his administration's support for requiring hospitals to disclose to the public serious medical errors, organizations representing hospitals and doctors mounted an offensive against the idea. Richard J. Davidson, president of the American Hospital Association, declared that "the idea that a mandatory reporting system is going to change behavior is naïve at best. You need to focus on making a cultural change in hospitals, to promote open discussion of errors, and that's not possible if some plaintiff's attorney is climbing on your back." Nancy W. Dickey, spokesperson for the AMA and its former president, stated flatly: "We are opposed to mandatory reporting. A number of states have mandatory reporting, and there's no evidence that they have greater safety or fewer errors."[48] The commission that accredited hospitals emphasized the need for "a blame-free, protected environment that encourages the systematic surfacing and reporting of serious adverse events."[49] Virtually alone among medical groups, the American Nurses Association supported reporting of serious errors and warned that confidentiality protections should be narrowly framed so that hospitals could not "hide or escape their accountability in health care errors."[50]

Public Disclosure versus Protection of Confidentiality

Within a few months, these major medical groups had succeeded in altering the terms of the national debate. Instead of promoting the compatibility of public reporting of serious errors with confidential reporting of near misses and minor mistakes, as the institute's report had done, they succeeded in reframing the issues, promoting the idea that public reporting for accountability would undercut the more important goal of confidential reporting for improved management. Instead of proclaiming the need to strengthen individual responsibility *and* improve systems of care, they charged that a culture of blame prevented hospitals from improving practices. "We have a blame and punishment society," declared JCAHO president O'Leary. "When something goes wrong, we want a hanging. That's not a climate that favors voluntary reporting of anything. We would want to see non-punitive and confidentiality measures."[51] These arguments were self-serving but they also reflected broad concerns. Some leaders of medical organizations believed that improvement had to grow out of collaborative efforts and could not be imposed by external pressures.[52] Others emphasized that primitive metrics and uneven rates of public reporting might mislead rather than inform. John M. Eisenberg, a respected physician who headed the Agency for Healthcare Research and

Quality, the federal entity charged with improving patient safety, believed that it was too soon to require public reporting of serious errors. "The evidence and experience with reporting systems is scattered and pretty rudimentary. We want to know more about how mandatory reporting has worked in states where it has been tried," he told Robert Pear of the *New York Times* soon after the Institute of Medicine issued its report.[53]

As these arguments were repeated by virtually all the major groups representing doctors and hospitals, they obscured two compelling reasons for public disclosure. First, patients, insurers, corporations, government entities, and other purchasers needed to know about large differences in rates of preventable errors among hospitals. The Harvard Medical Practice Study found that the portion of adverse events due to negligence varied from 1 to 60 percent at different hospitals. Negligence was much more common in government hospitals (36 percent of adverse events) than in nonprofit hospitals (25 percent of adverse events) or in teaching hospitals (11 percent of adverse events). Hospitals serving primarily minority patients had much higher than average rates of negligent care (37 percent of adverse events).[54]

Second, disclosure was needed to motivate hospitals to take action on safety issues, as the Institute of Medicine argued forcefully. Most hospitals in the United States faced rising costs and shrinking revenues. Emphasis on the *potential* for better information begged the question of why, without public pressure, executives would choose to adopt complex analytical processes and corrective measures when costs could be large, long-term savings remained speculative, and other priorities were compelling. For nearly a decade, large studies had shown high rates of death and injury from errors, but few hospitals had taken steps to change the system.

In addition, there were reasons to question the ideas that public reporting would increase lawsuits or drive reporting of errors underground. Albert W. Wu of Johns Hopkins University drew together findings suggesting that patients sued less frequently, not more frequently, if they were given an honest explanation of errors. The introduction of reporting of mortality in coronary-artery bypass surgery by doctor and hospital in New York had not increased lawsuits. Neither had a new system of rating physicians in Pennsylvania.[55] Perverse incentives created by the medical malpractice system remained a serious national problem, but two-thirds of states had already set legislative limits on the size of awards. Most capped noneconomic damages or total damages at less than $1 million, and some had also limited attorneys' contingency fees.[56]

Low reporting rates occurred with or without confidentiality. In Florida, where confidentiality was protected rigorously, only 5 to 10 percent of errors were reported to hospital administrators. A survey in 2000 by the National Academy of State Health Policy found no perceived difference between amounts of underreporting in states with strong protection of data and those with weak protection. Dennis O'Leary explained that the JCAHO, the commission that accredited hospitals, probably received reports of less than 1 percent of serious errors, even though individual reports were confidential.[57]

Some broad-based groups made the case for public reporting of errors. David Lansky, president of the Foundation for Accountability, argued that "the way to improve American health care is to measure which doctors, hospitals, and health plans do the best job, then provide that information to consumers so they can seek out the care that is best for them. Understanding your health care should be as easy as reading a nutrition label on a soup can or the fuel efficiency rating on a new car." Lansky worked to build support for broad measures of quality of care that patients could use to inform their choices of hospitals and health care providers.[58] The National Academy of State Health Policy was another group that argued forcefully for public reporting. Its director, Trish Riley, contended that reporting without identifying hospitals made it impossible for state officials to investigate incidents, validate data, and hold hospitals accountable for making improvements. It also made it impossible for consumers, investors, employees, or hospitals themselves to compare the safety of institutions.[59]

National Uniformity versus State Discretion

A second set of conflicts reflected familiar competition between national uniformity and variable state approaches. Oversight of hospitals and other health care providers was traditionally a state role and most state governments did not favor nationally standardized reporting of medical errors. State officials feared that standardization would lead to new national efforts to regulate quality of care and new unfunded responsibilities for states. They argued that each state should be free to choose priorities for reporting and that a diversity of approaches would foster innovation. Without standardized reporting, however, regulators, large purchasers, consumers, and hospital managers themselves would lack any means of comparing performance among institutions and tracking improvements over time.

For a generation, centrifugal forces had left fragments of information scattered among states. In the 1970s and 1980s the federal government, the nation's largest purchaser of health care, through the Medicare system, had delegated most quality-of-care oversight to the states. In the health care industry, where the dominant trend was toward concentration of ownership, managers relied increasingly on financial incentives and other decentralized means of encouraging attention to quality among their subsidiaries. Information about errors, if it existed at all, normally remained dispersed in medical records. Definitions and measures varied widely by specialty, hospital, and state. Information technology created opportunities to centralize and use data, but institutional problems remained and capital costs for systems to track errors and other quality improvement would be substantial.[60]

The Institute of Medicine's panel had proposed that states operate reporting systems for serious errors using nationally standardized formats. States could take the lead in analyzing causes and providing public access to reports, once they were confirmed. The federal government would provide funds for reporting and analysis and would collect information in any state that chose not to enact such a requirement. But even this degree of uniformity did not gain state support.

Government Officials Cede Leadership to Large Purchasers

Faced with these political cross-currents, neither Congress nor the executive branch took the kind of bold action recommended by the Institute of Medicine. By the fall of 2001 the Senate subcommittee on health had whittled broad proposals of individual senators into a compromise so limited that both supporters and opponents lost interest in it.

Cautious Steps by Federal Authorities

The executive branch used its enormous power as a provider of health care to take some modest steps. In 1998 Kenneth W. Kizer, under secretary for health in the Department of Veterans Affairs, had called for the department's 173 medical centers to initiate voluntary, confidential reporting of most medical errors. Under his leadership, the department devoted substantial resources to patient safety, including extra training for hospital staff, computerizing and bar-coding medication ordering, and using error reports to make changes in patient care.[61] The Department of Defense, which operated hospitals and clinics for military personnel and their families, took similar steps. In addition, the government required the 300 programs that provided health care for federal employees to initiate patient safety programs and disclose the elements of those programs to consumers.

Federal officials also took some steps to make better use of existing information, fragmentary though it was. In April 2001 Secretary of Health and Human Services Tommy G. Thompson directed federal agencies to combine and make accessible on the Internet federal, state, and private information about errors in medication and surgery, withholding names of doctors and hospitals.[62] The Food and Drug Administration continued important efforts to improve reporting of adverse events and labeling of drugs.[63]

The government did not, however, use its power as a purchaser of health care to provide patients with information about hospital safety. Medicare's peer-review system continued to encourage confidential investigation of errors, but for two decades the program had allowed doctors to veto disclosure of information even to individual patients. The government changed that rule only in 2001 in the course of settling a suit by the son of a Medicare recipient who died after an asthma attack. Henceforth, investigators would be required to tell patients the investigations' findings, whether they received "professionally recognized standards of health care," and whether doctors or hospitals had been subject to disciplinary actions.[64]

Limited Measures by States and Private Organizations

Most state-mandated reporting of errors remained a hollow shell. Initial bold commitments by state officials in response to the institute's report devolved mainly into mandates to study the problem further. Fifteen state legislatures took up patient safety measures, but the eight laws enacted by the fall of 2000 required mainly further analysis and tinkering with existing rules. Massachusetts and Missouri enacted whistleblower protection so that employees could not be penalized for reporting errors. South Dakota required more training in administering medication in some facilities. Washington, Florida, and New York envisioned broader changes but initially emphasized further study of the issues.[65] In thirty-five states serious errors were not required to be reported to public authorities at all. Among the fifteen that did require reporting, there was no consistency in the types of events or definitions and all the programs lacked resources to follow up on information received.[66]

National attention did spark some promising collaborative efforts. In Massachusetts, sixty-one of the state's sixty-eight hospitals formed a Coalition for the Prevention of Medical Errors in 1999 that set an agenda for short- and long-term reforms, despite the fact that two-thirds of the hospitals in the state were losing money. The Pittsburgh Regional Healthcare Initiative, with a membership of major insurers, hospitals, corporate purchasers, and civic leaders, urged hospitals to share data about medication errors and hospital-acquired infections and develop performance measures. The National Quality Forum, a public-private partnership created in 1999 to provide uniform definitions and measurements of health care quality, proposed standardized reporting of twenty-seven medical errors to state-run databases and recommended that institutions be identified, information be available to the public, and reporting become a condition for participation in Medicare. The JCAHO, the organization that accredited most of the nation's hospitals, adopted new safety standards in July 2001. The National Association of School Nurses and the American Academy of Pediatrics planned to publish voluntary guidelines to minimize medication errors in school health programs, and the American Hospital Association urged its 6,000 members to adopt the fifteen best practices for patient safety developed by the Massachusetts coalition.[67]

Finally, hospitals moved slowly toward the most basic provision of information: telling patients and their families about errors as soon as they occurred. Respected leaders in efforts to improve patient safety told Congress that the ethical obligation could not be compromised. "Every patient has a right to know if he or she has been injured by treatment, and whether the injury has been caused by an error or other breakdown of the system," Lucian L. Leape told members of the Senate committee on health in 2001. "Full and prompt disclosure is a moral obligation of both the hospital and the professional caregiver." In July 2001 the Joint Commission on Accreditation of Healthcare Organizations urged its member hospitals to provide patients with timely explanation of medical errors.[68]

Large Purchasers of Health Care Take the Lead

In the absence of government action, sustained pressure to reduce medical errors came from an unlikely source: business leaders. By 2000 eighty companies and public purchasers had joined the Leapfrog Group, the coalition of large purchasers sponsored by the Business Roundtable. These corporate leaders had several compelling reasons to reduce errors. First, the human toll on their employees was large and preventable. Second, with skilled workers in short supply, quality health care was a productivity issue as well as a benefits issue. Using the Institute of Medicine's estimates, the group calculated that medical mistakes might cause as many as one death and five injuries *each hour* among individuals covered by company plans. Third, errors contributed to the rapidly increasing cost of care by lengthening hospital stays and adding to needed procedures and medications. Members spent $45 billion annually on health care for their 25 million employees, retirees, and family members. General Motors, one of the group's members and the largest private purchaser of health care in the United States, spent $4 billion in 2000, 10 percent more than in 1999. Nearly $1 billion of that was spent on medications, 20 percent more than in 1999.[69]

Initially, the group looked for changes that would produce significant reductions in errors, could be introduced quickly, would be appreciated by patients, and could be easily monitored. It came up with three goals: referring patients to hospitals with the best outcomes for specific procedures, encouraging hospitals to adopt computerized entry systems for prescriptions, and assuring that intensive care units were staffed with physicians trained in critical care. Ultimately companies hoped to use these criteria to choose which hospitals to do business with.

Some members launched their own initiatives. Ford and General Motors mailed to employees in Cleveland, Atlanta, Buffalo, and other cities a consumer's guide that graded local hospitals on deaths, complications, and lengths of stay for common procedures. General Motors also launched a $15 million, three-year program to buy handheld computers for the 5,000 physicians that treated the company's employees, to provide automated entry of prescriptions and accessing of the latest medical literature and other data.[70] These corporate efforts followed the example of the Pacific Business Group on Health and other purchaser coalitions, which negotiated reduced premiums from providers in the early 1990s and went on to work on improving quality of care by obtaining improved data from hospitals and creating economic incentives to improve success rates.[71]

How hospitals and health care providers would respond to these new pressures remained uncertain. In most communities, participating employers represented a relatively small portion of health care consumers, many markets lacked significant competition among providers, and employee turnover reduced opportunities to recoup investments in patient safety. More than half of the nation's hospitals were in some kind of financial difficulty and all faced conflicting external pressures from federal and state regulators, oversight groups, labor unions, and many other sources, each with their own priorities. By 2001 the Leapfrog Group had begun to slow its timetable for action and acknowledge the need for more diversity in collaborative regional approaches to patient safety.

Incremental Approaches or Political Stalemate?

Two years after the public was alerted to serious risks from medical errors, a national consensus for action had splintered into an assortment of adjustments by federal agencies, modest actions by state governments, strengthened policies by oversight groups and trade associations, nascent collaborative efforts, specific demands by corporate purchasers for safer care, and an emphasis on further research. Proposals for new national laws to support mandatory reporting of serious errors and encourage voluntary, confidential reporting of minor incidents remained ensnared in intransigent political conflicts. Benefits of improved accountability conflicted with fears of increased litigation. Benefits of nationally uniform reporting conflicted with state discretion. A limited number of hospitals with unusual leadership and resources made impressive strides toward understanding the causes of errors and reducing them. Federal research funds launched promising efforts to improve understanding of errors. A few collaborative initiatives increased pressures for improvement. But overall, national and state policy remained roughly where it had been five years earlier.

Whether these actions represented early steps in an incremental approach to reducing medical errors or indications of an intractable political stalemate remained uncertain. John Eisenberg, who headed the federal agency responsible for improving patient safety during both the Clinton and the George W. Bush administrations, took the optimistic view that five years of further research would put the nation in a better position to construct effective information strategies to reduce errors. In the meantime, state actions, collaborative approaches, and successful pressure from corporate purchasers of health care could further national understanding of these risks and point the way to broader policies.

A more pessimistic view suggested that none of the providers, purchasers, oversight groups, consumers, or government authorities had lasting economic or political incentives to make substantial improvements in patient safety. For providers, identifying and correcting errors was costly, required professionals to change their ways, might reduce revenues, and would not necessarily improve their competitive position. For most purchasers, cost remained the driving consideration in choice of providers, most measures of patient safety remained primitive, and decisions that emphasized quality of care were often impractical. For professional societies and oversight groups, most of which received substantial funding from doctors or hospitals, effective error reduction was a time-consuming, expensive activity that outstripped current resources and created controversy among constituents. For government agencies, designing and carrying out strategies to reduce errors created formidable problems of measurement, workload, and political clashes. For consumers of health care, patient safety remained an enigma: hospital visits were rare and often unplanned events, judgments about risk were complicated by cognitive distortions, and informed choice was impeded by a lack of reliable information and other practical obstacles.

The Enigma of Information Use

A question that received surprisingly little attention in the national debate was whether individual consumers, large purchasers of health care, and hospitals themselves would make use of new information about errors if it existed. Early experience with various report cards that aimed to measure performance for hospitals and health care providers offered two insights. First, use of information about quality of care could not be taken for granted. Second, hospitals and health care providers sometimes had anticipatory reactions to public information. They took steps to improve safety, whether or not the public used the information to alter choices.

Early research suggested that public responses to information varied widely. In 2000 Martin N. Marshall reported on evaluations of seven report card systems in the *Journal of the American Medical Association*. In Pennsylvania, where disclosure of mortality rates associated with coronary bypass operations was required for each hospital, only 20 percent of patients interviewed in a telephone survey were aware of the rating system and fewer than 25 percent of those said that it had a significant impact on their choice of surgeon. In New York, on the other hand, hospitals and physicians with lower mortality rates gained market share when a similar disclosure requirement was introduced, and risk-adjusted mortality declined more rapidly than in any other state.

Employers apparently made limited use of report card data in these early years, basing choice of providers mainly on cost. A performance rating and accreditation system for health plans created by the National Committee for Quality Assurance was ranked as very important by only 11 percent of employers, for example. Use of report cards by physicians also appeared to vary widely. Thirty-eight percent of cardiologists in New York State used the disclosed mortality rates in making referrals, but only 2 percent of cardiologists and surgeons in Pennsylvania said that the influence of published mortality rates on referrals was significant. Many factors complicated questions of use. When asked why they did not make use of report card data, consumers cited lack of access to the data, lack of understanding, lack of interest, lack of trust in the data, and lack of meaningful choice. Only about 50 percent of employees of large companies had a choice among plans. Most people still relied on information from family or friends in evaluating the quality of doctors, hospitals, or plans.[72]

Interestingly, however, even when use was low, report cards spurred some hospitals to improve quality. In Missouri 50 percent of hospitals improved their quality of care after they were rated on their performance in obstetric procedures. Those in competitive markets were twice as likely to make improvements as those with monopolies. Risk-adjusted mortality from bypass surgery in New York hospitals decreased 41 percent in four years after hospital track records were published, according to one study. When Cleveland's Health Quality Choice program published mortality data for selected medical conditions and surgeries, significant and sustained reductions in risk-adjusted mortality for most conditions occurred.[73]

Technology's Promise

As computers and the Internet gained power, consumers of health care had reason to see them as a mixed blessing. People were increasingly concerned about whether providers would use technology to share confidential information about patients' illnesses and treatments with employers and insurance companies. At the same time, more and more patients were using the Internet to gain answers to pressing questions about health. The combination of better educated and better informed patients, the growing difficulty and cost associated with seeking advice from physicians, and the growth of user-friendly websites produced a new kind of populist medicine.

With decreasing amounts of time and effort, anyone with Internet access could gain the benefit of information previously available only to experts. Symptoms, choices of treatment, drug interactions, new studies, and ways to get experimental drugs were available to those willing to negotiate one of many popular websites. Chat rooms offered help from people with personal experiences as well as from medical authorities. Companies were working on electronic means for heart disease patients to transmit monitoring data to their physicians via the web. Nearly half the states offered some online information on doctors. Sites like Search-Pointe.com combined physician data from many government and private sources and charged a fee for it. With web-based advice proliferating, the nonprofit American Accreditation Health Care Commission offered a seal of approval for health care sites to guide consumers to reliable information (www.urac.org). By 2000 millions of Americans used the web to learn about their health problems.

In principle, technology could also resolve many of the issues that blocked access to information about patient safety. Hospitals' success rates with common procedures could be customized on websites to answer patients' specific questions in as much or little detail as they wished. Doctors' malpractice records could be moved from distant courthouses to instantly available databases. If hospitals remained unwilling to provide the information, patients could rate the performance of those with which they had experience. Drug interactions that caused many injuries could be checked easily by patients as well as doctors. Digital records, accessible via smart cards, could empower patients to more easily seek second opinions or change doctors. Nuanced portraits of hospitals could convey their strengths as well as their weaknesses. The degree of reliability of information about doctors and hospitals could be color coded. Fragmented safety data from many sources could be carefully integrated to produce composites and updated quickly.

Yet information about medical errors was slow to leap to the web. Political and institutional barriers blocked its path. Without the collection of basic information and standardization of definitions, no amount of technology could inform the public. With little information available, the chance of risks created from misinformation grew. In 2000 the federal General Accounting Office, Congress's investigative agency, reported that little was known about errors in medication, among the most common mistakes in hospitals, and they appeared to be increasing. Definitions varied widely and reliable information about their frequency and character was lacking. Both government and hospital tracking systems depended on voluntary reporting that detected only a small fraction of adverse events and were almost certainly unrepresentative. Even the number of deaths from medication problems remained unknown. Errors were increasing in part because doctors were writing more prescriptions, patients were taking more complicated combinations of drugs, and medications themselves were becoming more numerous and complex. Doctors ordered overdoses, underdoses, drugs with known interactions, or drugs for patients with documented allergies. Nurses administered the wrong drug, at the wrong time, or by the wrong means. Outside hospitals, patients themselves frequently erred in the doses or timing of medications. The benefits of information technology were slow to reach what the National Research Council called a "trillion dollar cottage industry."[74]

An Uncertain Future

Two years of national debate about medical errors produced remarkable changes in conventional wisdom but little progress in alerting patients to safety problems. Government officials, leaders of oversight groups, and many hospital administrators promoted the idea that most mistakes in treatment were products of persistent flaws in complex systems rather than simply one-time acts of carelessness by individuals. The idea that better understanding of these flaws and better management of complex systems could reduce deaths and injuries began to permeate the health care system.

At the same time, policymakers acknowledged that information strategies were not simply a choice between public disclosure and corporate confidentiality. Such strategies began to be viewed as versatile tools that could be calibrated to serve specific purposes by defining both the scope of data disclosed and intended audiences. Patients could be told about any error that affected them in order to uphold ethical standards. Hospitals could share among themselves and with oversight groups knowledge gleaned from minor errors and near misses in order to promote better management. The public could be informed about mistakes that caused death or serious injury to promote accountability. Information technology could enhance these strategies.

However, it remained uncertain whether and how fast advances in understanding and technology would translate into saved lives and reduced injuries in hospitals across the country. In 1999 medical experts and politicians had called for reducing medical errors by 50 percent in five years through the use of information strategies. Two years later, this goal was rarely mentioned. The specifics of national action remained contentious. Plans to strengthen state reporting systems were crippled by political obstacles and failure to commit public resources to the cause. Pressure from large purchasers of health care remained strong, but their lasting influence was uncertain. Interest by hospital managers in analyzing causes of errors and adopting corrective measures was countered by competing priorities and the financial insecurity of many institutions.

Pockets of innovation demonstrated some of the benefits of change but also provided a measure of the intractable gaps between promise and practice. Medical errors continued to draw national attention. In July 2001 an oxygen canister mistakenly left in the room was drawn toward a magnetic resonance imaging scanner in a Westchester County hospital, killing the patient being scanned, a six-year-old boy. The same month, a Philadelphia hospital reported that two patients may have died due to miscalculations in the amounts of a blood-thinning drug administered. Broader change by health care providers would require sustained leadership and unprecedented commitment of resources, a combination that could not be taken for granted in any industry.[75]

After more than a decade of work by medical experts and policy officials and two years of national attention, strategies to reduce errors had not yet been adopted by most hospitals or by state and federal governments. Americans still had access to less information about the safety of the hospitals where they sought care than about the cars they drove, the airplanes they flew in, and the places where they worked. If the Institute of Medicine was correct that "transparency is the route to accountability," little progress had been made.[76] At least in the short term, medical professionals' fears of embarrassment and increased liability proved stronger than the public's need for reliable information.

5 Disclosure as Social Policy

Knowledge will forever govern ignorance, and a people who mean to be their own Governours, must arm themselves with the power knowledge gives.

—JAMES MADISON*

The spread of disclosure systems to reduce risks has created a new technopopulism. The combination of new access to standardized information and new technology, especially the growth of the Internet, has set in motion an irreversible process that involves dangers as well as opportunities. Ordinary citizens can now do what government regulators have traditionally done: encourage manufacturers, food processors, hospitals, water authorities, and other large organizations to improve public health and safety. Armed with the facts, they create pressures for change through what they buy, how they invest, where they work, how they vote, and what groups they join. The expansion of the World Wide Web offers new ways to distribute and personalize information that automatically enhances the power of disclosure. Quick searches online to check contamination in drinking water, the rollover

*James Madison, letter to W. T. Barry, August 4, 1822, in Gaillard Hunt, ed., *The Writings of James Madison*, vol. 3 (G. P. Putnam, 1910), p. 103.

propensity of SUVs, toxic chemicals in neighborhoods, alternative products to meet nutritional goals, or the relative safety of hospitals are now feasible. Technopopulism is an optimistic notion: it expresses an belief that transparency can make life better for ordinary citizens.

But more information does not necessarily mean less risk. In practice, providing the public with facts to make decisions that translate into improved health and safety has proven surprisingly hard to do—and there are serious dangers in doing it badly. One problem is that the character and magnitude of risks are often uncertain. The health effects of most toxic chemicals remain open to question. So do many of the links between specific nutrients and chronic disease. The Institute of Medicine could only suggest that annual deaths from medical errors ranged somewhere between 44,000 and 98,000. Even when scientific consensus exists, reliable data are often scarce. Little is known about the exposure of the American public to toxic chemicals. How changes in eating habits reduce rates of disease is expressed in rough estimates at best. Collecting information about medical errors remains in its infancy. Finally, even good information will not automatically lead to good results. The paths through which information alters behavior are inherently difficult to predict. Corporations, other organizations, and individuals sometimes respond as expected. Often, they do not.

The Rise of Technopopulism

Despite these qualifications, the emergence of new systems of social disclosure does represent a major political innovation: something different that, for better or worse, is certain to endure. Policies as diverse as nutritional labeling, airline safety rankings, and reporting of workplace hazards share core characteristics. Stated simply, *such strategies employ government authority to require the standardized disclosure of factual information from identified businesses or other organizations about products or practices to reduce risks to the public.* Like the older populist measures of initiative and referendum, systems of social disclosure substitute direct democracy for deliberation. Levels of acceptable risk are set by the cumulative actions of consumers, investors, employees, voters, and members of advocacy groups.

As mainstream policy, these systems are something new. They differ from the plethora of report cards, rankings, and certifications produced by companies, trade associations, professional organizations, advocacy groups, and the media. Mandatory disclosure systems provide a legitimacy, permanence, and accountability that voluntarism lacks. Requirements emerge from contentious negotiations and carry the force of law. Standardized reporting allows users to evaluate the records of competing firms and products. Infractions lead to penalties, and requirements are enforced by courts. The government's authority to compel the collection and dissemination of information is central.

These new systems also differ from government's traditional collection of private-sector information. In the past, regulators collected the fragments of data they needed to set and enforce rules. Experts evaluated it. When information was made available to the public, it was usually as an afterthought or as a response to a "right-to-know" request. By contrast, the new disclosure systems are aimed at ordinary consumers and intended to inform comprehensively to change behavior. Information itself becomes the instrument of regulation. They also differ from familiar government-mandated warnings, which told people to fasten their seat belts, to keep household chemicals out of the reach of children, and that smoking may be harmful to their health. These messages provided the same general advice to everyone. By contrast, the new systems provide detailed information about specific companies and products, information that is intended to allow people with varied needs and values to make choices.

Paradoxically, this political innovation has been a product of political retrenchment and regulatory stalemate. Proposals emerged as pragmatic compromises when public action seemed imperative and other forms of regulation appeared infeasible. Each of the mandates examined in this book responded to a sudden new need. Congress required manufacturers to disclose routine toxic releases after a leak of poisonous gas killed more than 2,000 people near a pesticide plant in Bhopal, India. Nutritional labeling became law soon after food processors suddenly made bold health claims that left the public confused, inspired lawsuits, and triggered state labeling initiatives. Medical errors captured national attention when the Institute of Medicine found that thousands of Americans were killed annually by hospital mistakes.[1]

Surprisingly, the targets of new disclosure rules often ended up supporting them. New systems placed vast amounts of proprietary information permanently in the public domain. They threatened corporate reputations. They aimed to shift the balance of power, transferring some control over decisions about risks to the public at large. In a politically charged atmosphere, coalitions of consumers, public health organizations, labor unions, and others might impose such systems on unwilling businesses. But these cases suggest a more improbable reality: companies often lobbied for national disclosure requirements. They did so because they believed that disclosure could reduce the chances of tougher regulation, eliminate the threat of multiple state requirements, or improve competitive advantage.

When a Senate committee proposed that manufacturers reveal toxic releases, industry representatives worked to narrow but not to defeat the requirement. One national disclosure system seemed preferable to multiple state requirements or more onerous regulation. Likewise, large food processing companies and most trade associations supported national nutritional labeling as an alternative to multiple state requirements and new regulations, or a crackdown on health claims. Some also expected competitive gain from labeling as consumers, armed with accurate information, increased demand for authentically healthful products. Many hospitals and doctors favored limited reporting systems for medical errors. They saw them as means of revealing systemic problems that could be fixed, reducing political pressure for broader disclosure and staving off the possibility of further government regulation.

Pitfalls and Conflicts

To say that technopopulism is permanent is not to say that it will always succeed. For one thing, even with the aid of the Internet, communicating accurately about risks is complicated. The central question, whether new information reduces risk, has proven extraordinarily difficult to answer. Conflicts among affected parties counter disclosure's promise. Information that is incomplete, inaccurate, or out of date can do more harm than good. It can lead neighborhood residents to protest chemical discharges that are relatively benign while ignoring those that pose real threats. It can lead shoppers to choose products that increase rather than decrease their chances of getting heart disease or cancer. It can lead patients to choose hospitals where errors in medication or surgery are relatively common. Misplaced public pressure, in turn, can encourage manufacturers or hospitals to make changes that waste resources and lead to additional deaths and injuries.

The Problem of Communication

One pervasive problem is the way people commonly process information. Disclosure systems involve technical information communicated between experts and the general public. To work as intended, new knowledge must produce collective responses that, in turn, reduce risks. But that logic often collides with cognitive distortions. Three decades of empirical research by psychologists and economists have altered the classical view of the consumer's search for information. That view, as articulated in a 1961 essay by George Stigler on the economics of information, suggested that consumers would search for information until the value of the time they expended was equal to the benefits they gained.[2] However, later studies revealed that people often used shortcuts instead of rational searches to determine the importance of risks.

These shortcuts, called heuristics (from the Greek word *heuriskein,* to find), allow individuals to place new information in context. They simplify the complex array of large and small dangers in daily life and prevent information overload. But they can also interfere with an accurate understanding of those threats.[3] For example, people tend to overreact to risks associated with unlikely but frightening events, such as chemical accidents or airline crashes. They underestimate risks from probable but familiar events, such as smoking, eating foods high in saturated fats, or speeding on highways. They tend to assign disproportionate importance to risks of events that are easily brought to mind because of recent media coverage or local incidents. These distortions create gaps between public and scientific perceptions of risk.

As a result, whether and how new information is interpreted by public authorities is always an important issue, and one that causes controversy. Interpretation helps users convert data into usable knowledge. But when it can also influence markets, legislative action, or regulation, interest groups of all persuasions want to shape the presentation.

Disclosure often gives intermediaries new power. When government agencies have not interpreted data or made access user friendly, the media, advocacy groups, and business interests have filled the vacuum. Newspapers purchased the raw data on toxic releases from the Environmental Protection Agency, ranked polluters nationally and locally, and publicized the names of counties with the highest levels. Environmental groups and trade associations produced their own analyses and rankings. Likewise, public health groups, industry organizations, and companies all offered independent explanations of the significance of amounts of fat, salt, and other nutrients in processed foods. Hospitals have argued against translating complex data into rankings for safety or quality of care. But consumer groups, media organizations, and large employers have produced those rankings anyway. Increasingly, the result is a lively information marketplace, but not necessarily one in which accurate and complete accounts of risk prevail over those that are misleading, fragmentary, or self-serving.

Intractable Obstacles

These profiles provide some useful leads about when disclosure can work and when it cannot. They suggest a set of preconditions without which such systems may have no chance of succeeding. They point to the importance of each system's architecture. They shed light on the array of economic and political pathways through which new information exerts pressure for change and the central importance of reputation in organizations' responses. And they provide some evidence that the promise of disclosure can sometimes be fulfilled into practice.[4]

New information cannot always reduce risks. If information is already plentiful, consumers and investors are uninterested, or there is no feasible way to improve health and safety, public officials must look elsewhere for remedies. In each of these profiles, essential preconditions made disclosure at least a viable option. *Variable performance* among competing organizations made improvement plausible. An *information gap* concerning those risks existed. It was economically and technically feasible to *increase the supply* of information at a reasonable cost. There also existed an apparent *demand for information* from participants in markets or political processes, and *risks could be reduced* by target organizations within reasonable economic and technical limits. Measures could be developed that would not mislead, so that *communication was feasible* to inform a broad audience about risks. Finally, threats were not so severe that products needed to be banned or practices made illegal: *variable responses from target organizations were tolerable.*[5]

The profiles also illustrate how weaknesses in design can complicate effectiveness. Each system is created with a unique architecture. Scope, targets, metrics, and enforcement vary widely. (For a summary of architectural elements, see appendix.) The metric selected by Congress for disclosure of toxic chemicals made it impossible to judge changes in risks. The law required reporting only of total pounds of chemicals, with no adjustments for toxicity, exposure, and other variables. When releases of one chemical were reduced by substituting another, there was no way of knowing whether risks were increased or reduced. In addition, the system was structured so that the accuracy of reporting remained uncertain. Variable estimating techniques and limited enforcement cast doubt on the data submitted by manufacturers. The limited scope of nutritional labeling undermined its potential effectiveness as well. The government requirement left out fast-food establishments, grocery delicatessens, and restaurant meals—the sources of foods that were particularly high in nutrients that contributed to chronic disease. After six years of mandatory nutritional labeling, government researchers concluded in 2000 that it was not yet possible to determine whether the system had reduced health risks.

In principle, new information can produce both economic and political pressures for change. It can influence habits of individual or institutional customers, employment choices of workers, stock purchases by investors, and managers' calculations about improving efficiency, introducing new products, or otherwise gaining competitive advantage. Individuals or groups can use it to influence actions by elected representatives, appointed boards and commissions, regulators, enforcement authorities in agencies, or courts, or to influence boycotts, demonstrations, or other direct actions by citizens themselves. For a summary of

Table 5-1. *How Disclosure Systems Influence Actions of Target Organizations*

Economic pathways	Political pathways
Purchasing decisions	Legislative actions
Suppliers' actions	Votes (including initiative/referendum)
Investments	Decisions by boards and commissions
Employment competition	Regulations
Management initiatives	Enforcement
	Court action
	Boycotts, demonstrations

economic and political pathways through which new information creates such pressures, see table 5-1.[6]

In practice, however, paths from new information to reduced risks have proven remarkably circuitous. Reducing rates of disease through nutritional labeling, for example, required that individual shoppers be motivated to use new information, accurately understand it, compare products, reach decisions, and follow through with purchases. Company managers would have to track changing buying habits, understand them as reflecting preferences for reduced risks, decide to take action, have the wherewithal to do so, follow through, and come out with the impact they intended. Some shoppers reported that they stopped buying a product due to information they gained from nutritional labels. Similarly, some companies increased their marketing of relatively healthy products. But no one can be certain of how the two were linked and no one knows how much—if at all—these changes improved people's health.

These profiles also suggest that information that affects reputation may have particular power. Reputations can influence both politics and markets. Members of Congress or state legislatures, regulators, community groups, and voters weigh an organization's reputation when considering privileges or penalties. Customers, investors, and workers consider reputation when deciding what to buy or where to work.[7] When reputation was threatened by newly disclosed information, executives sometimes took preemptive action. Large chemical companies committed to cutting toxic pollution months before their releases were made public. Leading food processors introduced new lines of healthy products before consumers responded to nutritional labels. Companies respond early because they understand that reputation, always hard to gain, is increasingly easy to lose.[8]

For organizations that have worked to build national or international recognition, reputation is both more important and more volatile than in the past. In simpler times people judged the corner market or hardware store by the character of the owner or the quality and consistency of its products. Today, businesses are created, merge, change names, break apart, and disappear at an astonishing rate. Customers, employees, and investors are better educated, more aware of social risks, and less loyal to established brands. With more choices and time pressure than in the past, customers, workers, and investors make quick judgments about unfamiliar companies. Activists organizing boycotts, zoning officials approving expansion of a business, or voters concerned about corporate tax rates respond to and influence the way well-known companies are perceived compared to their competitors. The Internet can spread news of isolated corporate good deeds and misdeeds to a worldwide audience instantaneously. The increasing volatility of reputation can amplify the power of public access to information.[9]

Finding it harder to distinguish their brands by product or service quality, organizations strive to create broader images. Increasingly, these images implicitly or explicitly include social responsibility. Annual reports often tout concern for the environment, health, and safety. Many large corporations now issue separate environmental reports to publicize their policies and practices. "Community and environmental responsibility" is now one of eight factors *Fortune* magazine uses to rank the ten most admired firms in thirty-two industries, along with older measures such as management ability, product quality, long-term investment value, innovation, financial soundness, and ability to attract skilled workers.[10] This trend, too, increases the power of disclosure.

There is no doubt, for example, that government-mandated disclosure led several large corporations to undertake ambitious programs to reduce toxic releases. It also led the Chemical Manufacturers' Association to urge members to improve management of wastes. It led the Reagan administration to endorse the idea of new legislation to control toxic pollution, despite its general opposition to tightening environmental regulation.

Learning for the first time about toxic releases from nearby plants, community groups also made demands. Richard Mahoney, chief executive officer of the Monsanto Corporation when toxic releases were first made public, explained the local impact of disclosure on corporate executives by a simple proposition: every company operates at the sufferance of the community where it is located. Ultimately, that community, by actions large and small, influences the company's future. Actions can be as limited as a zoning approval for the expansion of a single plant or as broad as a boycott or call for new legislation. They can be as intangible as a change in the tenor of community relations or as concrete as a denial of water or sewer hook-ups, or public subsidies for new roads, or the imposition of new taxes.[11]

These profiles indicate the need to consider at least two aspects of firms' responses to disclosure systems over time. The first concerns anticipatory responses. In some circumstances, there may be a particularly strong incentive for firms to reduce risks after disclosure is a certainty but before it has produced an effect, as previously discussed. The second concerns changing responses over time. Some evidence suggests that incentives to reduce risks may diminish as disclosure becomes routine. Reductions in toxic releases were much slower in the last five years than they were in early years. Introduction of low-fat products was much slower in recent years than when nutritional labeling was new. The relative ease and low cost of reducing risks initially and responses of media, consumer groups, and competitors to surprising revelations may contribute to such changes.

Conflicts among Values and Interests

What is also clear is that technopopulism is not a goal in itself. The value of new public information needs to be weighed against other basic values. Each disclosure system is a compromise and the character of compromise matters. It determines whether the system is so misshapen that its potential effectiveness is crippled.

PROTECTING PROPRIETARY INFORMATION. Efforts to promote disclosure have often clashed with the importance of protecting trade secrets and other proprietary information. Both common law and statutory law in the United States have long recognized the importance of guarding trade secrets from public scrutiny. The rationale for such protection is that proprietary information is central to encouraging business innovation and healthy competition. General principles are well developed. Information is generally protected from disclosure as a trade secret when companies can document its importance to competition, show that they have made concerted efforts to protect it, and attest that no competitor has gained access to it.[12]

However, the precise scope, means, and burden of proof associated with protecting trade secrets have been among the most contentious issues in the construction of new disclosure systems. Industry insistence on strong procedures to protect trade secrets was the main obstacle to approval of disclosure of toxic releases. Ultimately, industry did not prevail in broadening trade secret protections but did prevail in invoking the importance of such secrets to narrow the scope of disclosure.

In fact, trade secrets represent a relatively small cluster of data at one end of a broad spectrum of information generated by organizations. At the other end of the spectrum is another small cluster of data that lies indisputably in the public domain. That includes basic financial information required by federal and state laws and health, safety, and environmental data required under traditional regulatory regimes. Disclosure systems focus on the vast amount of information that lies between these well-defined extremes. Organizations have long considered information in this middle ground proprietary. Proponents of disclosure argue that when it concerns risks to the public, more of it should move into the public domain.[13]

Conflicts over trade secrets and proprietary information have intensified as information technology has gained power. Industry groups have argued that business information needs more legal protection than in the past. Using computers and the Internet, they contend, competitors can more easily compile company information from a variety of public sources to produce composite clues about new products, manufacturing processes, and expansion plans, creating a kind of mosaic effect. Advocates of broader disclosure counter that public data concerning risks constitute a relatively unimportant source of intelligence for competitors; secrets are more likely to be leaked by company employees or consultants.[14]

GUARDING PERSONAL PRIVACY. Disclosure systems that reveal health and safety risks also have clashed with the importance of protecting personal privacy. Systems that aim to reveal hospital records concerning medical errors or workplace records of accidents often trigger debates about how and whether to protect victims' identities. Designers of such systems have arrived at pragmatic compromises. Systems to improve hospital safety have stripped records of patient identifying information as soon as investigations of mishaps are complete. Systems to improve aviation safety have stripped records of information about the person who reports unsafe situations. But the growing power of information technology to combine personal data from many sources is likely to intensify such conflicts in the future.

PROTECTING NATIONAL SECURITY. Disclosure of information about everyday risks raised concerns about national security long before the terrorist attacks of September 11, 2001. Information about risks that is made available to the public at large also becomes available to foreign governments, terrorists, or criminals. Law enforcement officials and some members of Congress have long argued that national security can be threatened by releasing facts about risks of chemical accidents, contamination of public water supplies, and vulnerabilities to nuclear power plants. In 1999 such concern led Congress to bar temporarily disclosure of chemical companies' worst-case scenarios in the event of accidents, as had been required by the 1990 Clean Air Act to help communities make contingency plans. Both the Federal Bureau of Investigation and the Central Intelligence Agency supported industry claims that such information (much of which was already available in public reports) could make it easier for terrorists to attack vulnerable targets.

The attacks on the World Trade Center towers in New York City and on the Pentagon in Washington, D.C., on September 11, 2001, heightened such concerns. The Environmental Protection Agency withdrew from its website information about accidents, risks, and emergency plans for factories that handle dangerous chemicals. Energy regulators removed reports on power plants, transmission lines, and transportation of radioactive materials. The Federal Aviation Administration stopped posting enforcement information about airline safety incidents and security breaches at airports. The U.S. Geological Survey took down reports on water resources and asked libraries to destroy all copies of a CD-ROM that described characteristics of reservoirs. Attorney General John D. Ashcroft issued a new policy that broadened the basis on which federal agencies could withhold any information from the public. Instead of showing "foreseeable harm," agencies needed to demonstrate only a "sound legal basis" for maintaining secrecy.[15] In a crisis atmosphere, the balance between the value of informing the public about health and safety risks and the value of guarding such information to protect national security tipped toward secrecy.

MINIMIZING GOVERNMENT-IMPOSED COSTS AND INTRUSIONS. Disclosure systems also add to the workload of public and private organizations. Manufacturers used that argument to convince Congress that annual disclosure of toxic releases should be based on estimates rather than additional monitoring. The Environmental Protection Agency, overworked and understaffed as a result of budget cuts during the 1980s, opposed the disclosure requirement altogether, in part because of the anticipated paperwork burden. When Congress debated nutritional labeling, representatives of the restaurant industry argued successfully against informing customers about amounts of fat, salt, and other nutrients in their meals, based on the costs of analyzing nutrients. Likewise, when Congress debated disclosure of medical errors, financially strapped hospitals pointed to the large costs in tracking errors, determining their causes, and taking corrective actions.

The costs associated with disclosure can be substantial. Information collected by one user is freely available to others. In those instances information has characteristics of what economists call a *public good*. The costs of disclosure vary widely, however, and may involve much more than number crunching. Consider the challenge of informing the public about food products that contain genetically modified organisms. Such a requirement would have required farmers and food processors to undertake expensive modifications in harvesting, transportation, and processing in order to keep crops of modified corn and wheat isolated.

At times, target organizations have also contended that public reporting conflicts with good management. Employees who would otherwise report safety problems might choose not to act if they thought their alert would be made public. Managers who would otherwise collect such information might be deterred if they thought it might lead to embarrassment or litigation. Designers of disclosure systems have acknowledged the legitimacy of this concern by constructing legal firewalls between confidential sharing of information about minor problems within organizations and public disclosure of incidents that cause serious harm. However, in some instances, most recently in efforts to inform the public about serious medical errors, arguments concerning the need to encourage voluntary and confidential reporting of safety problems have blocked public access altogether.

PRESERVING STATE AUTONOMY. Debate about disclosure systems has also featured clashes between the need for standardized reporting and traditional federalism concerns. Governors and legislatures resisted efforts by food processors to preempt state labeling laws. Many states already had requirements for nutritional labeling, some more stringent than proposed federal rules. Most states also joined hospitals and doctors in opposing nationally standardized reporting of medical errors. Some saw it as an opening wedge for federal intervention in an area of regulation traditionally controlled by states; others saw it as a limitation on state-set priorities.

PROTECTING COMMERCIAL SPEECH. Disclosure systems themselves can restrict free expression to some degree. Standardized formats may limit companies' efforts to explain the benefits of their products. Government-required definitions may restrict expansive advertising claims. Since such commercial speech is protected by the First Amendment to the Constitution, courts have established principles to circumscribe government restrictions. They are permissible only when the public interest is substantial, the action in question directly advances that interest, and the relationship between government means and ends is deemed reasonable.[16] When distributors of dietary supplements challenged the government's restrictions on the health claims they could make on labels when science was uncertain, the court sent the government back to look for labeling rules that would protect public health without interfering as much with companies' freedom of expression.[17]

WEIGHING INTERESTS. When disclosure systems have the potential to influence markets or collective action, organizations with much to lose or gain naturally seek to maximize their interests, just as they do with respect to other forms of proposed regulation. Such systems intentionally increase the costs of some activities and decrease the costs of others to further specific public purposes. If new information represents power to some interests, it nearly always represents a threat to others. It may improve the competitive position of some products while suggesting that others are less healthy or safe. It may make some cities or neighborhoods look like desirable places to live while suggesting that others have more contaminants in drinking water, toxic pollution, beach closings, or crime. It may benefit airlines that appear to have good track records on safety, processed foods that are low in fat or salt, or health care providers that make relatively few mistakes in prescribing medications at the same time as it impairs the market for other products or services. When finally approved, each disclosure system reflects the relative strength of conflicting interests that stand to gain or lose from new public access.

As these profiles illustrate, companies often work to weaken rather than defeat transparency. They have lobbied successfully to exclude facts that do not promote their interests, replace specific data with estimates, leave out clear statements about risk, define terms to gain competitive advantage, and introduce obstacles to accurate comparisons among companies or products. To avoid political controversy, Congress left out of the disclosure system for toxic chemicals much of the public health prob lem. Nutritional labeling left out nearly half of the public's food purchases, including fast food, restaurant meals, and prepared foods sold in grocery stores. It also placed little-tested dietary supplements and the meats that were substantial sources of saturated fat under particularly lenient disclosure rules. Just as congressional districts sometimes were drawn to strengthen the interests of individual politicians rather than reflect the functional boundaries of communities, public access to information has at times been gerrymandered in compromises that serve the interests of specific groups.

Once written into law, such compromises are hard to change. Like other forms of regulation, disclosure systems may fail to adapt to changing markets, science, or public agendas. Adaptive mechanisms have frequently been lacking, and vested interests have created political inertia. Disclosure of toxic chemicals from large factories has become viewed as less complete, as science has suggested that pollution from cars, trucks, buses, and small businesses represent important sources of toxic risks. Nutritional labeling limited to processed foods sold in grocery stores has become seen as less comprehensive, as Americans have spent a growing portion of their food dollar on carry-out, fast food, and meals eaten in restaurants, for which no labeling is required. Companies have resisted labeling revisions to reflect new science showing links between specific kinds of fat (trans fatty acids) and chronic disease. Once embedded in markets and political activities, disclosure systems become resistant to change.

Some Lessons from Experience

In the end, the design of new disclosure systems is a practical and political problem involving questions of what to reveal, to whom, and how. The advent of new information technologies has clearly changed what is possible. Not long ago complex information concerning risks was shared mainly with narrow and generally expert audiences, while only simple information was shared broadly. Personal computers and the Internet now make it possible to communicate vast amounts of data to broad audiences almost instantaneously. Interactivity provides the means to customize information for individual users and to display it in ways that are appropriate to different levels of literacy and knowledge.

As these profiles suggest, even disclosure systems designed as government reports and product labels have begun making the leap to the web. Community residents can search for information about local toxic releases by company, chemical, or health hazard by typing in their zip codes on government or privately designed websites. Doctors' and patients' questions about risks from side effects and interactions of prescription drugs, traditionally stated in the government-required fine print of package inserts, are increasingly answered online. In some health food stores and groceries information about benefits and risks of dietary supplements is provided in computer kiosks. Some cell phones and handheld computers include bar code readers that provide shoppers with detailed information about products through websites like BarPoint.com. In the next-generation World Wide Web envisioned by Tim Berners-Lee, its inventor, customers will be able to specify the characteristics of products and services they want and send software agents, or "shopbots," out to find them. The future possibilities are enormous.[18]

But new information technology—no matter how powerful—is not a solution in and of itself. No amount of technology can increase the scope or accuracy of data. Nor can it improve flawed metrics. Formidable design problems remain if disclosure is to become an effective means of reducing risks to the public. These profiles suggest some preliminary lessons about how the job can best be approached.

The design and evaluation of disclosure systems should follow a disciplined process. Legislators need to weigh the advantages and disadvantages of disclosure against those of alternative means of reducing risk. Such systems may be less costly and intrusive than convention regulation, but they inevitably involve trade-offs. The aberrant, the innovative, and the surprising can be lost when information is standardized. Trade secrets, personal privacy, and national security can be compromised when made public. Well-intentioned simplification can become rigid with age, establishing a tyranny of outdated benchmarks. Determining effectiveness is particularly difficult. The first step is to design systems to minimize practical problems. As a starting point, these cases suggest four general rules.

1. Match Disclosure to Risk

The potential effectiveness of disclosure requirements, like that of other forms of regulation, can be impaired by a scope that is too narrow. If systems are not matched to the dimensions of risks, they can increase overall hazards or channel too many resources to reducing relatively minor problems. To assure quick approval by Congress, the assortment of toxic chemicals initially targeted for national disclosure was limited to large manufacturers and derived by combining lists from Maryland and New Jersey. Everyone agreed that many toxic releases were not included. No one could tell whether manufacturers' substitutions of unlisted chemicals for those that were listed might increase real risks to the public instead of decreasing them. Likewise, nutritional labeling focused on products that amounted to only about half of food expenditures by consumers, and disclosure of medical mistakes focused on hospitals but not on doctors' offices and out-patient clinics.

This early experience reinforces two familiar lessons. First, distortions are a danger when regulations are directed at narrow fragments of perceived risks. Second, designers of these systems will increase chances of effectiveness by examining with care the context in which incentives will operate, searching in particular for possible unintended consequences.

2. Design for Accurate Metrics and Reporting

Flawed metrics distort incentives. As economist Tom Tietenberg has observed: "Inaccurate or partial information could be worse than no information at all to the extent that it promotes a false sense of security or it promotes unjustified fears. And firms have incentives to mislead the public either by overstating their environmental accomplishments or by selective omission."[19] The metric for toxic releases (total pounds for each chemical and facility) failed to account for variations in toxicity and exposure. But *any* measure of toxic risk today would be politically controversial and scientifically debatable. There are few, if any, perfect indicators of risk.

These profiles suggest the importance of two threshold questions. First, are chosen measures accurate enough initially to avoid serious distortion of incentives? Second, are they likely to improve? The development of accurate metrics is an evolutionary process. Even sophisticated systems improve over many years or decades. When Congress adopted the Securities Act in 1933, no single set of accounting standards was widely accepted. Until the 1970s and the creation of the Financial Accounting Standards Board (a private organization vested with standard-setting authority by the Securities and Exchange Commission), firms' executives chose among a variety of alternative standards that left ample room for self-serving reporting. Periodic scandals continue to furnish pressure for improvement. The bankruptcy of Enron in December 2001 provides a case in point. Disclosure requirements need monitoring and enforcement just as other regulatory systems do. The absence of resources to ensure accuracy and timeliness of data can make systems counterproductive.[20]

3. Recognize Disclosure as a Continuum

Most political debate has assumed that government-required access to information is an all-or-nothing proposition. But tiers of disclosure can be constructed to serve multiple purposes and reduce conflicts among values. Congress required that companies report "worst-case" accident scenarios to the public but limited some information to emergency response teams or local community groups in order to minimize risks of terrorism or other criminal acts. It required airlines to report serious safety incidents to the public but collect information about near misses and minor accidents confidentially, to encourage employee candor and voluntary action to prevent more serious accidents. For similar reasons, the Institute of Medicine recommended public reporting of deaths and serious injuries from medical errors but confidential reporting of minor mistakes. Sometimes tiers of disclosure open possibilities for reducing risks that would be foreclosed by a choice between disclosure to the general public and inaction.

4. Construct Dynamic Systems

Building in mechanisms for feedback and adaptation is important for two reasons. First, it is often in the interest of target companies to search for and find new loopholes. Regulators need to adjust rules frequently in order to protect the integrity of disclosure systems. Second, government rules need to adapt as public priorities, scientific knowledge, and markets change. Disclosure systems, like other forms of regulation, can lock in incentives for action that become counterproductive. Reports to the public about toxic releases have taken account only slowly of new knowledge about chemicals that accumulate in human tissue and about harmful effects of small quantities of lead and some other toxins. Labels on processed foods have not informed consumers about risks associated with added dietary supplements as new products entered the market or prepared them for the next step in biotechnology—foods that function as medicines. Seeking to avoid such pitfalls, the Institute of Medicine has made a recommendation that could be applied broadly: build in analysis and feedback, fund it generously, and use it to promote adaptation.[21]

This book could have been written three ways. It could have heralded new social disclosure systems as the most important innovation in domestic policy since financial disclosure transformed capitalism in the 1930s. It could have characterized new public access to information not only as a way to improve health and safety but also as a remedy for the costs, bureaucracy, and misfires of conventional regulation and as a cure for perennial distrust of government. It could have painted transparency as a means of exposing the corrupt and profit-driven motives of insensitive corporations, in order to enlighten citizens.

This book could also have been written as a chronicle of deception. It could have portrayed disclosure as a total sham. Its theme could have been the shameless efforts by self-interested politicians to provide the public with information that pretends to inform but really obfuscates. It could have featured the actions of so-called public interest groups beating up on evil corporations without real effect. It could have portrayed executives who have a stranglehold on legislators through campaign contributions pretending to be overwhelmed by disclosure demands while actually releasing information that is unintelligible, useless, misleading, and deceptive. It could have argued that no one pays attention to most of the information the government now places in the public domain. Most people have better things to do with their time. New demands for information would inevitably become meaningless paperwork requirements. It could have concluded that such pretended reforms amount to a kind of political theater, filled with posturing. Liberal groups combat corporations. Politicians represent the masses. Corporations reluctantly disgorge information that is useful. But none of this is true; the usual cast of characters is simply going through the motions.

There is some truth in each of these scenarios, but I have chosen instead to write about the more complicated reality. Democracy by disclosure has potential to reduce risks and improve democratic processes. It also has potential to deceive. A national learning process concerning its usefulness is under way. Systems adopted since the mid-1980s are approaching maturity. Optimistically, they may presage the gradual acceptance of a new way of approaching collective problems. During a time of retrenchment and regulatory stalemate, the American political system has turned up innovative remedies for difficult problems. Without broad debate or central direction, the government's enduring authority to require the dissemination of information has taken a legitimate place beside the government's authority to set standards and redistribute resources, as a way of reducing the risks of modern life. It is remarkable that Congress has wrested large quantities of previously proprietary information about risks from organizations and placed them in the public domain. In our system of government, new mainstream policies are rare.

However, a close look at three of the most important systems raises cause for concern. Conflicting values and interests have produced flawed metrics, fragmented requirements, and failure to adapt to scientific knowledge or changing markets. Disclosure systems have been systematically oversold. A disconnect has developed between broad claims by politicians that such systems reduce risks, promote informed choice, and further public participation in government and specific requirements that are limited in design, flawed in execution, and uncertain in effect.

The growing power of computers and the Internet represents both an opportunity and a threat. On the one hand, technology creates real possibilities for a transformation of social policy in the "Information Age." An expanding mosaic of reliable information about risk could influence both markets and politics. But it has also created more contentious polit ical issues and raised the possibility that the public's access to information may be reduced rather than expanded.

The importance of democracy by disclosure transcends national boundaries. The most important applications of these instruments of social change ultimately may take place in the international arena. In the United States, such systems supplement well-developed regulatory institutions that aim to reduce health and safety risks by means of rules and financial incentives. Internationally, however, developing countries have begun to see disclosure as a substitute for bureaucracy. International organizations have begun to see it as a substitute for sanctions.

That is all the more reason to draw lessons from early experience. For seventy years, disclosure systems have been employed to reduce financial risks to the public. Such systems have now been directed toward reducing health, safety, and environmental risks. Recognizing their power and limitations and addressing forthrightly conflicts among values and political interests are the next challenges.

The Architecture of Disclosure Systems

Providing public access to information is often thought to be a simple matter, especially compared to the complexities of traditional government regulation. But each requirement that employs disclosure as a means of reducing risks features a unique architecture, inevitably the product of political and administrative compromise. Architectural features are summarized below, together with illustrative examples and selected policy issues.

Purpose (*Why* disclosure?): Requirement includes stated regulatory objective.
Examples of purposes: To reduce risks of disease or accident.
Policy issue: Is purpose clear and specific, and is disclosure an appropriate regulatory tool to reduce the risk in question?

Targets (*Who* discloses?): Requirement aims to create incentives for specific categories of businesses or other organizations to change their practices.

Examples of targets: Businesses or other private organizations; public or quasi-public agencies; individuals.

Policy issue: Does disclosure system cover entities that are the main sources of risk?

Scope (*What* is disclosed?): Requirement specifies universe of substances or practices to be disclosed.

Examples of scope: Outcome measures (levels of toxic releases or medical mistakes); process measures ("organic" or "sustainable" practices); product characteristics (levels of fat and salt in processed foods, toxins in consumer products, or contaminants in drinking water).

Policy issue: Does the scope serve the purpose of disclosure?

Metrics (*How* is disclosure *framed*?): Requirement standardizes disclosure in content and reporting intervals for identified practices or products.

Examples of metrics: Quantitative measures; narrative descriptions; icons.

Policy issue: Does disclosure produce a reasonably complete indicator of risk that allows fair comparisons among sources and over time?

Vehicle (*How* is disclosure *communicated*?): Requirement specifies form of communication.

Examples of vehicle: Dissemination by government report; dissemination by target organization report or product label, using government ground rules.

Policy issue: Does vehicle of disclosure maximize accurate understanding?

Audience (Disclosure *to whom*?): Requirement defines intended audience.

Examples of audience: General public; emergency personnel; employees; community residents; oversight groups.

Policy issue: Is audience appropriate for risk reduction?

Enforcement (*How* is disclosure *enforced*?): Requirement includes provisions to ensure accurate, timely reporting.

Examples of enforcement: Penalties for nonreporting or inaccurate reporting; audits; citizen suits.

Policy issue: Do sanctions create adequate incentives for production of reliable information?

Notes

Chapter One

1. Joel Seligman, *The Transformation of Wall Street* (Northeastern University Press, 1995), pp. 1–38 (quotes, pp. 19, 20).

2. Brandeis noted that the Pure Food and Drug Act did not "guarantee quality or prices; but it helps the buyer to judge of quality by requiring disclosure of ingredients" (p. 103). Louis D. Brandeis, *Other People's Money*, 2d ed. (Frederick A. Stockes Company, 1932), pp. 92–108 (the reference to "social diseases," p. 92).

3. Ibid., p. 92.

4. Ibid., p. 98.

5. Ibid., pp. 104–05.

6. Ralph Gomory has explored the distinction between the known, the unknown, and the unknowable in a fascinating essay. Ralph E. Gomory, "The Known, the Unknown and the Unknowable," *Scientific American* (June 1995), p. 88.

7. Regulatory options have always been limited. The ways in which governments influence private sector decisions are circumscribed by constitutional limits and tend to reflect the tenor of particular times. The Constitution circumscribes regulatory actions by limiting federal powers and requiring due process and equal protection. As described by James Q. Wilson: "A liberal democracy erects, between the public and private sectors, barriers

that . . . require the government to respect certain matters as private and to impose legal controls on private action only for publicly agreed-on purposes and in accordance with due process of law." James Q. Wilson, *The Politics of Regulation* (Basic Books, 1980), p. vii.

8. Some of the ideas in this chapter are drawn from earlier work, including Mary Graham, *Information as Risk Regulation* (Institute for Government Innovation, John F. Kennedy School of Government, Harvard University, 2001); Mary Graham, "Toxic Releases: A Right to Know," *Environment* (October 2001), p. 8; and Mary Graham, "Regulation by Shaming," *Atlantic Monthly* (April 2000), p. 36.

9. For a provocative discussion on this dichotomy between the richness of information and its reach, see Philip B. Evans and Thomas S. Wurster, "Strategy and the New Economics of Information," *Harvard Business Review* (September–October 1997), p. 74.

10. Joseph E. Stiglitz, "On Liberty, the Right to Know, and Public Discourse: The Role of Transparency in Public Life," Oxford Amnesty Lecture, Oxford University, January 27, 1999 (www.worldbank.org/html/extdr/extme/jssp012799.htm).

11. In analyzing information gaps in markets, economist Joseph E. Stiglitz distinguishes information about characteristics of people, products, or assets from information about behavior. Joseph E. Stiglitz, "The Contributions of the Economics of Information to Twentieth Century Economics," *Quarterly Journal of Economics* (November 2000), p. 1441.

12. 66 Fed. Reg. 65536 (proposed December 11, 2001).

13. Details of the rollover resistance rating system can be found at www.nhtsa.dot.gov/hot/rollover.

14. Information on the specific absorption rates (SAR) for given cell phone models is available at www.fcc.gov/oet/#SAR. See, generally, U.S. General Accounting Office, *Telecommunications: Research and Regulatory Efforts on Mobile Phone Health Issues* (2001).

15. Residential Lead-Based Paint Hazard Reduction Act, 42 U.S.C. 4852(d).

16. Safe Drinking Water Act Amendments of 1996, 42 U.S.C. 201.

17. These are known as Hazard Communication Standards, 29 C.F.R. 1910.1200. For detailed accounts of efforts to combat "sweatshop" conditions, see David Weil, "Regulating Noncompliance in Labor Standards: New Tools for an Old Problem," *Challenge* (January/February 2002), pp. 47–74; and John D. Donahue, ed., *Making Washington Work* (Brookings/CEG, 1999), pp. 47–58.

18. Mary Beth Arnett, "Risky Business: OSHA's Hazard Communication Standard, EPA's Toxics Release Inventory, and Environmental Safety," *Environmental Law Reporter*, vol. 22 (July 1992), p. 10440. See, for example, Mass. Ann. Laws Ch. 21I § 10 (2001).

19. California Safe Drinking Water and Toxic Enforcement Act of 1986, Health & Safety Code, sections 25249 et seq.

20. 49 C.F.R. 830.5.

21. 14 C.F.R. 91.25.

22. Occupational Safety and Health Act (OSHA) of 1970, 29 U.S.C. 657, 673; and 29 C.F.R. 1904.39–1904.42.

23. 21 C.F.R. 201.57.

24. See Reporting On-Time Performance, 14 C.F.R. 234.4, and Baggage-Handling Statistics, 14 C.F.R. 234.6.

25. H.R. 1731 (107th Congress, 2001).

26. Home Mortgage Disclosure Act, 12 U.S.C. § 2801–10.

27. Requirements for disclosure by nonprofit organizations are set forth in 2 U.S.C. 441(b).

28. Stiglitz has suggested that in the field of economics, "perhaps the most important break with the past . . . lies in the economics of information. The recognition that information is imperfect, that obtaining information can be costly, that there are important asymmetries of information, and that the extent of information asymmetries is affected by actions of firms and individuals, has . . . provided explanations of economic and social phenomena that otherwise would be hard to understand." Stiglitz, "The Contributions of the Economics of Information to Twentieth Century Economics," p. 1441.

29. George A. Akerlof, "The Market for Lemons, Quality Uncertainty and the Market Mechanism," *Quarterly Journal of Economics* (August 1970), p. 488. In situations when information gathered by one user would be freely available to all, it has characteristics of what economists call a public good. No one has a strong incentive to collect and process it because no one can profit from it.

30. James D. Cox, Robert W. Hillman, and Donald C. Langevoort, *Securities Regulation Cases and Materials*, 2d ed. (Aspen Law & Business, 1997), pp. 3–4; Seligman, *The Transformation of Wall Street*, pp. 1–29, 49.

31. The statement was Adolf Berle's, a Roosevelt adviser with respected expertise in corporate finance. Seligman, *The Transformation of Wall Street*, p. 39.

32. Ibid., pp. 66–72 (quote, p. 66).

33. Upton Sinclair, *The Jungle* (Bantam Books, 1981), pp. 134–35; Richard Hofstadter, *The Age of Reform* (Vintage Books, 1955), pp. 173–98.

34. 49 U.S.C.S. 20133, and 49 C.F.R. 229.

35. 42 U.S.C. 4321–47.

36. The FDA took the position that the Food, Drug and Cosmetic Act of 1938 provided the authority for such action. 42 U.S.C. 6294.

37. Ibid.

38. The American Law Institute's Restatement of Torts provides that "[o]ne engaged in the business of selling products who sells a defective product is subject to liability for harm to persons or property caused by the product defect. A product is defective if, at the time of sale, . . . it is defective in design or is defective due to inadequate instructions or warnings. A product is defective because

of inadequate instructions or warnings *when the foreseeable risks of harm posed by the product could have been reduced by the provision of reasonable instructions or warnings* . . . and omissions . . . render the product not reasonably safe." (Emphasis added.) Restatement (third) of Torts 2 (c) (1998).

39. For example, alcoholic beverages must be labeled "Government warning: (1) According to the Surgeon General, women should not drink alcoholic beverages during pregnancy because of the risk of birth defects. (2) Consumption of alcoholic beverages impairs your ability to drive a car or operate machinery, and may cause health problems." 27 U.S.C. 215. Pursuant to 15 U.S.C. 1331 (a)(1). Cigarette packages must include labels such as "Smoking Causes Lung Cancer, Heart Disease, Emphysema, and May Complicate Pregnancy," "Quitting Smoking Now Greatly Reduces Serious Risks to Your Health," or "Smoking by Pregnant Women May Result in Fetal Injury, Premature Birth, and Low Birth Weight."

40. The Freedom of Information Act is codified at 5 U.S.C. 552.

41. For thoughtful discussions of innovation in government, see Alan A. Altshuler and Robert D. Behn, eds., *Innovation in American Government* (Brookings, 1997), pp. 38–67; and James Q. Wilson, *Political Organizations* (Princeton University Press, 1995), pp. 3–16.

Chapter Two

1. Richard J. Mahoney, "Monsanto Announces Program to Reduce Air Toxics by 90 Percent," *General Bulletin at Monsanto Company*, June 30, 1988, p. 2.

2. Emergency Planning and Community Right-to-Know Act of 1986, 42 U.S.C. 11023(j).

3. Personal communication with Richard J. Mahoney.

4. "Air Pollution: It's All Legal," *Newsweek,* July 24, 1989, p. 28.

5. Personal communication with Richard J. Mahoney.

6. Richard J. Mahoney, *The Anatomy of a Public Policy Crisis,* CEO Series Issue No. 4, Center for the Study of American Business (Washington University, May 1996), p. 1.

7. Tim Smart, "Pollution: Trying to Put the Best Face on Bad News," *Business Week,* July 17, 1988; "Air Pollution: It's All Legal"; Susan Rosegrant, *The Toxics Release Inventory: Sharing Government Information with the Public* (Kennedy School of Government Case Program, Harvard University, 1992), p. 12.

8. Personal communication with Richard J. Mahoney.

9. Ibid.

10. David Sarokin, "Environmentalism and the Right-to-Know: Expanding the Practice of Democracy," *Ecological Economics* (1991), p. 176.

11. U.S. Environmental Protection Agency (EPA), *1999 Toxics Release Inventory* (2001), E-7.

12. There was sad irony in this human toll. Construction of the Union Carbide plant had been promoted by India's government to increase yields of basic crops and create jobs in one of the country's poorest states. The plant manufactured a less toxic substitute for DDT called Sevin, a carbaryl pesticide endorsed by the Indian Council of Agricultural Research because of its ability to reduce by half insect damage to critical crops like cotton and lentils. By 1984, though, the plant was losing nearly $4 million a year. Drought had robbed farmers of resources to buy costly pesticides and advancing science had produced less toxic alternatives. Unless otherwise specified, this account of the accident at Bhopal is based on factual information included in National Research Council (NRC), *Tracking Toxic Substances at Industrial Facilities* (National Academy Press, 1990), p. 9; B. Bowonder, Jeanne X. Kasperson, and Roger E. Kasperson, "Avoiding Future Bhopals," *Environment* (September 1985), pp. 6–8; Stuart Diamond, "The Bhopal Disaster: How It Happened," *New York Times,* January 28, 1985, p. A1.

13. Leaders of Madhya Pradesh, India's largest state, of which Bhopal is the capital, approved the plant in 1975 and allowed it to be built on public land, exacting a rent of less than $40 an acre. The plant grew to occupy eighty acres. Union Carbide owned 50.9 percent of the operation; Union Carbide of India Limited owned the rest.

14. *Congressional Record,* December 19, 1985, p. S18389; NRC, *Tracking Toxic Substances,* p. 9; Stuart Diamond, "Problems at Chemical Plants Raise Broad Safety Concerns," *New York Times,* November 25, 1985, p. A1.

15. *A Legislative History of the Superfund Amendments and Reauthorization Act of 1986,* P.L. 99-499 (Congressional Research Service, 1990), p. 409.

16. Several thoughtful analyses of disclosure of toxic releases have been published recently. Among them are Bradley C. Karkkainen, "Information as Environmental Regulation," *Georgetown Law Journal* (January 2001), p. 259; Archon Fung, Bradley Karkkainen, and Charles Sabel, *Beyond Backyard Environmentalism* (Beacon Press, 2000); William F. Pedersen, "Regulation and Information Disclosure," *Harvard Environmental Law Review* (April 2000); Mark A. Cohen, "Information as a Policy Instrument in Protecting the Environment: What Have We Learned?" *Environmental Law Reporter* (April 2001), p. 10425; David W. Case, "The Law and Economics of Environmental Information as Regulation," *Environmental Law Reporter* (July 2001), p. 10773.

17. Maureen Smith and Robert Gottleib, "The Chemical Industry: Structure and Function," in Robert Gottleib, ed., *Reducing Toxics* (Island Press, 1995), pp. 209–32; Michael Shapiro, "Toxic Substances Policy," in Paul R. Portney, ed., *Public Policies for Environmental Protection* (Resources for the Future, 1993), pp. 195–206.

18. Smith and Gottlieb, "The Chemical Industry," pp. 218–19, 221.

19. Scientists disagreed about whether the death rate from "avoidable" cancers was increasing but agreed that exposure to toxic chemicals was a relatively small cause of such cancers, compared to diet and smoking. Shapiro, "Toxic Substances Policy," pp. 196–97.

20. Toxic Substances Control Act, 15 U.S.C. 2601 et seq.

21. Shapiro, "Toxic Substances Policy," pp. 206–37, citing National Research Council, *Toxicity Testing: Strategies to Determine Needs and Priorities* (National Academy Press, 1984).

22. Susan G. Hadden, *A Citizen's Right to Know* (Westview Press, 1989), pp. 19–28, 213–14; Mary Beth Arnett, "Risky Business: OSHA's Hazard Communication Standard, EPA's Toxics Release Inventory, and Environmental Safety," *Environmental Law Reporter* (July 1992), pp. 10467–68; Caron Chess, "Looking behind the Factory Gates; Right-to-Know Laws on Hazardous Substances," *Technology Review* (August 1986), p. 42.

23. The Freedom of Information Act is codified at 5 U.S.C. 552.

24. *A Legislative History of the Superfund Amendments*, pp. 1084–85; personal communication with David Sarokin.

25. New Jersey's industrial survey required manufacturing facilities and other industries, including transportation, electricity, gas, and sanitary services, to fill out a simple form listing any amount of toxic chemicals used or emitted as waste into water or air or on land. It was one of the first cross-media projects. A list of 155 chemicals was chosen for evidence of chronic health effects and production in commercial quantities in the United States or presence on the EPA's priority list. Results were available to the public. Regulations establishing the survey allowed firms to request confidentiality for trade secrets, proprietary information, or data related to national security, with the final decision resting with the state environmental agency. The state provided technical assistance to companies and conducted audits to verify information. Of 15,000 companies surveyed, 6,595 responded, and 1,312 of those reported using listed chemicals. Only 6 percent of those facilities—nearly all chemical manufacturers—requested confidentiality for business information, with 25 percent of such claims ruled invalid by the department. New Jersey Department of Environmental Protection, *The New Jersey Industrial Survey Project, 1979–1982*, Final Report (August 1986).

26. Two grants, totaling $140,000, from the EPA provided resources for the development of the New Jersey industrial survey, some of which was carried out under contract by Rutgers University, and for analysis of the data. Ibid, p. 76.

27. Personal communication with David Sarokin.

28. Personal communication with Ronald Outen.

29. *A Legislative History of the Superfund Amendments*, pp. 606, 1083 (quotes, p. 1083).

30. Personal communication with Ronald Outen.

31. Personal communication with David Sarokin.

32. Personal communication with Linda Fisher. The Senate committee emphasized that "[m]odification of the existing [government] system to accommodate information obtained under this section can be accomplished within three months at a cost of approximately $50,000, according to the EPA." *A Legislative History of the Superfund Amendments*, p. 607.

33. *A Legislative History of the Superfund Amendments*, p. 1084.

34. Manufacturers were defined as any business included in Standard Industrial Classification (S.I.C.) codes 20 through 39. *A Legislative History of the Superfund Amendments*, p. 1083.

35. U.S. Environmental Protection Agency (EPA), *Toxics in the Community: The 1989 Toxics Release Inventory National Report* (1991), p. 19.

36. 53 Fed. Reg. 4523 (February 18, 1988).

37. U.S. Environmental Protection Agency, *Taking Toxics Out of the Air* (1998), p. 3.

38. An amendment by Rep. Robert Edgar (D-Pa.) and Rep. Gerry Sikorski (D-Minn.) to include chemicals that posed serious chronic health risks passed by only one vote. The Edgar-Sikorski Amendment added chemicals that were dangerous due to chronic exposure to the provision to list chemicals with health effects from acute exposure, because people have a "right to know they are being exposed to chemicals that could potentially kill them, regardless of whether they die instantly or over a decade," as Rep. Edgar put it. The amendment passed 183-166 late on December 5, 1985, was reconsidered, and passed 212-211 a few days later. *A Legislative History of the Superfund Amendments*, pp. 1093–95, 4195–206.

39. EPA, *Toxics in the Community: 1989 Toxics Release Inventory*, p. 18.

40. Environmental leaders in the George H. W. Bush administration championed the emerging idea of pollution prevention. In January 1988, months before companies reported on releases of toxic chemicals for the first time, Lee Thomas, administrator of the EPA, declared pollution prevention a government priority. In November 1989, shortly after the first Toxics Release Inventory (TRI) report was released, his successor, William K. Reilly, emphasized that "there is growing recognition that traditional approaches, which stress treatments and disposal after pollution has been generated, have not adequately dealt with existing environmental problems." Allan R. Gold, "Dealing with Pollution Before, Not After, It Happens," *New York Times*, November 20, 1989, p. A19. In 1990 Congress passed the Pollution Prevention Act, aimed at redirecting all federal environmental efforts toward reducing pollution at the source. 43 U.S.C. § 13101.

41. A release was defined as "any spilling, leading, pumping, pouring, emitting, emptying, discharging, injecting, escaping, leaching, dumping, or disposing

into the environment (including the abandonment or discarding of barrels, containers, and other closed receptacles)." Emergency Planning and Community Right-to-Know Act of 1986, 42 U.S.C. 11049(8).

42. For example, New Jersey required reporting of toxic chemical use and included a procedure for making claims of confidentiality. But less than 1 percent of data submitted had been claimed to be confidential. NRC, *Tracking Toxic Substances*, p. 67.

43. Emergency Planning and Community Right-to-Know Act of 1986, 42 U.S.C. 11023(l).

44. NRC, *Tracking Toxic Substances*, pp. 67–69. This episode represented a fragment of a larger debate. Throughout the 1990s manufacturers also argued that chemical use was unrelated to risk and was therefore not a public concern. Proponents of pollution prevention countered that use often created risks when products containing toxic chemicals were disposed of, and manufacturers should take responsibility for those risks.

45. Emergency Planning and Community Right-to-Know Act of 1986, 42 U.S.C. 11023(a).

46. Ibid., 42 U.S.C. 11023(g)(2).

47. NRC, *Tracking Toxic Substances*, p. 31.

48. National Research Council, *Understanding Risk* (National Academy Press, 1996), pp. 14–16.

49. Emergency Planning and Community Right-to-Know Act of 1986, 42 U.S.C. 11023(f).

50. Ibid., 42 U.S.C. 11023(b).

51. Ibid., 42 U.S.C. 11023(j).

52. Ibid., 42 U.S.C. 11023(j). The Senate committee bill had also emphasized public accessibility, requiring that an 800 number be staffed 24 hours a day and that the number be "computer accessible" to expand "the population that can gain meaningful access to information." *A Legislative History of the Superfund Amendments*, p. 602.

53. Emergency Planning and Community Right-to-Know Act of 1986, 42 U.S.C. 11042.

54. Ibid., 42 U.S.C. 11045–46.

55. Philip Shabecoff, "Industry to Give Vast New Data on Toxic Perils," *New York Times*, February 14, 1988, p. A1.

56. Rosegrant, *The Toxics Release Inventory*, p. 7.

57. U.S. Environmental Protection Agency, "Toxic Chemical Release Reporting: Proposed Rule," 52 Fed. Reg. 21165–66 (June 4, 1987). It should be noted that reports based on actual monitoring would have been far more costly. The EPA later estimated that companies spent an average of fifty person hours per report.

58. 605.3 Fed. Reg. 4500 (February 16, 1988). The rule set out the reporting form to be used by companies and provided detailed guidance about who had to report and what events had to be reported. It interpreted terms used by Congress, such as *release, environment,* and *process,* and provided guidance for reporting chemical mixtures, determining reporting thresholds, claiming trade secrets, and estimating releases where monitoring data were not available.

59. Instead, government officials prepared to respond to anticipated requests from industry or environmental groups to add or delete chemicals. As it turned out, such requests were slow in coming. Six months after the law was enacted, only five such petitions had been filed with the agency. Mark A. Greenwood and Amit K. Sachdev, *A Regulatory History of the Emergency Planning and Community Right to Know Act of 1986: Toxic Release Inventory,* prepared for the Chemical Manufacturers Association (Ropes & Gray, 1999), p. 4.

60. Smart, "Pollution: Trying to Put the Best Face on Bad News," p. 76.

61. Personal communication with Susan Hazen. Agency leaders may have had other motivations as well. Charles Elkins, the program's first director, believed it was critical to the legitimacy of the disclosure system for the EPA to avoid getting "between the data and the public." There may also have been an agency interest in not blunting the shock effect of the numbers. "I told the chemical industry, 'I'm not going to solve your problems. Don't count on me to protect you from the public reactions,'" Elkins recalled later. Rosegrant, *The Toxics Release Inventory,* p. 9.

62. U.S. General Accounting Office (GAO), *Toxic Chemicals: EPA's Toxic Release Inventory Is Useful but Can Be Improved* (June 1991), pp. 49–52. The agency worked to improve accuracy by means other than enforcement, however. It sent data back to companies for verification, worked to improve the accuracy of its own data entry, and developed electronic means to check for inconsistencies in industry data. Greenwood and Sachdev, *A Regulatory History,* p. 6.

63. Rosegrant, *The Toxics Release Inventory,* p. 10.

64. GAO, *Toxic Chemicals,* p. 11.

65. Personal communication with David Sarokin. Officials considered whether to develop and maintain a database in-house; contract with a private firm or non-profit organization, such as a university; or negotiate an agreement with another governmental entity. The EPA sought participation of industry representatives and citizen groups in that discussion and hired consultants to consider how to make information accessible in a cost-effective way that would meet the needs of the most users. Citizen groups had urged the EPA to develop and manage the database to minimize costs and maximize convenience to users and ease of integration with other EPA data.

66. Personal communication with Gary Bass, OMB Watch; Greenwood and Sachdev, *A Regulatory History,* pp. 7–8; Rosegrant, *The Toxics Release Inventory,* pp. 16–17.

67. Smart, "Pollution: Trying to Put the Best Face on Bad News," p. 76.

68. Norman L. Dean, Jerry Poje, and Randall J. Burke, *The Toxic 500: The 500 Largest Releases of Toxic Chemicals in the U.S., 1987* (National Wildlife Federation, August 1989); Philip Shabecoff, "U.S. Calls Poisoning of Air Far Worse Than Expected and Threat to Public," *New York Times,* March 23, 1989, p. B11.

69. GAO, *Toxic Chemicals,* pp. 74–76.

70. Rae Tyson and Julie Morris, "The Chemicals Next Door," *USA Today,* July 31, 1989, p. A1.

71. Dan Whipple, "Casper Industries Emitting Hundreds of Tons of Toxics: No One Knows How They Affect Residents' Health," *Sunday Star Tribune,* July 10, 1988, p. 1; Don Michak, "Experts See Risks in Air Emissions," *Journal Enquirer,* July 28, 1988, p. 5.

72. Mark A. Stein, "Group Cites High-Tech Firms' Pollution," *Los Angeles Times,* August 3, 1988, p. 1.

73. Smart, "Pollution: Trying to Put the Best Face on Bad News," p. 76.

74. Shabecoff, "U.S. Calls Poisoning of Air Far Worse Than Expected," p. B11; Tyson and Morris, "The Chemicals Next Door," p. A1.

75. Richard C. Paddock, "Beginning Today, Businesses Must Warn Customers on Dangerous Toxic Chemicals," *Los Angeles Times,* February 27, 1888, p. 31.

76. Cass Peterson, "W.R. Grace Pleads Guilty to Lying on Chemical Use," *Washington Post,* June 1, 1988, p. A3.

77. Robert C. Percival, Alan S. Miller, Christopher H. Schroeder, and James P. Leape, *Environmental Regulation,* 2d ed. (Aspen Law and Business, 1996), pp. 520–22.

78. Denise Kalette and Rae Tyson, "Special Report: Tracking Toxics," *USA Today,* July 31, 1989, p. A1.

79. Charles L. Elkins, "Toxic Chemicals, the Right Response," *New York Times,* November 13, 1988, sec. 3, p. 3.

80. Kalette and Tyson, "Special Report: Tracking Toxics," p. A1.

81. "Air Pollution: It's All Legal," p. 28.

82. EPA, *Toxics in the Community: 1989 Toxics Release Inventory,* p. 1.

83. EPA, *1999 Toxics Release Inventory,* pp. E-7–E-9.

84. GAO, *Toxic Chemicals,* p. 24.

85. EPA, *Toxics in the Community: 1989 Toxics Release Inventory,* pp. 310–13.

86. The law declared that "only as a last resort" should waste be disposed of or released into the environment. Pollution Prevention Act of 1990, 42 U.S.C. SS.13101-13109. Quoted language is from 13101(b).

87. Reilly, who had gained wide respect as head of the Conservation Foundation and the World Wildlife Fund, was appointed EPA administrator by President George H. W. Bush in 1989.

88. Rosegrant, *The Toxics Release Inventory,* p. 15; U.S. Environmental Pro-

tection Agency, *Oral History Interview—4: William K. Reilly* (September 1995); U.S. General Accounting Office (GAO), *Toxic Substances: EPA Needs More Reliable Source Reduction Data and Progress Measures* (1994), p. 2.

89. Executive Order 12,856 (August 3, 1993); the EPA had asked federal facilities to report voluntarily in 1988 but few complied. GAO, *Toxic Chemicals,* p. 28.

90. Executive Order 12,969 (August 8, 1995).

91. U.S. Environmental Protection Agency, *1997 Toxics Release Inventory* (1999), p. 1–3.

92. 64 Fed. Reg. 58666, October 29, 1999.

93. Inform, Inc., *Toxics Watch 1995* (1995), pp. 419–28.

94. Known as Proposition 65, this requirement was adopted by voters in 1986 by a margin of more than 2 to 1. California Safe Drinking Water and Toxic Enforcement Act of 1986, California Health & Safety Code, sections 2549.5–2549.13.

95. EPA, *Toxics in the Community: 1989 Toxics Release Inventory,* p. xvii. For a more detailed account of pollution disclosure requirements adopted by other countries, see Bradley C. Karkkainen, "Information as Environmental Regulation," *Georgetown Law Journal* (January 2001), pp. 347–50.

96. An exchange with reporters, April 22, 1997; *Weekly Compilation of Presidential Documents,* vol. 33, no. 17 (1997).

97. EPA, *1997 Toxics Release Inventory,* Appendix B-1.

98. Ibid., pp. 1–6.

99. Amoco Corp. and EPA, *Amoco-U.S. EPA Pollution Prevention Project, Yorktown, Virginia* (January 1992), pp. 2-4–2-5.

100. GAO, *Toxic Substances,* pp. 14–16.

101. The EPA used a random sample of more than 1,200 facilities. Seventy percent of respondents said changes in production levels were partly responsible for release declines; 24 percent said that changes in estimation accounted for some release declines; and 48 percent said that factors such as changes in reporting guidance or interpretation accounted for some declines. U.S. Environmental Protection Agency, National Advisory Council for Environmental Policy and Technology, *Transforming Environmental Permitting and Compliance Policies to Promote Pollution Prevention* (1993).

102. Thomas E. Natan Jr. and Catherine G. Miller, "Are Toxics Release Inventory Reductions Real?" *Environmental Science and Technology,* August 1, 1998, p. 368.

103. The GAO noted that it was not possible to tell whether reported reductions were due to changes in chemical use or to changes in production levels, whether substitutions were more or less harmful to human health or the environment, or how much of which chemicals were embedded in products. GAO, *Toxic Substances,* pp. 12–16 (quote, p. 16).

104. EPA, *Toxics in the Community: 1989 Toxics Release Inventory*, p. xvi.

105. EPA, *1997 Toxics Release Inventory*, pp. 1–6.

106. U.S. General Accounting Office (GAO), *Environmental Information: Agencywide Policies and Procedures Are Needed for EPA's Information Dissemination* (1998), p. 3.

107. Charles L. Elkins, "Risk Communication: Getting Ready for 'Right to Know,'" *EPA Journal* (November 1987), pp. 23, 25.

108. The term *release*, invented by Congress, also did not tell people much that was useful. It included a multitude of events, each of which had different implications for human health and the environment. Events included release of chemicals directly into air or water, disposal in landfills, injection into underground wells, or storage. They included emissions from smokestacks and drainpipes, as well as fugitive air emissions and run-off into lakes and streams. They included not only routine discharges but also accidental spills or leaks, and they included events that occurred at the plant site or "off-site releases" (meaning toxic waste that is shipped elsewhere for disposal).

109. National Academy of Public Administration, *Setting Priorities, Getting Results: A New Direction for EPA* (1995), p. 102.

110. GAO, *Environmental Information: Agencywide Policies and Procedures Are Needed*, p. 4.

111. There is a fundamental problem, which researchers have not yet overcome, in using disclosed data, with all its known limitations, as a metric by which to judge companies' reduction of toxic releases. I am grateful to Cary Coglianese for this insight.

112. Shameek Konar and Mark A. Cohen, "Why Do Firms Pollute (and Reduce) Toxic Emissions?" Working paper, Vanderbilt University, March 1997.

113. Seema Arora and Timothy N. Cason, "An Experiment in Voluntary Environmental Regulation: Participation in EPA's 33/50 Program," *Journal of Environmental Economics and Management* (May 1995), pp. 271–86.

114. James T. Hamilton, "Exercising Property Rights to Pollute: Do Cancer Risks and Politics Affect Plant Emission Reductions?" *Journal of Risk and Uncertainty* (August 1999), pp. 105–24.

115. Marianne Lavelle, "Environmental Vise: Law, Compliance," *National Law Journal*, August 30, 1993, pp. S1–9.

116. James T. Hamilton, "Pollution as News: Media and Stock Market Reactions to the Toxics Release Inventory Data," *Journal of Environmental Economics and Management* (January 1995), pp. 98–113.

117. Shameek Konar and Mark A. Cohen, "Information as Regulation: The Effect of Community Right to Know Laws on Toxic Emissions," *Journal of Environmental Economics and Management* (January 1997), p. 109.

118. Some of the material in this section was previously published in Mary Graham and Catherine Miller, "Disclosure of Toxic Releases in the United States,"

Environment (October 2001), p. 8. Trends documented with disclosed data are qualified by accuracy and scope limitations discussed elsewhere in this chapter.

119. Data cited in this section are drawn from EPA, *1999 Toxics Release Inventory.*

120. Natan and Miller, "Are Toxics Release Inventory Reductions Real?" figure 2 and p. 372.

121. J. Clarence Davies and Jan Mazurek, *Pollution Control in the United States* (Resources for the Future, 1998), p. 274.

122. The Cumulative Exposure Project recognized that people tend to be exposed to toxic chemicals in many ways, from different pollutants, and from a variety of sources. It aimed to identify the most serious exposures and the most affected communities in order to develop better policy. Technically, the project would combine measured and modeled concentrations in air, food, and drinking water with human activity and consumption patterns. Using data on air toxics from the TRI, the project would estimate outdoor concentrations of 148 hazardous air pollutants regulated under the Clean Air Act and use computer models to track their dispersion in the atmosphere. Officials in the Office of Policy Planning and Evaluation, which launched the project, believed that it would make possible comparisons among concentration among regions, states, and census tracts. Applying benchmarks for carcinogens and noncarcinogens would allow estimates of where health risks occurred. GAO, *Environmental Information: Agencywide Policies and Procedures Are Needed,* pp. 9–10.

123. The Relative Risk-Based Environmental Indicators Project was the most ambitious of the EPA's projects in terms of assessing risk. Initiated by the Office of Pollution Prevention and Toxics, it attempted to rank risks from toxic chemicals. A computer model would assign numbers to risk elements (amount, toxicity, and exposure) and allow analysis by medium, chemical, geographic area, industry, and facility. Intended as a risk-screening tool and not as a means of assessing risks to individuals or communities, the project relied heavily on assumptions about individual sites for which information was unavailable. The agency expected that results would be used to track trends, rank releases for purposes of strategic planning, target enforcement and compliance, and increase community-based environmental protection. In 1998 the model was being tested in states and regions, initially limited to air toxics. Ibid., pp. 8–9.

124. The Sector Facility Indexing Project combined extensive information about the environmental performance of specific facilities with population statistics of surrounding communities. Initiated by the Office of Enforcement and Compliance Assurance in 1995, it provided information on 600 facilities in auto assembly, iron and steel production, petroleum refining, pulp manufacturing, and primary smelting and refining of several metals. Consolidating data from different sources, it disclosed location, production or capacity, population statistics, permits, inspections, compliance records, releases, and spills. The EPA planned to

evaluate the project and consider expanding it to add other sectors and more data. Ibid., pp. 7–8.

125. Mark Greenwood, *Governmental Accountability for Environmental Information Policy* (Ropes & Gray, 1999), pp. 1–11.

126. Mark A. Greenwood, Kelly B. Kramer, and Amit K. Sachdev, *Protection of Sensitive Business Information at the Environmental Protection Agency,* prepared for the Chemical Manufacturers Association (Ropes & Gray, 1998), pp. 91–103.

127. U.S. General Accounting Office (GAO), *Environmental Information: EPA Could Better Address Concerns about Disseminating Sensitive Business Information* (June 1999), pp. 11–12; Greenwood, Kramer, and Sachdev, *Protection of Sensitive Business Information,* p. 6; GAO, *Environmental Information: Agencywide Policies and Procedures Are Needed,* p. 3.

128. Kline & Co., *Economic Espionage: The Looting of America's Economic Security in the Information Age* (Chemical Manufacturers Association, 1997).

129. GAO, *Environmental Information: EPA Could Better Address Concerns,* pp. 4–6. The GAO also concluded, however, that the EPA could do a better job of protecting sensitive information by developing agencywide procedures and standards and recommended that the agency also establish a broad-based information "users' group" to provide regular feedback.

130. Under 1990 amendments to the Clean Air Act, about 30,000 factories were required to disclose to the public worst-case scenarios of risks that could occur in the event of chemical accidents.

131. U.S. Environmental Protection Agency, *Security Study: An Analysis of the Terrorist Risk Associated with the Public Availability of Offsite Consequence Analysis Data under EPA's Risk Management Program Regulations* (1997), p. 10.

132. Testimony of Paul Orum, coordinator of the Working Group for Community Right-to-Know, before the Subcommittee on Health and the Environment of the House Commerce Committee, February 10, 1999.

133. Chemical Safety Information, Site Security and Fuels Regulatory Relief Act, P.L.106-40; and www.rtknet.org.

134. Graham and Miller, "Disclosure of Toxic Releases in the United States," p. 8. The Scorecard website is www.scorecard.org.

135. The RTK Net can be accessed at www.rtknet.org.

136. The EPA provides user-friendly access to data about toxic releases and other environmental information through its envirofacts website, www.epa.gov/enviro.

137. The American Chemistry Council website can be accessed at www.Americanchemistry.com.

138. John H. Cushman Jr., "Gore Asks Chemical Industry to Test for Any Toxic Effects," *New York Times,* April 22, 1998, p. A24; GAO, *Environmental Information: EPA Could Better Address Concerns,* p. 7.

Chapter Three

1. The White House meeting is described in Marian Burros, "U.S., Ending Dispute, Decides What Food Labels Must Tell," *New York Times,* December 3, 1992, p. A1; Peter Barton Hutt, "A Brief History of FDA Regulation Relating to the Nutrient Content of Food," in Ralph Shapiro, ed., *Nutrition Labeling Handbook* (Marcel Dekker, Inc., 1995), pp. 17–19; and background interviews with some participants. A detailed account of the meeting is offered by then–FDA administrator David Kessler in *A Question of Intent* (Public Affairs, 2001), pp. 67–71. Other persons attending the meeting reportedly included Vice President Dan Quayle, the president's chief of staff, James A. Baker 3d, and Robert B. Zoellick, a member of Baker's staff.

2. Kessler, *A Question of Intent*, pp. 56–57.

3. Burros, "U.S., Ending Dispute," p. A1.

4. U.S. Department of Health and Human Services (DHHS), Public Health Service, *The Surgeon General's Report on Nutrition and Health* (GPO, 1988), p. 1.

5. Chronic diseases include heart diseases, cancer, diabetes, obesity, osteoporosis, dental caries, and chronic liver and kidney diseases.

6. The label read: "You'll find no cereal has more fiber than Kellogg's All-Bran. . . . The National Cancer Institute reports that research may suggest eating the right foods may reduce your risk of some kinds of cancer. Here are their recommendations: eat high fiber foods." Label template obtained from the Kellogg Corporation.

7. Congress defined drugs as "articles intended for use in the diagnosis, cure, mitigation treatment, or prevention of disease." 21 U.S.C.A. 321(g)(1)(B). The House Report for the 1990 labeling legislation observed that "very few, if any, disease claims were made prior to 1984. Until that time, the FDA took the position that the statement that a food could prevent a diseases was tantamount to a claim that the food was a drug." House Report No. 101-538 (June 13, 1990), p. 9.

8. "Disease-Specific Health Claims on Food Labels: An Unhealthy Idea," House Report No. 100-561 (August 4, 1988), p. 5.

9. The proposed rules were published in 52 Fed. Reg. 28843 (August 4, 1987). Beginning in the 1970s the FDA had allowed some health claims by failing to take action against them but continued to crack down on others. The agency did not try to stop companies from repeating on product labels the American Heart Association's advice to reduce dietary cholesterol and saturated fats to reduce risk of heart disease. But in 1976 the FDA stopped a campaign by the ITT Continental Baking Company and its Fresh Horizons bread that claimed that a high fiber diet was linked to decreased risk of colon cancer. "Disease-Specific Health Claims on Food Labels," pp. 3–7.

10. Zachary Schiller, Russell Mitchell, Wendy Zellner, Lois Therrien, Andrea Rothman, and Walecia Konrad, "The Great American Health Pitch," *Business Week,* October 9, 1989, p. 119.

11. For accounts of expansive health claims in the 1980s, see, for example, "FDA's Continuing Failure to Prevent Deceptive Health Claims for Food," House Report 101-980 (November 14, 1990), pp. 6–7; Schiller and others, "The Great American Health Pitch," p. 119; and Richard M. Cooper, "History of Health Claims Regulation," *Food Drug Cosmetic Law Journal* (November 1990), p. 66.

12. Kessler, *A Question of Intent,* p. 7.

13. Schiller and others, "The Great American Health Pitch," p. 119.

14. As would be true nearly a hundred years later, when nutritional labeling was proposed, the powerful food industry formed an unlikely alliance with reformers. Confronted with diverse and conflicting state requirements aimed at abuses, the industry supported national regulation of food labeling. Detailed accounts of early food labeling can be found in Alfred D. Chandler Jr., *The Visible Hand: The Managerial Revolution in American Business* (Belknap Press, 1977), pp. 233–34, 293–96; DHHS, *The Surgeon General's Report on Nutrition and Health,* pp. 24–46; Institute of Medicine (IOM), *Food Labeling: Toward National Uniformity* (National Academy Press, 1992), p. 42–46.

15. The Federal Food, Drug, and Cosmetic Act of 1938, 21 U.S.C. 321(n), 343. For accounts of these developments, see DHHS, *The Surgeon General's Report on Nutrition and Health,* pp. 29–46; Institute of Medicine (IOM), *Nutrition Labeling: Issues and Directions for the 1990s* (National Academy Press, 1990), pp. 55–57.

16. Despite scientists' growing knowledge of causes of infectious diseases, few vaccines and treatments were available. Antibiotics would not be widely available until the 1950s. These developments are chronicled in IOM, *Food Labeling,* pp. 44–46; DHHS, *The Surgeon General's Report on Nutrition and Health,* pp. 31–46; Hutt, "A Brief History of FDA Regulation," pp. 8–9; Pauline M. Ippolito, "How Government Policies Shape the Food and Nutrition Information Environment," *Food Policy* 24 (1999), pp. 295–306.

17. DHHS, *The Surgeon General's Report on Nutrition and Health,* pp. 1–6, 18, 696–99 (quote, p. 697).

18. National Research Council (NRC), *Diet and Health: Implications for Reducing Chronic Disease Risk* (National Academy Press, 1989), pp. 655–58.

19. IOM, *Nutrition Labeling,* pp. 87–88; Institute of Medicine (IOM), *Ensuring Safe Food* (National Academy Press, 1999), pp. 52–55; Schiller and others, "The Great American Health Pitch," p. 119; Lorna Aldrich, "Consumer Use of Information: Implications for Food Policy," *Agricultural Handbook,* no. 715 (Food and Rural Economics Division, Economic Research Service, U.S. Department of Agriculture, undated), pp. 2–9.

20. IOM, *Nutrition Labeling,* pp. 94–96; IOM, *Food Labeling,* pp. 50–51; Schiller and others, "The Great American Health Pitch," p. 119; Julie Kosterlitz, "The Food Lobby's Menu," *National Journal,* September 29, 1990, p. 2334.

21. IOM, *Nutrition Labeling,* pp. 1–2, 55–56 (quote, p. 2).

22. IOM, *Food Labeling,* pp. 52–53.

23. 21 C.F.R. 101.9(8)(i) (sodium) and 51 Fed. Reg. 42584 (November 25, 1986) (cholesterol proposal).

24. "FDA's Continuing Failure to Prevent Deceptive Health Claims for Food," pp. 6–8. IOM, *Nutrition Labeling,* pp. 148–49 (fast food settlement).

25. Bruce Silverglade, *The Fight for Food Labeling Reform—An Insider's Perspective* (Center for Science in the Public Interest, undated), pp. 1–2.

26. In two scathing reports, the House Government Operations Committee charged that the decision on health claims had been "usurped by political appointees in the Office of Management and Budget" and that political interference had encouraged food companies to flood the marketplace "with a barrage of false and misleading health claims." "Disease-Specific Health Claims on Food Labels: An Unhealthy Idea," pp. 30–32 (quote, p. 32); and "FDA's Continuing Failure to Prevent Deceptive Health Claims for Food," pp. 8–22 (second quote, p. 22).

27. *Congressional Record,* July 27, 1989, p. S8994.

28. On February 13, 1990, as Congress was debating the issue, the FDA proposed to introduce roughly the same labeling system administratively. 55 Fed. Reg. 5176 (February 13, 1990). The proposed rule allowed disease-specific health claims for links between calcium and osteoporosis, sodium and hypertension, fats and heart disease or cancer, and fiber and cancer or heart disease. "FDA's Continuing Failure to Prevent Deceptive Health Claims for Food," pp. 8–12.

29. Marian Burros, "Push Is on for Nutrition Labeling," *New York Times,* March 8, 1989, p. C1.

30. See, for example, "Nutrition Labeling and Education Act of 1989: Hearing on H.R. 3028 before the Subcommittee on Health and the Environment of the Committee on Energy and Commerce," 101st Cong. (1989), pp. 84–96 (statements of John Cady, president of the National Food Processors Association, and Sherwin Gardner, vice president for science and technology, Grocery Manufacturer's Association), 224–34 (statement of J.B. Cardaro, president of the Council for Responsible Nutrition), 246–47 (statement by the Food Marketing Institute).

31. Kosterlitz, "The Food Lobby's Menu," p. 2334.

32. W. John Moore, "Stopping the States," *National Journal,* July 21, 1990, p. 1758.

33. The law provided that such exceptions could be made if they did not cause violation of federal law or unduly burden interstate commerce, and served a purpose not met by the law itself. 21 U.S.C. 343-1(b). Provisions are summarized in IOM, *Food Labeling,* pp. 28–30; for the Bush administration's position, see 55 Fed. Reg. 5184 (February 13, 1990).

34. Commercial speech receives limited protection under the First Amendment of the Constitution. The test for government regulation of commercial speech was set forth in *Central Hudson Gas & Elec. Corp. v. Public Service Commission*

of New York, 447 U.S. 557, 566 (1980). See also *Board of Trustees of State University of New York* v. *Fox*, 492 U.S. 469, 477 (1989) (holding that government regulation of commercial speech need not be the "least restrictive means" as long as fit is reasonable); *Pearson* v. *Shalala*, 164 F.3d 650, 655–56 (1999) (applying the *Central Hudson* test to potentially misleading health claims about dietary supplements).

35. "FDA Proposals to Permit the Use of Disease-Specific Health Claims on Food Labels: Hearing before the House Subcommittee on Human Resources and Intergovernmental Relations of the House Committee on Gov't Operations," 101st Cong. (1987).

36. This was a standard proposed by the FDA in February 1990. Health claims are defined as statements on packaging that link the product to prevention of a specific health risk or disease. Statutory language is quoted from 21 U.S.C. 343(r)(1)(8).

37. Sources for this section include IOM, *Nutrition Labeling*, pp. 254–69; Center for Science in the Public Interest, *Food Labeling Chaos* (1989), pp. 10–13.

38. Alan S. Levy, Sara B. Fein, and Raymond E. Schucker, "Performance Characteristics of Seven Nutrition Label Formats," *Journal of Public Policy and Marketing* (Spring 1996), pp. 1–15. "Many people say they want and would use the largest amount of information offered, but tests often find that the preferred amount of information leads to poorer performance. The implicit theory that underlies stated preferences in these cases (i.e., more information must be more useful) is demonstrably wrong" (p. 9).

39. See, for example, "Nutrition Labeling and Education Act of 1989: Hearing," pp. 84–96, 246–47.

40. IOM, *Nutrition Labeling*, pp. 59–62 (describing alternative labeling approaches); Ippolito, "How Government Policies Shape the Food and Nutrition Information Environment," pp. 295–306; American Dietetic Association, "Nutrition Education for the Public," *Journal of the American Dietetic Association* (1996), pp. 1183–87; Richard A. Williams, "Consumer Response to Changes in Food Labeling: Discussion," *American Journal of Agricultural Economics* (December 1992), pp. 1213–14.

41. 21 U.S.C. 343(q)(5)(A).

42. IOM, *Nutrition Labeling*, pp. 90–91, 144–50.

43. IOM, *Nutrition Labeling*, pp. 144–49, 273–74, 285–87. See also "The Impact of the Nutrition Labeling and Education Act of 1990 on the Food Industry," *Administrative Law Review* (Fall 1995), p. 608; and 21 U.S.C. 343(q)(5)(D)-(E).

44. Instead of issuing formal rules, the Department of Agriculture gave companies guidance about its labeling policies through policy memoranda and a handbook. Labeling was a relatively minor part of the work of the department's Food Safety and Inspection Service. In 1990 less than two dozen employees reviewed

130,000 labeling requests each year. By contrast, the Food and Drug Administration, which regulated most other processed foods, issued labeling policies via formal rules that were rarely changed. IOM, *Nutrition Labeling*, pp. 52–54.

45. *Congressional Record*, October 24, 1990, p. S16607.

46. Ibid., p. S16611.

47. Signing statement, P.L. 101-535, *Weekly Compilation of Presidential Documents*, vol. 26 (1990), p. 1795.

48. House Report No. 101-538 (June 13, 1990), p. 8.

49. These provisions are set forth at 21 U.S.C. 343(q)(1).

50. House Report No. 101-538, pp. 17–19.

51. 21 U.S.C. 343(q)(1).

52. 21 C.F.R. 101.9 (1993).

53. 21 U.S.C. 343(b)(1)(A).

54. Cost estimates come from the Food and Drug Administration, *Regulatory Impact Analysis of the Proposed Rules to Amend the Food Labeling Regulations*, RIN 0905-AD08, 56 Fed. Reg. 60856 (November 27, 1991), pp. 3, 17–18. Estimates did not include the cost of reformulated products.

55. Brenda M. Derby and Alan S. Levy, "Do Food Labels Work?" in Paul N. Bloom and Gregory T. Gundlach, eds., *Handbook of Marketing and Society* (Sage Publications, 2001), pp. 391–92.

56. Christine Moorman, "Market-Level Effects of Information: Competitive Responses and Consumer Dynamics," *Journal of Marketing Research* (February 1998), pp. 82–98; "The Impact of the Nutrition Labeling and Education Act of 1990 on the Food Industry," pp. 605–22. Since the law did not take effect until 1994, its relationship to some of these trends is uncertain.

57. Constance J. Geiger, "Health Claims: History, Current Regulatory Status, and Consumer Research," *Journal of the American Dietetic Association* (November 1998), pp. 1312–22. See also Alan R. Kristal and others, "Trends in Food Label Use Associated with New Nutritional Labeling Regulations," *American Journal of Public Health* (August 1998), pp. 1212–15. From 1993 to 1996 the portion of women surveyed who usually used labels increased from 34 to 43 percent, and men, from 16 to 27 percent.

58. 21 U.S.C. 343(r)(3).

59. 21 C.F.R. 101.72–78.

60. "Position of the American Dietetic Association: Functional Foods," *Journal of the American Dietetic Association* (1999), pp. 1278–85; Chris Adams, "Splitting Hairs on Supplement Claims," *Wall Street Journal*, February 22, 2000, p. B1.

61. Ippolito, "How Government Policies Shape the Food and Nutrition Information Environment," pp. 295–306 (quote, p. 303); U.S. General Accounting Office (GAO), *Food Safety: Improvements Needed in Overseeing the Safety of Dietary Supplements and "Functional Foods"* GAO/RCED-00-156 (2000), pp.

23–25; Geiger, "Health Claims: History, Current Regulatory Status, and Consumer Research," pp. 1312–22.

62. GAO, *Food Safety: Improvements Needed,* pp. 21–22.

63. Food and Drug Modernization Act of 1997, 21 U.S.C. 343 r(3).

64. One-third of the product labels making health claims linked diets low in saturated fat or cholesterol to reduced risk of heart disease and most of those included endorsements by the American Heart Association or other organizations. Susan J. Brecher and others, "Status of Nutrition Labeling, Health Claims, and Nutrient Content Claims for Processed Foods: 1997 Food Label and Packaging Survey," *Journal of the American Dietetic Association* (September 2000), p. 1057.

65. *Durk Pearson and Sandy Shaw, American Preventive Medical Association and Citizens for Health* v. *Donna E. Shalala,* 164 F.3d 650 (January 15, 1999).

66. Dietary Supplement Health and Education Act of 1994, 21 U.S.C. 321 et seq.

67. Sources for this account include the Institute of Medicine, *Ensuring Food Safety* (National Academy Press, 1999); Senate Report on the Dietary Supplement Health and Education Act of 1994, 103-410 (October 8, 1994); Alan C. Miller, "The Potent Politics of Vitamins, *Los Angeles Times,* July 2, 1994, p. A1; and Hutt, "A Brief History of FDA Regulation," pp. 17–19.

68. Labels are quoted from "The New Foods: Functional or Dysfunctional?" *Consumer Reports on Health* (June 1999), p. 1; and Julian E. Barnes and Greg Winter, "Stressed Out? Bad Knee? Relief Promised in a Juice," *New York Times,* May 27, 2001, p. A1.

69. See, for example, Senate Report on the Dietary Supplement Health and Education Act of 1994; and "Herbal Supplements: What's in the Chips?" *Consumer Reports* (December 2000), p. 8. It is important to distinguish little-tested herbal products from well-understood vitamins and minerals, which scientists discovered had new benefits. Research suggested that calcium could help prevent osteoporosis, that folic acid (a B vitamin) could reduce risks of neurological birth defects, and that vitamin E could reduce risks of heart disease, for example.

70. GAO, *Food Safety: Improvements Needed,* pp. 16–18; "Herbal Supplements. What's in the Chips?" p. 8; "Does the Supplement You Buy Contain What Its Label Says?" *Tufts University Health and Nutrition Letter,* October 2000, p. S1; Amanda Spake, "Natural Hazards," *U.S. News and World Report,* February 12, 2001, p. 43; Robert Pear, "Tighter Rules Are Sought for Dietary Supplements," *New York Times,* April 17, 2001, p. A10.

71. GAO, *Food Safety: Improvements Needed,* pp. 14–15; Greg Winter, "F.D.A. Warns Food Companies about Herbal Additives," *New York Times,* June 7, 2001, p. C1.

72. GAO, *Food Safety: Improvements Needed,* pp. 6–9; "Position of the American Dietetic Association," pp. 1278–80.

73. For accounts of these developments, see William H. Langridge, "Edible Vaccines," *Scientific American,* September 2000, p. 66; Juan Enriquez and Ray A. Goldberg, "Transforming Life, Transforming Business: The Life-Science Revolution," *Harvard Business Review* (March–April 2000), p. 96 et seq.

74. These new products were often referred to, together with foods enriched with vitamins or minerals and foods to which herbs or other dietary supplements have been added, under the umbrella term *functional foods.* For a useful account of the separate categories of products, see "Position of the American Dietetic Association," pp. 1278–85. Marketing of early products proved problematic. Disappointing sales led Kellogg to remove its Ensemble line from grocery shelves after less than a year on the market.

75. GAO, *Food Safety: Improvements Needed,* pp. 13–15; "Position of the American Dietetic Association," pp. 1278–85. If substances were classified as additives, another regulatory category, they required a long and expensive safety review. Traditionally, the FDA had also approved a category of medical foods, sold without a prescription but labeled to say that they should be eaten only under a doctor's supervision.

76. Patricia Callahan and Scott Kilman, "Seeds of Doubt: Some Ingredients Are Genetically Modified Despite Labels' Claims," *Wall Street Journal,* April 5, 2001, p. A1.

77. For a more detailed discussion of these issues, see David Greenberg and Mary Graham, "Improving Communication about New Food Technologies," *Issues in Science and Technology* (Summer 2000), pp. 42–48; and National Research Council, *Genetically Modified Pest-Protected Plants: Science and Regulation* (National Academy Press, 2000).

78. "FDA to Strengthen Pre-Market Review of Bioengineered Foods," FDA press release, May 3, 2000. Products labeled "organic" already had to be produced without genetically modified organisms under the Federal Organic Foods Production Act of 1990, 7 U.S.C. 6501.

79. Marian Burros, "F.D.A. Throws Its Best Pitches for Food Label," *New York Times,* May 1, 1994, p. 1.

80. NRC, *Diet and Health,* p. 5; see also IOM, *Nutrition Labeling,* p. 64.

81. The pioneering work on understanding cognitive distortions is Daniel Kahneman, Paul Slovic, and Amos Tversky, *Judgment under Uncertainty: Heuristics and Biases* (Cambridge University Press, 1982). Applications to nutritional labeling are described in Joanne F. Guthrie, Brenda M. Derby, and Alan S. Levy, "What People Know and Do Not Know about Nutrition," U.S. Department of Agriculture, Economic Research Service, 1999, pp. 250–51; Aldrich, "Consumer Use of Information," pp. 8–9; and Edward Groth III, "Risk Communication in the Context of Consumer Perceptions of Risks," Consumers Union (www.consumersunion.org/food/riskcomny598.htm, accessed July 2001).

82. Walter Willett, chairman of the Department of Nutrition at Harvard's School of Public Health, told the *Wall Street Journal*: "It has become like a religious crusade. The claims that we are having a calcium emergency and we need to increase calcium intake simply are not based on sound data. There's equally strong and sometimes better data that show there could be harm in increasing calcium." Tara Parker-Pope, "Flood of New Products May Push Some to Get Too Much Calcium," *Wall Street Journal,* June 2001, p. B1.

83. "Dietary Fat Makes a Comeback," *Tufts University Health & Nutrition Letter,* July 2001, pp. 4–5.

84. Aldrich, "Consumer Use of Information," pp. 2–9.

85. U.S. Department of Agriculture, *Food Review,* January–April 2000, p. 31; IOM, *Ensuring Safe Food,* pp. 52–55. The Economic Research Service (ERS) of the Department of Agriculture provided a more detailed analysis in 1999 of trends in meals eaten away from home. Defining away-from-home foods to include carry-out meals eaten at home, the ERS estimated that away-from-home meals accounted for 27 percent of total meals in 1995, up from 16 percent in 1977–78, but nearly 40 percent of fat consumption. Biing-Hwan Lin, Joanne Guthrie, and Elizabeth Frazao, "Away-From-Home Foods Increasingly Important to Quality of American Diet," Information Bulletin No. 749, Economic Research Service, U.S. Department of Agriculture, January 1999.

86. Aldrich, "Consumer Use of Information," pp. 2–7 (quote, p. 7).

87. Derby and Levy, "Do Food Labels Work?" pp. 372–83 (quote, p. 384). See also Kristal and others, "Trends in Food Label Use," pp. 1212–15; and Lauren Haldeman and others, "Development of a Color-Coded Bilingual Food Label for Low-Literacy Latino Caretakers," *Journal of Nutritional Education* (May/June 2000), pp. 152–60 (on the challenges that labeling presents to immigrant groups).

88. Derby and Levy, "Do Food Labels Work?" pp. 380–81.

89. Estimates are derived from the Department of Agriculture's Continuing Survey of Food Intakes by Individuals (CSFII). Cecilia Wilkinson Enns and others, "Trends in Food and Nutrient Intakes by Adults: NFCS 1977–79, CSFII 1989–91, and CSFII 1994–95," *Family Economics and Nutrition Review,* vol. 10, no. 4 (1997), pp. 2–15; see also Aldrich, "Consumer Use of Information," pp. 16–17; Derby and Levy, "Do Food Labels Work?" pp. 387–90.

90. Jeffrey A. Tannenbaum, "Fat-Free Store Tries to Gain Weight as U.S. Gets Greasy," *Wall Street Journal,* February 13, 2001, p. B2. Results are from surveys by ACNielsen and NPD Group Inc.

91. Shoppers who said they sought out low-fat products declined from 81 to 77 percent; those who sought out low-cholesterol products declined from 70 to 60 percent; and those who sought out low-salt products declined from 61 to 53 percent. Derby and Levy, "Do Food Labels Work?" p. 390.

92. Geiger, "Health Claims: History, Current Regulatory Status, and Consumer Research," p. 1312 (quote, p. 1316).

93. "Nutrition Takes Center Stage on National Agenda," *The Nation's Health,* July 2000, p. 1; Ippolito, "How Government Policies Shape the Food and Nutrition Information Environment," pp. 295–306.

94. Greg Winter, "F.D.A. Survey Finds Faulty Listings of Possible Food Allergens," *New York Times,* April 3, 2001, p. C1; Greg Winter, "Tighter Standard on Food Labeling Is Set by Industry," *New York Times,* May 31, 2001, p. A1.

95. Amanda Spake, "Walter Willett: The Real Skinny on Dietary Fat," *U.S. News and World Report* (December 25, 2000–January 1, 2001), p. 60. The proposed rule for trans fat labeling can be found in Food Labeling: Trans Fatty Acids in Nutrition Labeling, Nutrient Content Claims, and Health Claims, 64 Fed. Reg. 62746 (proposed November 17, 1999).

96. GAO, *Food Safety: Improvements Needed,* pp. 12–26 (quote, p. 25).

97. Ibid., pp. 12–26 (quote, p. 26).

98. Thomas E. Weber, "The New Way to Shop: Why Marketers Covet Spots on Your Key Ring," *Wall Street Journal,* March 26, 2001, p. B1. The site was withdrawn when the start-up firm that produced it shut down in 2001; Stephen A. Brown, *The Explosion of the Bar Code* (Harvard University Press, 2000.)

99. The SlimFast website is www.SlimFast.com; Saul Hansell, "Marketers Find Internet Opens New Avenues to Customers," *New York Times,* March 26, 2001, p. C1.

100. Julian E. Barnes, "Study Finds Inaccurate Labels on Health Bars," *New York Times,* October 30, 2001, p. A12.

101. Comments of the American Dietetic Association on proposed FDA structure/function regulations for dietary supplements, FDA Docket No. 98N-0044 (August 14, 1998). See also the association's comments on the Report of the Commission on Dietary Supplement Labels (August 14, 1998). Both are summarized in "Position of the American Dietetic Association," pp. 1278–85.

102. Tufts University evaluates nutritional websites at www.navigator.tufts.edu.

103. Tom Weir, "Scanning the Future," *Supermarket Business,* October 15, 2000, pp. 34–36; Quentin Hardy, "Scanned Goods," *Forbes,* October 30, 2000, pp. 354–56.

104. Hansell, "Marketers Find Internet Opens New Avenues to Customers," p. C1.

105. Ibid.

106. The jurisdiction of federal agencies over claims made on the World Wide Web was already an issue. In February 2001 the FDA challenged a claim on Ocean Spray's corporate website that its juices may help the body fight cancer or lower cholesterol. A spokesman for the National Food Processors Association warned that "they have fired a shot across our bow." Greg Winter, "F.D.A. Action Could Change Food Marketing on the Web," *New York Times,* February 14, 2001, p. C11.

Chapter Four

1. Lawrence K. Altman, "Big Doses of Chemotherapy Drug Killed Patient, Hurt 2nd," *New York Times,* March 24, 1995, p. A18.

2. Sarah Glazer, "Medical Mistakes," *CQ Researcher* (February 25, 2000), pp. 139–60.

3. The Institute of Medicine defined errors as failures of planning or execution of a medical treatment. Errors were a subset of adverse events, defined as injuries attributable to medical management rather than to a patient's underlying condition. Errors are also referred to as preventable adverse events. Institute of Medicine (IOM), *To Err Is Human: Building a Safer Health System* (National Academy Press, 1999), pp. 23–30.

4. Ibid., pp. 22–42. Richardson is quoted in Robert Pear, "Group Asking U.S. for New Vigilance in Patient Safety," *New York Times,* November 30, 1999, p. A1.

5. IOM, *To Err Is Human,* pp. 1–3.

6. Ibid., pp. 3–13 (quote, p. 3).

7. Glazer, "Medical Mistakes," pp. 137–60.

8. Ibid.

9. For further overviews of medical errors as a policy issue, see Agency for Healthcare Research and Quality, *Translating Research into Practice: Reducing Errors in Health Care* (U.S. Department of Health and Human Services, April 2000) (www.ahrq.gov/research/errors.htm); *Report of the President's Advisory Commission on Consumer Protection and Quality in the Health Care Industry* (July 1998), ch. 10. For details of the debate about error rates, see Clement J. McDonald, Michael Weiner, and Siu L. Hui, "Deaths Due to Medical Errors Are Exaggerated in the Institute of Medicine Report," *Journal of the American Medical Association* (July 5, 2000), pp. 93–95; Lucian L. Leape, "Institute of Medicine Medical Error Figures Are Not Exaggerated," *Journal of the American Medical Association* (July 5, 2000), pp. 95–97; and Troyen A. Brennan, "The Institute of Medicine Report on Medical Errors—Could It Do Harm?" *New England Journal of Medicine* (April 2000).

10. Personal communications with Howard H. Hiatt and Lucian L. Leape.

11. The study examined 30,121 randomly selected admissions at fifty-one hospitals in New York State in 1984. Researchers reviewed each record to determine whether adverse events had occurred and whether such events were caused by negligence. Adverse events were defined as prolonged hospitalization or disability at discharge due to medical management. Negligence was defined as care that fell below the standard expected of the average qualified physician in that specialty. Dr. Leape has suggested that negligence rates may not be reliable. For detailed accounts of this study, see Troyen A. Brennen and others, "Incidence of

Adverse Events and Negligence in Hospitalized Patients: Results from the Harvard Medical Practice Study I," *New England Journal of Medicine* (February 7, 1991), p. 370; IOM, *To Err Is Human,* pp. 23–30; Lucian L. Leape and others, "Preventing Medical Injury," *QRB* (May 1993), p. 144. See also Paul C. Weiler and others, *A Measure of Malpractice* (Harvard University Press, 1993), pp. vi–xiv; and L. L. Leape and others, "Adverse Events and Negligence in Hospitalized Patients," *Iatrogenics* (1991), pp. 17–21.

12. The results of this study are described in Eric J. Thomas and others, "Incidence and Types of Adverse Events and Negligent Care in Utah and Colorado," *Medical Care* (March 2000), pp. 261–71; IOM, *To Err Is Human,* pp. 25–27.

13. The nuclear reactor at Three Mile Island overheated on March 28, 1979, because regulators failed to tell operators about sticky valves, faulty maintenance left the system vulnerable, and poorly designed temperature gauges and control panels were misread. The *Challenger* space shuttle exploded on January 28, 1986, seconds after its launch from the Kennedy Space Center in Florida, because Morton Thiokol, the principal contractor for the shuttle's rocket, reportedly ignored nine years of evidence that the o-rings that stopped jet fuel from leaking frequently came unsealed, safer designs were rejected, the weather was unusually cold, and a last-minute effort by Thiokol's chief engineer to stop the launch failed. James Reason, *Human Error* (Cambridge University Press, 1990), pp. 164–65, 251–54.

14. Mikel Harry and Richard Schroeder, *Six Sigma* (Currency Publishers, 2000), pp. 8–19.

15. Lucian L. Leape, "Error in Medicine," *Journal of the American Medical Association* (December 21, 1994), pp. 1851–56.

16. See, for example, David C. Classen and others, "Computerized Surveillance of Adverse Drug Events in Hospital Patients," *Journal of the American Medical Association* (November 27, 1991), p. 2847; David W. Bates, Lucian L. Leape, and Stephen Petrycki, "Incidence and Preventability of Adverse Drug Events in Hospitalized Patients," *Journal of General Internal Medicine* (June 1993); "Putting Adverse Drug Events into Perspective," *Journal of the American Medical Association* (January 22/29, 1997), pp. 341–42.

17. Leape is quoted in Sheryl Gay Stolberg, "The Boom in Medications Brings Rise in Fatal Risks," *New York Times,* June 3, 1999, p. A1. By the late 1990s nearly half of Americans took prescription drugs, spending about $100 billion a year on them. In 1998 there were 2.78 billion prescriptions written, compared to 2.03 billion in 1992 and an estimated 4 billion by 2005. With more patients taking more drugs, harmful interactions, allergies, tolerance problems, and misdoses became more common. U.S. General Accounting Office (GAO), *Adverse Drug Events* (January 2000), pp. 1–7; statement by Janet M. Corrigan, director of the Board on Health Care Services, Institute of Medicine, Senate Hearing, Committee on Aging, May 3, 2001.

18. In 1998 the National Patient Safety Foundation brought together experts in cognitive psychology, organizational behavior, and performance evaluation to continue this work. The workshop noted parallels between systems to improve airline safety, worker safety, and medical errors. National Patient Safety Foundation, *Report from Workshop on Assembling the Scientific Basis for Progress on Patient Safety* (1998).

19. M.R. Chassin, R.W. Galvin, and the National Roundtable on Health Care Quality, "The Urgent Need to Improve Health Care Quality," *Journal of the American Medical Association* (September 16, 1998), pp. 1000–05 (quote, p. 1000).

20. The report, "Quality First," is available at www.hcqualitycommission.gov/final.

21. Report of the Quality Interagency Coordination Task Force to the President, "Doing What Counts for Patient Safety: Federal Actions to Reduce Medical Errors and Their Impact" (February 2000), pp. 10–12; Robert Pear, "Clinton to Order Steps to Reduce Medical Mistakes," *New York Times,* February 22, 2000, p. A1.

22. Other federal oversight systems were designed for narrow purposes. In 1986 Congress required hospitals to share names of doctors who had been denied privileges for more than thirty days and to check on license suspension and malpractice suits before hiring physicians. A National Practitioner Data Bank and state medical boards collected and disseminated such information. However, medical boards varied widely in the degree to which they encouraged reporting, and lobbying by the medical groups limited public access to the data. Jill Rosenthal and Trish Riley, *Patient Safety and Medical Errors* (National Academy for State Health Policy, March 2001), p. 19; Glazer, "Medical Mistakes," pp. 137–60.

23. Other federal programs required manufacturers to report any adverse events associated with the use of medical devices and blood products and encouraged voluntary, confidential reporting of infections acquired in hospitals and of problems with medical products, but they were not aimed at revealing patterns of errors in treatment. GAO, *Adverse Drug Events,* pp. 9–11; IOM, *To Err Is Human,* p. 80.

24. Lynda Flowers and Trish Riley, *State-Based Mandatory Reporting of Medical Errors: An Analysis of Legal and Policy Issues* (National Academy for State Health Policy, March 2001), pp. 14-15 (quote, p. 37); Jill Rosenthal and others, *Current State Programs Addressing Medical Errors,* National Academy for State Health Policy, January 2001, pp. 4–8; Rosenthal and Riley, *Patient Safety and Medical Errors,* pp. 21–22.

25. Jennifer Steinhauer and Ford Fessenden, "Medical Retreads: A Special Report—Doctors Punished by State but Prized at the Hospitals," *New York Times,* March 27, 2001, p. A1.

26. Leape and others, "Adverse Events and Negligence in Hospitalized

Patients," p. 17. See also Paul C. Weiler, Joseph P. Newhouse, and Howard H. Hiatt, "Proposal for Medical Liability Reform," *Journal of the American Medical Association* (May 6, 1992), p. 2355.

27. Institute of Medicine (IOM), *Crossing the Quality Chasm* (National Academy Press, 2001), p. 45.

28. IOM, *To Err Is Human,* p. 82.

29. Classen, "Computerized Surveillance of Adverse Drug Events in Hospital Patients," p. 2847.

30. IOM, *To Err Is Human,* pp. vii–viii, 175–78 (quote, p. vii).

31. Ibid., p. 74.

32. Testimony of Donald Berwick, Hearing on Medical Errors, Senate Committee on Health, Education, Labor, and Pensions, February 16, 2000.

33. By the late 1990s the system received more than 30,000 reports a year and the safety record for commercial aviation had improved markedly. The system operated on an annual budget of about $2 million. IOM, *To Err Is Human,* pp. 82–83.

34. Ibid., pp. 59–64.

35. Ibid., p. 7.

36. Ibid., p. 88.

37. Ibid., p. 18.

38. Ibid., pp. 7–8 (quotes, p. 7).

39. Ibid., pp. 23–24, 73–93.

40. Testimony of Berwick, Hearing on Medical Errors. For discussion of public response to the IOM's report, see the introductory section of this chapter.

41. Statement by President Bill Clinton, February 22, 2000; Quality Interagency Coordination Task Force, "Doing What Counts for Patient Safety," pp. 55–56.

42. For a summary of legislation proposed in the 106th Congress, see Howard Isenstein, "One More Time: Key Legislators Join Effort to Reduce Medical Errors," *Modern Physician,* July 1, 2000, p. 28.

43. Quality Interagency Coordination Task Force, "Doing What Counts for Patient Safety," pp. 6–10, 30–31 (quote, pp. 30–31).

44. Lynda Flowers and Trish Riley, *How States Are Responding to Medical Errors: An Analysis of Recent State Legislative Proposals* (National Academy for State Health Policy, September 2000), p. 3.

45. Rosenthal and Riley, *Patient Safety and Medical Errors,* pp. 25–26.

46. Testimony of Dennis O'Leary, Joint Commission on Accreditation of Healthcare Organizations, Hearing on Medical Errors, Senate Committee on Health, Education, Labor, and Pensions, February 22, 2000.

47. Testimony of Arnold Milstein on behalf of the Business Roundtable, Hearing on Reducing Medical Errors, Senate Committee on Health, Education, Labor, and Pensions, January 26, 2000 (www.leapfroggroup.com). This collaboration by

large purchasers built on a decade of efforts to control costs and improve the quality of care. In the 1990s some large companies required disclosure of performance data by the hospitals and health maintenance organizations to which they referred their employees, for comparisons of costs and quality. Xerox, IBM, and General Motors were among the thirty companies that required disclosure of standardized quality and consumer satisfaction data for plans that competed for their employees' business. They made efforts to couple these report cards with financial incentives for employees to choose high-quality, low-cost plans. Thomas Bodenheimer, "The American Health Care System—The Movement for Improved Quality of Health Care," *New England Journal of Medicine* (February 11, 1999), p. 488; Jason Ross Penzer, "Grading the Report Card: Lessons from Cognitive Psychology, Marketing, and the Law of Information Disclosure for Quality Assessment in Health Care Reform," *Yale Journal on Regulation* (Winter 1995), p. 207.

48. Pear, "Clinton to Order Steps to Reduce Medical Mistakes," p. A1.

49. Testimony of O'Leary, Hearing on Medical Errors.

50. Testimony of Mary Foley, American Nurses Association, Hearing on Reducing Medical Errors, Senate Committee on Health, Education, Labor and Pensions, January 26, 2000.

51. O'Leary is quoted in Peter T. Kilborn, "Ambitious Effort to Cut Mistakes in U.S. Hospitals," *New York Times,* December 26, 1999, A1.

52. See, for example, comments of Dennis O'Leary on new patient standards (www.jcaho.org/news [July 2, 2001]).

53. Robert Pear, "U.S. Health Officials Reject Plan to Report Medical Errors," *New York Times,* January 24, 2000, p. A1.

54. Troyen A. Brennan and others, "Hospital Characteristics Associated with Adverse Events and Substandard Care," *Journal of the American Medical Association* (June 26, 1991), p. 3265.

55. In 1987 a Veterans Administration medical center in Lexington, Kentucky, instituted a policy to disclose errors to patients and their families and offer assistance in filing claims. The new policy was an attempt to take a proactive approach to errors, following two losses in malpractice suits that totaled more than $1.5 million. A comparison of seven years of malpractice payments at that center and comparable Veterans Administration centers without the disclosure requirement policy found that the new policy was not associated with higher malpractice payments. The Lexington center negotiated more settlements and reduced legal expenses. Albert W. Wu, "Handling Hospital Errors: Is Disclosure the Best Defense?" *Annals of Internal Medicine* (December 21, 1999), p. 970; Steve S. Kraman and Ginny Hamm, "Risk Management: Extreme Honesty May Be the Best Policy," *Annals of Internal Medicine* (December 21, 1999), p. 963.

56. *Report of the President's Advisory Commission on Consumer Protection and Quality in the Health Care Industry,* ch. 10.

57. Anna Polk, director of Florida's reporting system, told *National Journal* reporter Marilyn Serafini in February 2000 that confidentiality "hasn't worked. We see instances of injuries all the time that were not reported." Marilyn Werber Serafini, "First, Do No Harm," *National Journal*, February 19, 2000, p. 542. See also comments of Dennis O'Leary on new patient standards (www.jcaho. org/news [July 2, 2001]); and Jill Rosenthal and others, *Current State Program Addressing Medical Errors* (National Academy of State Health Policy, 2001), pp. 66, 82.

58. David Lansky, "Can Consumers Judge?" *Blueprint* (Spring 2000) (www.ndol.org/blueprint [June 2001]).

59. Flowers and Riley, *State-Based Mandatory Reporting of Medical Errors*, p. 39.

60. David Blumenthal, "The Future of Quality Measurement and Management in a Transforming Health Care System," *Journal of the American Medical Association* (November 19, 1997), p. 1622.

61. Donald F. Phillips, "New Look Reflects Changing Style of Patient Safety Enhancement," *Journal of the American Medical Association* (January 20, 1999), p. 217.

62. This information was posted at www.hhs.gov.

63. Statement of Tommy G. Thompson, Hearing, Senate Committee on Health, Education, Labor and Pensions, May 24, 2001; the FDA also required reporting of problems in the quality of blood products and began a pilot project to encourage voluntary reporting of deaths, injuries, and close calls associated with medical products.

64. "Medical Errors: New Medicare Policy Mandates Disclosure," *American Health Line*, National Journal Group, January 2, 2001.

65. Flowers and Riley, *How States Are Responding to Medical Errors*, pp. 2–4.

66. Jill Rosenthal, Trish Riley, and Maureen Booth, *State Reporting of Medical Errors and Adverse Events: Results of a Fifty-State Survey* (National Academy for State Health Policy, 2000).

67. The National Quality Forum's report is available at www.qualityforum.org.

68. Quote is from the prepared statement of Lucian L. Leape before the Senate Committee on Health, Education, Labor and Pensions, May 24, 2001; JCAHO's new policy is summarized by the organization's president, Dennis O'Leary (www.jcaho.org/news [July 2, 2001]).

69. Testimony of Milstein, Hearing on Reducing Medical Errors.

70. Ibid.; Robin F. DeMattia, "Getting into the Game: Employers Want Their Chance to Shape and Improve the Quality of Care," *Modern Physician*, April 1, 2001, p. 21; personal communication with Arnold Milstein, spokesman for the Leapfrog Group and medical director, Pacific Business Group on Health; Leapfrog Group reports are posted at www.leapfroggroup.com.

71. Sarah Glazer, "Rating Doctors," *CQ Researcher* (May 5, 2000), p. 394; Bodenheimer, "The American Health Care System—The Movement for Improved Quality of Health Care," p. 488.

72. Martin N. Marshall and others, "The Public Release of Performance Data: What Do We Expect to Gain? A Review of the Evidence," *Journal of the American Medical Association* (April 12, 2000), p. 1866; see also Bodenheimer, "The American Health Care System—The Movement for Improved Quality of Health Care," p. 488, and Henry J. Kaiser Family Foundation, *National Survey on Americans as Health Care Consumers: An Update on the Role of Quality Information* (www.kff.org [June 2001]).

73. Marshall, "The Public Release of Performance Data, p. 1866.

74. National Research Council, *Networking Health* (National Academy Press, 2000), pp. 13, 35, 60, 66, 81 (quote, p. 13); GAO, *Adverse Drug Events*, pp. 6–7, 11–15.

75. Patient errors in 2001 were reported in Cinda Becker, "Accepting Responsibility: Two Hospitals Admit Central Roles in Recent Deaths," *Modern Healthcare,* August 6, 2001, p. 4.

76. IOM, *Crossing the Quality Chasm*, p. 80.

Chapter Five

1. In each instance, seemingly sudden action in fact reflected years of preparatory steps. By the time Congress required disclosure of toxic releases, Maryland, New Jersey, Massachusetts, California, and Pennsylvania had enacted laws requiring industry to alert the public to industrial hazards. By the time Congress required nutritional labeling, government agencies and private groups had been working on the idea for more than two decades. By the time Congress took up the issue of medical errors, fifteen states had adopted various reporting requirements, and leaders in the medical profession had spent more than a decade developing proposals for disclosure of such risks.

2. George J. Stigler, "The Economics of Information," *Journal of Political Economy* (June 1961), p. 213.

3. Some researchers have emphasized that such shortcuts are not irrational but reflect the fact that experts tend to rely on quantitative risk assessments while consumers rely on a broader spectrum of experience, emotion, and judgment. Cultural differences, individual psychology, and social milieu also play a role. This section provides a brief summary of a rich body of research. It draws on information from these central sources: National Research Council, *Improving Risk Communication* (National Academy Press, 1989); Wesley A. Magat and W. Kip Viscusi, *Informational Approaches to Regulation* (MIT Press, 1992), pp. 1–17; W. Kip Viscusi, "Alarmist Decisions with Divergent Risk Information,"

Economic Journal (November 1997), p. 1657; Daniel Kahneman, Paul Slovic, Amos Tversky, *Judgment under Uncertainty: Heuristics and Biases* (Cambridge University Press, 1982), p. 7; W. Kip Viscusi and Wesley A. Magat, *Learning about Risk: Consumer and Worker Responses to Hazard Information* (Harvard University Press, 1987), pp. 1–12; Baruch Fischhoff, "Managing Risk Perceptions," *Issues in Science and Technology* (Fall 1985), p. 83; Stephen Breyer, *Breaking the Vicious Circle: Toward Effective Risk Regulation* (Harvard University Press, 1993), pp. 33–38; Richard Zeckhauser, Ralph L. Kenney, and James K. Sebenius, *Wise Choices: Decisions, Games and Negotiations* (Harvard Business School Press, 1996), pp. 5–41.

4. The issue cannot be avoided, however. Legislators have obligations to conserve public and private resources. In approving new laws, they make choices about which public actions are most likely to reduce risks while minimizing regulatory burdens and promoting other important values. When disclosure systems aim to regulate, they cannot escape close scrutiny.

5. Some of these factors are suggested in U.S. Environmental Protection Agency, Science Advisory Board, *Integrating Environmental Decision-Making in the 21st Century* (1999), ch. 7. Further research would be needed to determine whether such factors amount to preconditions of broad applicability.

6. Economist Tom Tietenberg has identified five channels through which disclosure of environmental information influences corporate action. They are product markets, capital markets, labor markets, the judicial system, and legislative action and private enforcement. Tom Tietenberg, "Disclosure Strategies for Pollution Control," *Environment and Resource Economics* (1998), p. 587.

7. Reputation is one of the most important assets of any organization but one of the least amenable to measurement. Traditional notions of corporate goodwill measure only the amount by which the purchase price of a company exceeds the value of its tangible assets. See Charles J. Fronbrun, *Reputation: Realizing Value from the Corporate Image* (Harvard Business School Press, 1996). A discussion of reputational capital, including the concept of goodwill, appears at pp. 81–108.

8. In a special report, the *Economist* concluded that these trends make brands "highly effective tools through which to bring about change." "Who's Wearing the Trousers?" Special Report: Brands, *The Economist*, October 8, 2001, p. 26. See also Clive Smallman, Andrew Robinson, and Gareth John, "Unhealthy Attitudes That Endanger Good Performance," *Financial Times*, special section on mastering risk, part 5, May 23, 2000, p. 12.

9. Large corporations are not the only organizations to value their images and respond to new information about risks. Hospitals and health care providers compete for patients and staff on the basis of their reputation, universities compete for students and professors, environmental groups and other consumer organizations compete for members, government agencies compete for employees and resources, and communities compete for residents and businesses.

10. Fronbrun, *Reputation: Realizing Value from the Corporate Image*, pp. 6–7, 182–83.

11. Monsanto's response to disclosure of toxic releases is described in detail in chapter 2.

12. See, for example, the Freedom of Information Act's provisions on trade secrets, 5 U.S.C. 552(b)(4).

13. See, generally, Anne Wells Branscomb, *Who Owns Information? From Privacy to Public Access* (Basic Books, 1994), chapter 9.

14. U.S. General Accounting Office, *Environmental Information: EPA Could Better Address Concerns About Disseminating Sensitive Business Information* (1999), p. 15.

15. See, for example, "Terrorism: The Aftermath: Hill, Activists Fear Bush Using Security Issue to Limit Data, EPA Rules," *Environmental Policy Alert*, October 31, 2001, pp. 40–42.

16. These principles are articulated in two Supreme Court cases: *Central Hudson Gas & Electric Corp.* v. *Public Service Commission*, 447 U.S. 557, 566 (1980); and *Board of Trustees of State University of New York* v. *Fox*, 492 U.S. 469, 470 (1989).

17. For a full discussion of this issue, see chapter 3.

18. Berners-Lee and his colleagues envision a next-generation "semantic web" in which Extensible Markup Language (XML) and Resource Descriptive Frameworks (RDFs) will allow data from diverse sources to be shared automatically. See, for example, Tim Berners-Lee, James Hendler, and Ora Lassila, "The Semantic Web," *Scientific American*, May 2001, p. 36. For an account of the evolving use of barcodes, see Stephen A. Brown, *Revolution at the Checkout Counter* (Harvard University Press, 1997), pp. 224–46; Alan L. Haberman, ed., *Twenty-Five Years behind Bars* (Werthheim Publications/Harvard University, 2001); Leslie Kaufman, "Speaking in Bar Code," *New York Times*, October 6, 2000, p. B1; and Mark Fischett, "Quick Scan," *Scientific American*, May 2001, p. 88.

19. Tietenberg, "Disclosure Strategies in Pollution Control," p. 591.

20. The slow improvement of accounting standards is described in Joel Seligman, *The Transformation of Wall Street* (Northeastern University Press, 1995), pp. 48–49, 197–201, 551–54.

21. Institute of Medicine, *To Err Is Human: Building a Safer Health Care System* (National Academy Press, 1999), pp. 67–68, 156–57.

Index